THE ATTEMPTED

ERASURE

OF THE KHOEKHOE AND SAN

Jacob Cloete

SUN MeDIA

The Attempted Erasure of the Khoekhoe and San

Published by African Sun Media under the SUN MeDIA imprint
Place of publication: Stellenbosch, South Africa

First edition 2023

ISBN 978-1-998951-42-0
ISBN 978-1-998951-43-7 (e-book)
https://doi.org/10.52779/9781998951437

Set in Gudea 10.5/14

Cover design, typesetting and production by African Sun Media
Cover image courtesy of Ben Mcrae Photography.

SUN MeDIA is an imprint of African Sun Media. Academic and general works are published under this imprint in print and electronic formats.

This publication can be ordered from:
orders@africansunmedia.co.za
Takealot: bit.ly/2monsfl
Google Books: bit.ly/2k1Uilm
africansunmedia.store.it.si (e-books)
Amazon Kindle: amzn.to/2ktL.pkL
JSTOR: https://bit.ly/3udc057

Visit africansunmedia.co.za for more information.

Contents

Act 1: The Set-up

Act 2: The Confrontation

Act 3: The Resolution

Acknowledgements

Several people and organisations supported me in writing this book. Before I thank them, I must acknowledge my late grandparents' role in my life. Their early education before I encountered Western education laid the foundation of my worldview. It instilled in me a critical spirit and not to be ashamed of my culture and experiences. I would also like to thank my family, especially my first Aunt, Johanna Maarman – for her patience when I repeatedly asked about our family history.

Firstly, a special thank you to Prof Vivienne Lawack for her continued support. This book would not have seen the light if she did not recognise the potential. When everyone rejected me, she offered to sponsor the project. I also want to thank her for allowing me to be myself at work. Allowing myself to be myself allowed me to write, think, and research. She also continuously pushed me to finish the book and talked about the launch when I could not see the book launch. Her support gave me hope and the courage to finish the book.

Secondly, I want to thank two friends in particular. They are Dr Lorato Mokwena and Simone Momplé. They walked alongside me while I was writing this book. They saw my lows and my highs. To Dr Mokwena, knowing that I always had your support allowed me to push through and complete the book. I also want to thank you for reading the manuscript and the feedback you gave me. It sharpens my argument. Thank you for taking me on your many research trips. Those research trips helped me also to continue and finish my research. You are appreciated.

Thirdly, I want to thank many Khoekhoe and San leaders and activists with whom I shared many conversations. Allow me to mention a few. Ant Florence Filton, your drive and passion for the culture sparked the renewed pride with which many children and adults perform the *ǀKhâba ra*. I do not know where we would have been if it was not for you. Oom George Slaverse, who knew the *ǀKhâba ra* better than anyone, may your spirit rest in peace. I treasure our many conversations at the "riel dance" competitions. You and Oom Peter Takelo always made sure that everyone approached the *ǀKhâba ra* with seriousness. It was always more than a dance for you and Oom Peter, and you ensured people knew it. Oom Piet *!Aru ǀ'Khuisi* and Oom Hans Springbok, I appreciate you for reawakening my first education that was dormant. When we talk, it is like speaking to my late grandfather. I also want to thank Danab Bradley van Sitters, whose Khoekhoegowab class I greatly enjoyed. You awaken the spirit of my grandmother in me. By teaching me the language, I could access my childhood memories and the education my grandmother gave me throughout my life.

Fourthly, I must thank many of my colleagues who read parts of this book and who gave me sometimes hard but generous feedback. Amongst the many, I must mention Prof William Ellis. Our conversations were instrumental in carefully thinking about the Khoekhoe and San's past, present, and future in South Africa. He lent me many of his books and suggested so many others I must read. I want to thank my colleagues, Cynthia Kros and Pervaiz Khan, at Wits University for giving me the platform to present three of the chapters of this book at the Reframing Africa Workshop in 2018, 2019, and 2020. I thank my colleagues at the Centre for Humanities Research, especially the Communicating the Humanities film class, for your input, guidance, and support in creative endeavours. Those endeavours led me to the three limitations. Thus, without that platform, the three limitations would have never seen the light.

Fifth, a special thank you to the Centre for Humanities Research for funding my first trip to Barrydale. If it was not for that trip, I would have never heard of and experienced the Barrydale rock art. A chapter in this book is based on my experiences in Barrydale. In particular, I want to thank Prof Jane Taylor and Prof Maurits van Bevendoncker.

Finally, I did not write this book alone. Many people influenced and contributed during the writing process. I am aware of this, and I would like to thank everyone who contributed towards completing this book. I appreciate it dearly.

Preface

This book is primarily influenced by three events. The first event is the #RhodesMustFall and #FeesMustFall movements, which rocked the foundation of Higher Education in post-apartheid South Africa. These movements started the year after I enrolled for my PhD at the University of the Western Cape. Since my dissertation focused on the ongoing conflict in the Great Lakes region in Africa, I was able to distinguish the various forms of violence that made this such a ground-shifting event. I recognised the invisible structural violence of Higher Educational institutions that triggered these movements. I also saw and experienced the physical and overt acts of violence by the police and students. However, it quickly became apparent to me, where I saw two sides of the same coin, that many of my colleagues in Higher Education did not share my balanced view of the violence.

The second event was the screening of *Strike a Rock* at the Centre for Humanities Research at the University of the Western Cape. The screening took place in 2017, during the third year of the ongoing #FeesMustFall protests on campuses across South Africa. *Strike a Rock* is a documentary film about a group of women in Nkaneng in the aftermath of the 2012 Marikana massacre. While many of my colleagues welcomed the film, I was critical of its portrayal of black children. I did not like how black children were used as props to employ an emphatic response from the audience.

Additionally, for me, the film perpetuated a specific image of black people in South Africa, and this was a result of a longer colonial tradition where the camera was used to inflict an incredible amount of suffering on the indigenous people of South Africa. This tradition was perverted and pornographic in nature. These images stripped the indigenous of their agency, presenting them as subjects of research, pity, or pain. If it were not for *Strike a Rock* and the fallout after the screening, I would have never taken up documentary filmmaking. Documentary filmmaking enabled me to tell a different story about the marginalised in society. I now use the lens creatively to tell the story of the struggles of university students, communities, and people in general. I tell stories that liberate them from the popular pity and suffering trope.

The third and most significant event was growing up in Namaqualand. I was born and raised on a farm called Kwanous. My grandparents, who were farm workers, raised me. On this farm, I was introduced to my Khoekhoe identity – an identity that the education system, society, and the state stripped from me. I remember my grandmother always told us that she was a "Baster" (Mixed), and my grandfather always told us that his father spoke a language with clicks in it.[1] However, my great-grandfather refused to teach him (grandfather) and his siblings the language. Whilst my grandmother grew up in Namaqualand in the Kamiesberg, my grandfather grew up in the "Boesmanland" (Bushmanland). They lived and negotiated their existence in these two regions. For them, this was home.

Even though my grandparents were classified by apartheid as "Kleurling" (Coloured), it was always foreign to them. They never used the "coloured" identity to refer to themselves, their family, or their ancestors. Instead, they kept their Khoekhoe ("Hotnot") identity alive.[2] My grandfather's task was to teach the ancient knowledge of the veld, and my grandmother's task was to teach us some aspects of the religion and customs of the Khoekhoe. Many of their teachings contained traces of the "Hotnotstaal" (the "Hottentot" language). My grandmother, in particular, used many of the phrases and words when she taught aspects of the Khoekhoe's "voorgebruike" (customs) and "bygelowe" (religion). I once asked her where these words came from, and she told me it was the "Hotnotstaal".[3]

My grandparents trusted traditional medicinal practices more than modern Western medicine. Growing up, the medicine I was exposed to was traditional medicine. For every ailment, there was a traditional medicine that could treat it. My grandmother taught me the different medicinal plants and their purposes. She also showed me how to prepare and administer it. My grandfather made sure that we were exposed to the culture. He ensured that we knew what the ǀkhâba ra was and that we had a sense of belonging that reached far beyond the farm.

I encountered another view of our values when I entered the basic education system. It was also here that I encountered the "backward" and "uncivilised" "Hottentot" and "Boesman" figures. At school, I realised that people who lived in towns looked down on us. Many called us "Boesman" or "plaasjapie". In the basic education system, my first education (the education of my grandparents)

[1]   In Namaqualand, "Baster" or Bastard was still widely used when I was growing up. It was a reference to people's Griqua ancestry. However, it is now considered a derogatory term among the Griqua people. You rarely hear this word in Namaqualand these days.

[2]   "Hotnot" is a shortened version of "Hottentot". "Hotnot" and "Hottentot" are derogatory terms and are no longer openly used in South Africa.

[3]   It was only much later that I learned that "Hotnotstaal" was a reference to either Khoekhoegowab or Namagowab. Khoekhoegowab means the Khoekhoe language, whereas "gowab" means language. Namagowab thus means the Nama language. Scholars consider Khoekhoegowab the official and standardised version of the Khoekhoe language. In contrast, Namagowab is considered one of the dialects of Khoekhoegowab (Fredericks, 2013).

was rendered backwards and discarded. Instead, we were forced to learn of the arrival of Jan van Riebeeck and the "civilising" mission he started. We were conditioned to accept everything that was written in textbooks. Your grades and progress in the basic education system depended on how well you could recite what was written in these textbooks. And slowly but surely, the erasure of my "Hotnot" and "Boesman" past occured. It had to make space for the "Kleurling" (Coloured) identity. They wanted us to be ashamed of our ancestry so we could reject it. We had to make space for the so-called coloured identity, a civilised version of the "Hotnot" or "Boesman". This version made the Khoekhoe and San landless figures with no history or real sense of belonging to South Africa.

When I entered the university system, I realised they appropriated the knowledge of the Khoekhoe and San. The university is the custodian of the knowledge my grandparents taught me. Some academics and disciplines are the authoritative voices on the Khoekhoe and San knowledge systems. It became clear that the university was complicit in the attempt to erase the Khoekhoe and San identities, religion, and culture. Some universities are now the custodians and beneficiaries of the Khoekhoe and San artefacts and knowledge systems. However, they were unsuccessful in their attempted erasure because the religion, the customs, the language, and the knowledge system survived on the margins of the colonial and apartheid state. It has been passed down from one generation to the next.

This book is partly an autoethnographic account and revisits each of these events and shows how those events contributed to my struggles with the university, the "coloured" identity, and the attempted erasure of the Khoekhoe and San identities in South Africa. Furthermore, it is written as a decolonised text and does not follow the structure of a classic academic text. The book instead follows the narrative structure of a documentary film.

Act 1
The Set-up

1

The Three Limitations

In April 2017, I attended the documentary film *Strike a Rock* screening.[1] The film is an exposé of the lives of two women in the aftermath of the 2012 Marikana Massacre in Nkaneng. The film is about friendship, hardship, and the lack of accountability for the victims of the Marikana massacre. The film borrowed its title from the well-known struggle song "Wathint' Abafazi, Wathint' Imbokodo", which means "you strike the women, you strike the rock." The film frames Nkaneng as another poor and hopeless informal settlement. This framing of Nkaneng and the people appearing in the film did not sit well with me. Since a question-and-answer session followed the film, I decided to raise my concerns about the film with the Director.

For me, one of the biggest concerns was around the dignity of the subjects who appeared in the film. There were three striking scenes with undertones of "poverty porn." In one scene, the main character puts peanut butter on her daughter's bread. The problem with this scene was that her daughter's face was in the frame of the shot.[2] There was also a scene where she was dishing her daughter soft mealie meal porridge with no sugar or milk and another of people living in Nkaneng queuing alongside a Gift of the Givers truck. The framing of Nkaneng as an informal settlement and these scenes aimed to show how difficult life is for people in Nkaneng.

The question, for me, was whether there had to be scenes of black children with no agency to convey this message. It did nothing to the main narrative of the film. The main narrative thread of the film is centred around the women of

---

[1]   Aliki Saragas, *Strike A Rock* (South Africa, 2017).
[2]   After the screening, the face of the child was blurred out for the festival screenings.

Nkaneng's struggle to get Lonmin to compensate them for the 2012 Massacre. However, the scene of the black child was needed to establish a troubling subtext. The film's subtext is that of the "poor black African" whom a black government abandoned, and it was the same government responsible for the massacre. The film showed the apology of President Jacob Zuma. Yet, there was no apology from Lonmin or any white benefactors of Lonmin. White people were strikingly absent in the film, especially the white Lonmin mineworkers and their children. With this in mind I asked the filmmaker: "Did you consider filming the children of white miners and contrast that with the black children who appeared in the film?" I never got an answer to my question.

The second issue I had was regarding the violence the film produced. At the time, I was busy studying the ongoing conflict in the Great Lakes region in Africa. It was for my doctoral dissertation. To make sense of the ongoing conflict in the Great Lakes region in Africa, I had to make sense of the violence. I learned that violence manifested physically and structurally, leaving lasting psychological effects on the victim. I realised that the film had a relatively narrow interpretation of violence. To me, it was clear that the filmmaker was unaware of the violence the film produced. For example, there was a scene of a sexually abused teenage girl. A group of Nkaneng women talked to her about the incident while it was filmed. Watching her, I could sense her shame, yet this was showcased to an audience. That particular scene also left me with two questions. First, why couldn't the filmmaker recognise the violence the camera inflicted? Second, did the teenager see a psychologist? Once again, this scene did not aid the film's main narrative.

It was clear to me that I experienced the film differently than my white colleagues in the room. For example, during the question-and-answer session, one of my white colleagues stated that the people in Marikana were traumatised by the killing. Yes, the Marikana Massacre was a traumatic event. However, in reality, Black people lived in a traumatised state before the Marikana event. Let us not forget that colonialism and apartheid were two very traumatising events for Black people in South Africa's history.[3] The violence of colonialism and apartheid was physical and structural, leaving lasting psychological scars. More importantly, since 1994, it has been difficult for Black people to escape the lasting structural violence of apartheid. Many of us are still trapped in

---

[3] When "black" is written with the small letter "b" in this book, it refers to Steve Biko's notion of "black" in Black Consciousness. Biko's (2017) notion of black in "black" Consciousness included all oppressed groups in South Africa. When "Black" is written with a Capital letter "B", it refers to the apartheid and post-apartheid states' racial classification. Also note that where "White" and "Coloured" are written with capital letters they refer to the racial classification of the colonial, apartheid and post-apartheid states.

the violent neighbourhoods that apartheid created, and this violence is still affecting us. Thus, the structural violence institutionalised during these oppressive periods did not cease to exist after 1994. Moreover, one white colleague went as far as to say that the film "beautifully and brilliantly depicted the life of women in Nkaneng." What is beautiful about structural violence? I grew up in places like Nkaneng. I knew there was nothing beautiful about structural violence.

After I raised my concerns, some audience members felt that the Director did not need to answer my question because I was "out of line." As a result, I was shut down, or dare I say "cancelled". Afterwards, several people came to speak to me about my concerns, and others came to put me in my place. So it seemed. White women, for example, outright rejected my concerns. They responded that I missed the gendered lens of the film. For them, my critique was supposed to take a gendered lens and not a racial lens. Since a woman made the film, and it was about women. Consequently, as a male, I did not know what I was talking about. They indirectly implied that I, a so-called coloured man, do not have a right to critique a film about women, especially if a woman made it. They presuppose that gender is a greater historical injustice in South Africa than race.

I respected their points of view, but it did not make sense how white women and feminists, in particular, could argue that gender was the greater historical injustice and that they were oppressed as much as I was.[4] I wanted to say: You were not as oppressed as my grandmother, mother or grandfather. Growing up, I did not see White women working in the kitchens of black women and living in the shacks as my mother and grandmother did. I also did not see White women working in the gardens of black men, calling them "baas" (Master) and "nooi" (Madam) or sitting at the back of the "bakkie" while black men sat in front. White women at a particular time in South Africa's history were the oppressors, and they participated in the oppression of black people. This oppression was racial, and it superseded gender. It struck me that they viewed me as the aggressor and threat. I was the subtext the film already established. It made me wonder where this fear came from. Why am I seen as the aggressor? Why were they blind to the violence the Director inflicted on Black people?

---

[4]   After the screening, several White women came to me with this argument.

More troubling for me were those who agreed with me and shared my concerns about the film but were too scared to raise their concerns during the question-and-answer. Needless to say, this group of people was black. It was interesting to see how they looked around to ensure nobody was close enough to hear them agree with me.

Voyeurism and the "White Saviour Complex"

I realised that documentary films like *Strike a Rock* contributed to the post-apartheid structural violence in South Africa. That contribution comes in the form of voyeurism or the unintended pornographic power relationship these films create. A relationship that intentionally or unintentionally created pornographic subjects of poor black people. For example, I was made a pornographic object by white students in 1993. Our principal informed us that students would visit the Catholic Church in Rietpoort, and our task as the school was to welcome them. Rietpoort is a Catholic missionary established in 1912 and was the only one in the region with a monastery and boarding school. Since I lived on a farm, I was in this boarding school. We practised several songs in a guard of honour leading up to their visit. They were visiting Rietpoort in the winter, and they arrived in the late afternoon. They took photos of us as we stood in our raggedy clothes in that cold winter afternoon sun. Some also gave us the food they had with them. After that, they left, and I soon forgot this had happened.

However, the memory of this incident only returned in 2013 when I attended a photo exhibition at the District Six Museum Homecoming Centre in Cape Town. The exhibition told a story of how people used to live in District Six before the forced removals. Several colleagues and I had an interesting discussion that evening. We discussed what we saw at the time as a growing trend in Cape Town: township tours. We discussed how the "African safari" changed. In the 20th century, safaris into the wilderness were a fashionable trend enjoyed by the upper classes. The upper class used to go into the natural habitat of wild animals and take explicit and hard-core photos of animals. Once they had their photos, they returned to their social circles and revelled in their pornographic content. And a century before them, it started with the explorer Henry Morton Stanley. He was among the first explorers to take a camera with him as he explored tropical Africa (Killingray & Roberts, 1989). Over time, a new trend started, "slumming".

In South Africa, "slumming" is known as "township tours" (Huysamen et al., 2020). Slum tourism or "slumming" dates as far back as the Victorian age in London. During this period, the upper classes of society actively engaged in slumming, where slumming is considered to be the desire among the upper class to experience first-hand the conditions of the poor (Koven, 2004; Nead, 2005). Freire-Medeiros is critical of slum tourism because it frames poverty as a product "for consumption through tourism at a global scale" (Freire-Medeiros, 2009, p. 586). In this instance, township tours frame poverty outside its colonial and apartheid context. And more importantly, for me, humans are made subjects of "poverty porn". "Poverty porn could be any type of media, which exploits the poor's condition to generate the necessary sympathy or support for a given cause" (Kaskure, Nadezda, & Jana Krivorotko, 2014, p. 5). This act of turning a camera on a poor subject to create sympathy is a demonstration of power, and this creates a voyeuristic relationship between the poor and the tourist.

Even though some people might argue for the economic benefits of "township tourism", poverty is at the heart of this practice. This is the ethical dilemma township tourism presents. Through township tourism, the upper class observe poor Black people in their "natural habitat". They want the "township experience." During township these tours, they take photos from their vehicles. Sometimes these vehicles are always higher than the 'poor township' subject. They sometimes look down on a very powerful position. The photos they take are explicit and of hard-core poverty. These photos are a means to arouse sympathy but not necessarily to act (Freire-Medeiros, 2009; Huysamen et al., 2020).

If they do act, they suffer from what is known as the "white saviour complex." White Saviour complex or WSC is when a white person tends to be the saviour and lift the poor and oppressed of supposed poverty (Cowden, 2020; Straubhaar, 2015). The "white saviour complex" is a psychological residue of the age-old civilising mission during colonial times.[5] McCurdy (2016) links WSC to imperialism and Cowden (2020) to neo-colonialism. Therefore, "a nobody from America or Europe can go to Africa and become a godlike savior or, at the very least, have his or her emotional needs satisfied. Many have done it under the banner of 'making a difference'" (Cole, 2012, cited in Straubhaar, 2015, pp. 384-385). In 2019, the story of Renee Bach surfaced. For years, Bach ran a centre for malnourished children in Uganda. Bach presented herself as a doctor but was only a high school graduate and did not have any medical

---

[5]   Chapter 3 goes into more detail.

training. Between 2010 and 2015, 105 children died in Bach's centre (Aizenman & Gharib, 2019). Therefore, the WSC is the tendency of white people to try to save the unfortunate Black person, even if it means killing them.

Another example would be the case of Nkosikho Mbele. In May 2019, Mbele helped a distressed white woman who ran out of petrol and forgot her bank card at home. The petrol attendant decided to pay for the petrol. Later that day, the woman posted on a social media site about Mbele's good deed. She asked people to support her crowdfunding campaign. She aimed to raise R100 000. It quickly reached national and international news agencies, surpassed the initial goal and reached close to R500 000. Her good deed quickly overshadowed Mbele's. Mbele became the one in need of rescuing – a saviour.

This "complex" is always accompanied by photos of well-doing. In these photos, the white person sometimes appears beside a Black person in a less dignified manner. These photos rob the Black person of any dignified portrayal of self. For example, there are several photos of Mbele in his petrol attendant uniform juxtaposed with his smiling and well-dressed "saviour". Reading and following these incidents, I could not help but draw the similarities they shared with *Strike a Rock.*

The Three Limitations and the Postcolonial Archive

Given the fallout of *Strike a Rock,* I decided to study the cause of voyeurism or the unintended pornographic power relationships in certain documentary films. So, I participated in the Centre for Humanities Research's documentary film course. Once I completed the course, I formed part of the Communicating the Humanities documentary film group, where we discussed how documentary filmmaking could help academia rethink the Humanities. Part of the requirement to be part of the group is to actively engage in documentary filmmaking. I was particularly interested in the power relations between the filmmakers and those they are filming. As I started making documentary films, I realised there was a thin line between voyeurism and documentary. My investigation led me to "discover" three inherent limitations of documentary filmmaking. These three limitations are (1) the selectiveness of the frame, (2) the subjectivity of the audience, and (3) the invisibility of the filmmaker. These limitations sometimes create an unintended pornographic relationship or voyeurism.

I wondered whether I could work with or resolve these three limitations when making a documentary film. So, I set out to use the three limitations as a conceptual approach when making documentary films. I also intentionally decided to focus on marginalised rural communities in South Africa. I wanted to see if I could overcome the three limitations and present the people I am filming in a dignified manner. I also wanted the audience to notice and experience these limitations. For example, one of the films, Ending and Beginning, combines and uses all three limitations to tell the story of a rural community, a filmmaker and the students of #FeesMustFall.

During this journey, I also realised that the three limitations provided a conceptual approach to unmasking structural violence in Higher Education in South Africa. In October 2018, I presented a paper at the annual *Re Framing Africa* photo and film workshop at Wits University. The workshop title was "Re Framing Africa: Restructuring the Self". One of the workshop themes focused on "How do we reclaim the archive even if it was not made with us in mind? Exploring the ways African filmmakers have or are repurposing the archive".

My paper was titled "The Second Limitation: the archive, voyeurism and the problematic black figure". I argued that it is difficult to reclaim and restructure the Self without dealing with the custodian of the postcolonial archive. The custodian of the postcolonial archive is the university. For me, the university is a colonial institution that remains untransformed, and its lack of transformation results from coloniality.[6] In Africa, the Self (postcolonial subject) was trapped in the subliminal colonial power relations of coloniality. I proposed that we use the three limitations of documentary filmmaking as a conceptual approach to unmasking the subliminal power relations in which the university in Africa and the postcolonial archive came into existence.

Since archivisation informs history, archivisation also starts with Van Riebeeck's arrival at the Cape. This is evident from the classification of the indigenous people of South Africa. For example, the Khoekhoe and San are seen as "pastoralists" or "hunters-and-gatherers". This classification, which the university is mainly responsible for, strips them of their history and advances the Hegelian notion of what constitutes civilisation, progress, and modernity. Before Van Riebeeck, the Khoekhoe and San people also preserved their history, educated their children, and had laws and a religion that regulated their broader society. Colonialism and colonisation stripped them of their culture, philosophy, and religion. It stripped them of all those components

---

[6]   A discussion on coloniality will follow in Chapter 3.

that form complex human relations and societies. The Khoekhoe and San were rendered "savages," "hunters-and-gatherers", or "pastoralists", thus uncivilised, without an archive.

Thus, colonialism's first attempt was to destroy the history of Africa. Hegel, after all, wrote that Africa had no history. His work and that of John Locke justified missionaries and colonialists to enslave and colonise Africans. Hegel argues that through slavery, the African will desire the European's (Master's) level of "civilisation." This desire, Hegel argues, will set the slave on the path to emancipation. Hence, the "civilisation" of the indigenous erased a large part of their pre-colonial history. The history before Van Riebeeck was cast in a "hunters-and-gatherers" or "pastoralists" frame, a frame the university created to classify the indigenous people of South Africa. This archive keeps indigenous people in the "uncivilised" and "savage" frames.

However, the indigenous peoples of South Africa were not "uncivilised" and "savage" people. On the contrary, they were as civilised and human as their European, Arabian, American, and Asian counterparts. For example, pre-colonial archivisation in South Africa took place at various sites. Take the ǀkhâba ra, for example. The ǀkhâba ra is a Khoekhoe dance, and it is considered one of the oldest dances in South Africa. This dance is still practised today. Since choreography is the notation of dancing, the ǀkhâba ra wrote a historical record of the Khoekhoe people in their bodies. Hence, the ǀkhâba ra preserved the memories and histories of the colonised in the bodies of the colonised.

However, colonialism and colonisation's attempt to exterminate the Khoekhoe people failed and the dance was passed down to generations. This dance preserved the history of a people on the margins of the colonial and apartheid state. Hence, when destroying the African archive was unsuccessful, the credibility of the African archive was questioned. Africa's history was always treated with scepticism and suspicion by European and colonial scholars because African archivisation did not resemble European archivisation. European archivisation disputed Africa's historical records. If not in a library or museum, the historical record was "questionable." However, European writers and scholars conveniently ignored the skewed power relations that brought their archives into existence. European elites created archives to preserve and tell their side of history, erasing the "common folk" from history (Derrida, 1998).

Another example of a pre-colonial archive is any site of rock art. There is already excellent and very prominent scholarly work on rock art, but they do not treat rock art sites as pre-colonial archives. They treat them as archaeological sites and not archives. Archaeology destroys these archives and removes the information from its original context. The data collected by archaeologists ends up in museums and universities. Ironically, the same institutions question the credibility of African archives.

Furthermore, most scholarly works on rock art follow either an interpretive or narrative approach, and these works are more interested in rock art images. In addition, the interpretive and narrative approaches have become the dominant lens through which rock art is encountered and analysed. The work of a few scholars presumes a level of authority over the analysis of rock art in Southern Africa. The indigenous' voice is largely absent from these scholarly works and begs the question: Is a reading of rock possible outside the interpretive and narrative approaches, which do not render it as the work of "hunters-and-gatherers" but as a people that has a philosophy, religion, laws, and customs. In Chapter 2, I will return to this question.

I believe a different reading of rock art is possible if one uses the three limitations as a conceptual approach. The three limitations will help unmask coloniality in the interpretation and analysis of rock art. For example, unlike Western paintings, rock art has no physical frame. Framing it will destroy the art. In addition, if one attempts to take a photo of rock art, the camera's lens frames the art and excludes some figures or symbols from the frame. In addition, when rock art is analysed by drawing on Western epistemologies, it reveals a European conceptual lens through which sensemaking occurs. These epistemologies still primarily treat rock art as the work of "hunters-and-gatherers" and make it "inferior" and "backward" compared to Western paintings.

Clarifications of Concepts

This book does not want to reproduce the excellent work of many scholars. Over the past 40 years, some scholars have done excellent work in writing against the erasure of Khoekhoe and San. Notably of these scholars are Bredenkamp (1980, 1981), Abrahams (1994, 2000), Besten (2006), Adhikari (2014), Mellet (2020) and Bam (2021). These scholars made sure to write against the erasure of the Khoekhoe and San people in South Africa. They also openly questioned the "coloured" identity and highlighted many problematic areas in this identity construct.

This book is about how the Khoekhoe and San were framed in colonial and apartheid texts and how that contributed over time to their erasure. The framing of the Khoekhoe and San laid the basis or the justification for the violence that contributed to their attempted erasure. When the "coloured" frame was institutionalised, it took on the structural nature that the descendants of the Khoekhoe and Saw are facing now. However, before I commence this argument, I must clarify some concepts I use in this book.

Erasure and Genocide

Erasure in this book does not mean *genocide*. I think Adhikari (2014), in *Anatomy of a South African Genocide: The Extermination of the Cape San People,* successfully argued for a case of genocide regarding the Cape San peoples during Dutch and British colonial rule. However, a shortcoming of Adhikari's (2014) work is to limit his investigation to the San people. The Khoekhoe were also subjects of genocide.

Furthermore, I intentionally steered away from using the concept of *genocide* in this book. As a scholar on the ongoing conflict in the Great Lakes region in Africa, I know how contentious the concept of *genocide* is. For example, Mahmood Mamdani, in *Good Muslim, Bad Muslim: America, the Cold War, and the Roots of Terror,* explained this contention at length. Instead, I decided to focus on erasure. My work compliments the work of June Bam in her book *Ausi Told Me: Why Cape Herstoriographies Matter.* I am aware that Bam, in *Ausi Told Me,* discusses seven types of "concomitant erasures within the ecology of indigenous knowledge in the Cape context" (Bam, 2021, p. 141). My book does not speak or position any of these forms of erasures. I am more concerned with bureaucratic erasure and how it builds institutions to continue the erasure of the Khoekhoe and San people. Colonial and apartheid racial classification led to social stratification, which led to certain groups' discrimination. Therefore, colonial and apartheid racial classification erased Khoekhoe and San people by forcefully including them in the "Coloured" racial classification.

Furthermore, with their taxonomical classification of the indigenous people, universities aided the colonial and apartheid state in the bureaucratic erasure of the Khoekhoe and San. According to (Mellet, 2020, p. 18), "In the colonial academic world went a step further and intellectually wiped out the existence of the San and the Khoekhoe in the interest of the colonial government by asserting that these peoples no longer existed except in the form of a genetic fingerprint" (Mellet, 2020, p. 18). The pseudo-scientific tests conducted on the Khoekhoe and San were to prove that they were genetically distinct and inferior to white people. Museums and university disciplines are created around this "scientific" endeavour (Skotnes, 1996). As Mellet points out, this led to their de-Africanisation.

As you will see in the forthcoming chapters, stripping the Khoekhoe and the San of their land was the start of erasing their identity. Missionary societies also played a significant part in erasing Khoekhoe and San identities in South Africa. Before the "Coloured" classification, "Hottentot" erased various Khoekhoe and San groups into one category. "Khoisan" also contributed, and "Coloured" finally erased the indigeneity of the descendants of the Khoekhoe and San people.

Khoekhoe and San

Before the widespread usage of Khoekhoe (Khoikhoi)[7] and San, the racial categories of "Hottentot" (Khoekhoe) and "Bushman" (San) were used. "Hottentot" and "Bushman" were used to describe the "inferiority" and "primitivism" of the Khoekhoe and San peoples. Since many scholars became aware of the derogatory association of these racial categories, they were replaced with Khoekhoe (Khoikhoi) and San. The Khoekhoe (Khoikhoi) and San framing were supposed to be more positive.

However, San is a problematic term for me because of its negative meaning and effect on people's lives. I know this term erased many identities of the Bushman people. "San" in Namagowab (the Nama language) means "gatherer" and was attributed to people who did not have livestock and had a different way of living than the Khoekhoe. Therefore, even though the title of this book has "San" in it, know that I am uncomfortable using the term "San." I am only using it because it is an indigenous phrase many people classified as San have accepted.

Another problematic term for me to use is "Bushman." Some scholars in the university view the terms "Bushman" and "Bosjesmans" as derogatory. For them, the acceptable term in academic writing is San. However, not all the people the university classifies as San want to be identified as San because of its derogatory meaning in Namagowab. In this sense, San is offensive to some "Bushmen" groups. They preferred to be called "Bushman" or "Boesman" (Ellis, 2015). Personally, my encounter with the term was never positive. Whenever I was called "Boesman", it was always to render me subhuman. It was intended to strip me of my humanity and give my offender the upper hand. Thus, for me, it was always negative.

---

[7] In this book, I have decided to use Khoekhoe instead of Khoikhoi. Khoekhoe is the correct linguistic pronunciation (Fredericks, 2013). It is also my attempt to move away from the crystallised conception of the Khoekhoe in History and Anthropology.

Khoekhoe

Scholars write Khoekhoe differently in various texts. For example, Nienaber (1989) uses Khoekhoen, Biwa (2006), Khoekhoe, Fredericks (2013), Khoe, Adhikari (2014), Khoikhoi, Barnabas and Miya (2019), Khoekhoe, Mellet (2020), Khoe, and Bam (2021) Khoena. The reason for the different applications and writing of "Khoekhoe" is that scholars come from different disciplines and have preferences. Khoikhoi was an older version of Khoekhoe before linguistics pointed out that it is not "oi" but "oe" in Khoekhoegowab (Frederick, 2013, p. 10). The "oe" sounds a lot like "oi" in Afrikaans. In Khoekhoegowab, the -o and -e are pronounced separately, and if one says it fast, it sounds like "oi".

In addition, Nienaber (1989) has pointed out that the -n of Khoekhoen indicates the plural form for a community (nation / "volk"). Hence, San ends with an -n. Nienaber also explains that some scholars are writing Khoekhoe without the -n, which is incorrect. Hence, he used Khoekhoen. However, in the Khoekhoegowab dictionary, Haacke (1999) defines Khoekhoen as people speaking Khoekhoegowab. Therefore, there seems to be a differentiation between Khoekhoe and Khoekhoen based on who speaks the language and who identifies as Khoekhoe.

Interestingly, Bam (2021) believes that "Khoena" is a gender-neutral way to refer to the Khoekhoe; since Khoekhoe means "men of men." However, Haacke in Fredericks (2013, p. 9) points out that "men of men" is merely a reduplication of the root for "person". Therefore, the best and closest translation would be a *proper human being*. In addition, Haacke (1999) points out that Khoen is the gender-neutral term in Khoekhoegowab. In addition, Haacke (1999) indicated that *people* in Khoekhoegowab can be written as Khoen or as *!haos*. However, *!haos* also means clan, family, family line, or tribe.

I have to note that in Khoekhoegowab, the -s at the end of a word indicates the female gender, -b the male gender, -i is gender neutral, and as mentioned earlier, -n indicates plural. Interestingly *!haos* end with -s which indicates the female gender. This left me with an interesting question: Since some words in Khoekhoegowab are culturally predetermined, why did the Khoekhoe gender the name of the tribe? I think this needs further research.

San

We encounter the San via colonial texts. One of the first encounters is through the Sonqua. From Van Riebeeck's account, it is clear that the Dutch found several indigenous groups at the Cape. These groups were the Sonqua,

Goringhaicona, Goringhaiqua, and Gorachouqua. Biwa (2006, p. 17) argues that "qua" in "Namaqua" is a corruption of "khoe"; hence she, in her dissertation, uses "Namakhoeland" instead of "Namaqualand". Biwa explains that "Namakhoeland in Khoekhoegowab means 'land of the Nama people', and describes the historical place where the Nama people lived and still live up to this day" (Biwa, 2006, p. 17). Hahn's (1888) research on the language of the Khoekhoe indicated that the Khoekhoe spoke the same language with slight variations in dialect. According to Hahn (1881, p. 3), "Sā(n) consequently would mean Aborigines or Settlers proper." Hahn (1881, p. 3) also explains that "Sonqua" can also be written as "Sa-n or Sa-gu-a". Abrahams (1994, p. 36) notes that Van Riebeeck's Journal clearly stated that the Sonqua also owned cattle and were accustomed to trading annually. Nienaber (1989, p. 18) indicates that Sonqua were also referred to as "Bergh-hottentoos" (Mountain Khoekhoe), which is an indication that lines between Khoekhoe and Sonqua were blurred. Thus, if "qua" is a corruption of "Khoe", it would mean the "Sonqua" were Khoekhoe. Considering this, one can argue that "Sonqua" could mean Sā(n)khoe, meaning the Aborigines or Settlers proper of the area.

As mentioned earlier, *people* in Khoekhoegowab can also mean !*hoas*. I support Biwa's observation that -*qua* is a corruption of Khoe. Still, as I explained earlier, people in Khoekhoegowab can also mean !*haos*. To me, -*qua* could be a corruption of !*haos*. If that is the case, Sonqua could be written as *Sa(n)!haos?*, meaning the people originally inhabiting the Cape. Thus, San ending with -n could also be interpreted as the original inhabitants.

"San" also means "gatherer" and "first inhabitant" and was attributed to people who did not have livestock and had a different way of living than the Nama (Bredekamp, 1981, p. 11). San is also a derivative of Sonqua. Abrahams (1994) argues that since their cattle were taken from them after the war, the Khoekhoe in the Peninsula had "to subsist solely on hunting-and-gathering." The following question captures the theory that Abrahams explores: Could it be that the Khoekhoe and the San were of a larger pre-colonial homogeneous society? If so, can we consider this society as "Khoisan"? Even though this is a very persuasive argument, it does not account for the different linguistic, cultural, and religious practices between the Khoekhoe and San.

A more recent argument is the genetic argument to prove that San is genetically the oldest community in South Africa. Mellet (2020) uses the genetics argument as a premise to treat the San as a separate entity from the Khoekhoe. He argues that "all other African communities also have old San communities as part of their genetic, ancestral and cultural heritage. As such, the San represent the cement that binds us in a strong, uniting pan-African heritage that is greater than ethnic division or 'race' constructs" (Mellet, 2020, p. 32). Even though Mellet (2020, p. 32) carefully argues that "diverse San societies began to emerge from the L-0d, L-0k and L-0d1" Homo sapiens, I feel uncomfortable using this argument. I am afraid that racist scientists with a sleight of hand can use this argument to strengthen their racist evolution theory of race. Mellet (2020) stresses that all humans are related to the San. However, the discrimination the San experienced during colonialism and at the hands of scientists was to show that they did not evolve as much as the rest of humanity, that human beings consisted of different races and that these races could be placed on a civilisation ladder. This was, after all, the reason inhumane experiments and measurements were taken of the San to prove this "civilisation ladder" theory. I am writing this book to expose the long trajectory of that discourse. If we are not careful, the genetics argument might play right into the hands of the old racial scientists. They argued that race was biological and not political, social, or cultural.

I am also aware that many San, were forcefully incorporated into the colonial servant class as "Hottentots." San who were incorporated into the colonial labour force were also liable to be categorised as "Hottentot and to thus develop a 'Hottentot' identity" (Besten, 2006, p. 24). As you would see later in this book, *The Hottentot Proclamation of 1809* had a far-reaching effect on the psyche of the Khoekhoe and San people. The "Hottentot", or "Hotnot", became the servant class of white colonists. Thus, those indentured lost their group identity and were made into a "Hottentot" and later "Hotnot." A "Hotnot" has a "baas" (Master) – someone who could exploit their labour cheaply and who could enforce a master-slave relationship. Scholars often miss that "baas" and "hotnot" identities are still alive in South Africa, and the "baas-hotnot" relationship is still operational. Hence, the master-slave sensibility is still present in South Africa. The "baas" sensibility of white people indicates that they still have the psyche of the master and treat people who are not classified as white as their "servants".

"Khoisan" (Khoe–San)

I use Khoekhoe and San in this book instead of "Khoisan" (Khoe-San). I believe the Khoekhoe and the San were two distinct pre-colonial political, religious, and cultural entities. However, it must be noted that pre-colonial identity was fluid, and people could move between various subject identities (Besten, 2006).

Moreover, the term "Khoisan" did not exist pre-colonial. As pointed out by many scholars, it was invented to describe two very different groups of people (Barnabas & Miya, 2019; Besten, 2006; Gordon, 2009; Kuper, 2007). However, for me, the term "Khoisan" is problematic. The term "Khoisan" was coined by Leonhard Schultz-Jena. He was a zoologist and racial scientist. This term was used in a biological sense. According to Gusinde (1953, p. 24):

> Leonhard Schultze had coined the term "Khoi-san" for the Bushman and Hottentot races. The older and more popular term to identify these races was "the yellow people." This refers to the light skin color which distinguishes the Bushmen and Hottentots from their neighbors, the Hererors and Bantu-negroes. Their yellow skin color and small stature were used as criteria for genetically grouping the Bushmen and Hottentots with the Pygmies of the tropical forest areas of central Africa.[8]

More problematic for me is that Schultze conducted his "research" during Namibia's infamous Nama, San, and Herero genocide. He even accompanied the German troops in their last flanking movement that led to the death of Hendrick Witbooi. He also accompanied "Hauptmann Ludwig von Estorff in his famous tracking expedition, which pursued fleeing Nama and their allies to Rietfontein in the southern Kalahari" (Gordon, 2009, p. 44). Thus, many of Schultze's "research subjects" were prisoners of war. According to Gordon (2009, p. 45):

> Schultze measured some ninety characteristics, including such arcana as breast circumference, while the genitalia of his twelve female subjects enjoyed special emphasis. Six people measured in southern Botswana (Lehututu or Letlake Pan), together with three Namib Bushmen, constituted the "Bushman" sample.

Schultz-Jena's notion of "Khoisan" combined erased two distinct pre-colonial societies into a single racial category." In addition, Schultze also assisted the infamous Dr Bofinger with experimenting on the Nama and Herero people in these death camps (Mellet, 2020, p. 36). Finally, Isaac Schapera much later adopted the "Khoisan" frame as the racial lens through which he looked at the Khoekhoe and San (Gordon, 2009; Kuper, 2007). Thus, for me, "Khoisan" erases. This term subjected the Khoekhoe and San people to an inferior racial position.

I must note that Adhikari (2014) and Abrahams (1994) use "Khoisan" positively. Adhikari (2014) shows that a "Khoisan" identity can be constructed if one considers that the Khoekhoe and San joined forces against colonial expansion into Khoekhoe and San territories. It was during the resistance and

---

[8]   The term is found in "Zur Kenntnis des körpers der Hottentotten und Buschmänner" (1928) by Leonhard Schultze.

later during the "apprenticeship" or indenture system (inboekstelsel) and at the missionary societies that the difference between Khoekhoe and San started to disappear. It was also on the farms and the missionary societies that they were later entered as "Coloured".

However, I cannot entirely agree with Abraham's deployment of "Khoisan" when suggesting, "We are of them but are not them" (Abrahams, 1994, p. 14). The conflation of Khoekhoe and San into one category obscures that the Khoekhoe was divided into various sub-groups. For example, there was the Nama, !Kora (Koranna people),[9] Griqua, Hessequa, etc. and some groups like the Nama and Griqua never lost their identity. Furthermore, in apartheid and post-apartheid South Africa, the Khoekhoe and the San do not see themselves as interrelated. For example, in Namaqualand, Bushmanland, and the Kalahari, the distinction between "Boesman", "Hotnot", and "Baster" is quite clear.

In addition, Abrahams (1994) argued that the Khoekhoe and the San were not separate groups and used the phrase "Khoisan". With her doctoral dissertation on Sarah Bartmann, Abrahams admitted that she found 'Khoisan' problematic and decided to use Khoekhoe instead (Abrahams, 2000). In both dissertations, Abrahams went to great lengths to show the fluidity of identity and the possibility of a universal Khoekhoe identity. Bam (2021, p. 150) shares the same sentiment as Abrahams. "Today, there is still an assumption that the San or Bushmen people are separate from the Khoi or 'Coloured'. Therefore, groups continue to internalise these racial binaries within themselves, even though they are identity frontiers created by colonialism and apartheid" (Bam, 2021, p. 150). Both Abrahams and Bam do not account for the differences in languages, culture, and religious practices between the Khoekhoe and San. They argue from the present when the "coloured" identity has already erased various identities. This is a conceptual mistake. If one considers the work of Hahn (both cite Hahn's work), then one would be aware that in the pre-colonial era, various languages distinguished between a group that was classified as San or "Boesman" and Khoekhoe or "Hottentot". Some of the languages and cultural practices still exist. They were not completely erased. Therefore, their historiographies do not account for these groups' language, religious, and cultural differences.

However, one can deploy Adhikari's (2014) and Abrahams' (1994) arguments to replace the "coloured" identity in South Africa. Still, there is a limitation to this argument. Before the *Population Registration Act in 1950*, people were

---

[9]   Hahn (1881) writes *!Kora* or *!Koras* when referring to the group.

still classified as Nama, Griqua, "Boesman", etc. Even though the Act of 1950 erased these classifications, these identities did not cease to exist. They resisted the classification and are still resisting the re-classification into "Khoisan." Therefore, I must point out that "Khoisan" also erases because it combines two distinct political, cultural, and religious societies.

Finally, there is a danger regarding substituting "Khoisan" for "Coloured". If we are not careful, "Khoisan" will potentially become the placeholder for the "coloured" identity with all its racial prejudice towards Black people in South Africa. Adhikari (2002, 2004) already pointed out this danger.

"Khoisan revivalism"

What appears to be a Khoisan resurgence or revivalism in academic discourse undermines the struggle and resistance of many Khoekhoe and San people. The Khoekhoe and the San were part of apartheid and colonial South African societies. Their identities, language, culture, and religious practices never ceased to exist. They were just bureaucratically erased. Hence, I do not share the views of Adhikari (2004), Barnabas and Miya (2019), Veracini & Verbuyst (2020), and Verbuyst (2022). For me, "Khoisan revivalism" is yet another frame born in the university that contributes to the erasure of the Khoekhoe and San people in South Africa (see Chapter 5 for a discussion on "Khoisan revivalism"). I cannot entirely agree with Adhikari that some "coloured" people tried "to re-invent a Khoisan ethnic identity" (2004, p. 170) after 1990. The Khoekhoe and San identity were always there; it was just located in the "Hottentot", "Boesman", Nama, Griqua, among others, identity constructs. Even though scholars ceased to use the "Hottentot" and "Bushman" categories, that did not mean the people ceased to exist in society. These racist constructs are still widely used in South Africa.

Since the Khoekhoe and San were bureaucratically erased by apartheid, they vanished from the collective consciousness of South African society. This contributed to the notion Bam (2021) encountered in Europe that they are extinct. Hence, the "resurgence" of Khoekhoe and San culture, religion, and languages must baffle many South Africans. Suddenly the Khoekhoe and San are in the media and speaking Afrikaans and English. They do not look like the archetypes that colonialism and apartheid imprinted on the consciousness of South African society. What people do not realise is that many descendants of the Khoekhoe and San "do not need to 'revive' the memory because they did not lose their culture and identity. Instead, they kept it alive under difficult and impossible circumstances" (Mellet, 2020, p. 19). Keeping their identity, culture, religion, and languages alive under impossible circumstances is what this book is about. For example, Chapter 4 highlights how they kept their culture and knowledge alive despite their oppression.

Methodology

I know of the firsthand rejection of academics when students in 2015 called for the decolonisation of the university in South Africa. From 2016 to 2020, I attended many seminars, conferences, and workshops that tried to grapple with what it means to decolonise the university. Consequently, I started writing this book during the FMF. In 2018, I also ran a reading group for student support staff to grapple with how we could decolonise student affairs in South Africa. I started the reading group because, at my university, the student affairs practitioners were left out of the conversation. Therefore, the students' call to "decolonise the university" heavily influences this book.

A decolonised methodology would give voice to the "voiceless", especially those who were and still are marginalised in the university. It will attempt to free those objectified through research and allow them to speak and be heard. However, for this to be possible, Tuhiwai Smith suggests that we constantly rework our understanding of the impact of imperialism and colonialism on those objectified through research. Tuhiwai Smith also suggests that we use a language of critique that demands an investigation into how we are colonised and what it means for our past, present, and future (Tuhiwai Smith, 2012, p. 25).

There is a need for the marginalised and objectified to tell and write our own stories, our versions in our own ways, for our own purposes. This approach is what Tuhiwai Smith (2012) calls "researching back" and "writing back". As the colonised, we have a right to tell our own version of colonisation. However, we also must use research methodologies that make sense to us. Research methodologies that would reverse the skewed power relations that exist between the university, the global north, and those objectified through research.

Tuhiwai Smith (2012, p. 20) observes, "Imperialism frames the indigenous experience". This observation is mainly true in written text and the media. However, my response to this observation would be: "It does not have to." We can write our own stories. But then again, a counter response could be, "The master's tools will never dismantle the master's house." In response, I would say: "It was not the master's tools in the first place." The tools were developed in Africa, the Middle East, India and China before they became the foundation of Western civilisation (Bernal, 1987; Diop, 2012; Du Bois, 2007). Therefore, "Decolonisation, however, does not mean and has not meant a total rejection of all theory or research or Western knowledge. Rather, it is about centring our concerns and world views and the coming to know and understand theory and research from our own perspectives and for our own purposes" (Tuhiwai Smith, 2012, p. 41).

Furthermore, I do not feel represented by the current body of work on the Khoekhoe, San, and "coloured" identities. According to Tuhiwai Smith (2012, p. 37), "So, reading and interpretation present problems when we do not see ourselves in the text. There are problems, too, when we do see ourselves but can barely recognise ourselves through the representation." The Khoekhoe and San cannot be reduced to "hunters-and-gatherers" or "pastoralists" in texts. These are frames that hurt. Many might say that I am represented. Yes, I know that many indigenous writers have written on some of the topics I am addressing in this book. However, that does not stop me from extending or challenging their work. If that is the expectation, I think it reinforces the power relationship between the university and those objectify through research. I think that would go against the decolonising effort.

But then again, the decolonisation effort is going against the grain and challenging the power relations in the university. Hence, decolonising the university is not in the interest of many stakeholders. Tuhiwai Smith (2012, p. 37) states, "Another problem is that academic writing is a form of selecting, arranging and presenting knowledge. It privileges sets of texts, views about the history of an idea, what issues count as significant; and, by uncritically engaging in the same process, we too can render indigenous writers invisible or unimportant while reinforcing the validity of other writers." If we are serious about decolonising higher education in South Africa, we cannot privilege some texts and views about the history of an idea over others, even if it means that marginalised writers have written those texts. We are then reinforcing the validity of some writers over others.

This brings me to the next point: writing brings forth violence; as Tuhiwai Smith puts it, writing can be dangerous. Tuhiwai Smith (2012, p. 37) states, "Writing can also be dangerous because we reinforce and maintain a style of discourse which is never innocent." Writing about the peoples of Africa was never in the interest of Africans. It was in the interest of the colonial power. Being part of the university, I am aware of my privileged position. I know that what I write yields extreme power, and if I get it wrong, it will be difficult to undo. So, how do the colonised or marginalised scholars write? I think the approach that would best suit my purposes with this book is the notion of "researching back" and "writing back".

Linda Tuhiwai Smith, in *Decolonizing Methodologies: Research and Indigenous Peoples,* explains that "research back" and "writing back" can be seen in the same tradition as "talking back". This is an attempt for the colonised and marginalised to recover themselves (Tuhiwai Smith, 2012). However, I am also aware of a proverb in my community, "'n Stil bek is 'n heel bek." This proverb can be translated as: it is better to keep quiet than say anything. This proverb gives one a glimpse of the psychological disposition in my community. Years of oppression taught them that it was best to keep quiet because those who spoke out were subjected to violence. Hence, it would be better for them to shut their mouths than to speak out against injustice. This sentiment can be expressed by another saying in my community "Jy kan nie terug praat teenoor die baas" (You cannot talk back to the *baas*). The history of this country shows us that whenever the colonised dared to speak out, they could lose their lives like Biko and many before him. Hence, I am aware that "researching back" and "writing back" are not without consequences.

However, not "researching back" and "writing back" also have consequences, which are transferred from one generation to the next. In a recent documentary, Bergsig, Christopher Tarentaal explains that "'n Stil bek is 'n heel bek" results in a traumatised life. It creates unbearable pain for young "coloured" people in Calitzdorp. This, in turn, leads them to life on the periphery of society. It is our responsibility as colonised and marginalised researchers to give voice to the voiceless in society.

Autoethnography

In this book, I combine discourse analysis with autoethnography. Adams et al. (2015, p. 1) state that with "autoethnography, we use our experience to engage ourselves, others, culture(s), politics, and social research." Central to autoethnography is the researcher's personal experiences and how the researcher and society intersect. Nevertheless, autoethnographic accounts must maintain methodological rigour even though they draw on emotion, the self and creativity (Adams et al., 2015, p. 1). Hence, in this book, I am balancing autoethnography with discourse analysis.

Furthermore, the "autoethnographic means sharing politicized, practical, and cultural stories that resonate with others and motivating these others to share theirs" (Adams & Jones, 2011, p. 111). Both my grandparents can be considered illiterate to Western standards of education. My great-grandmother passed away when my grandmother was still a little child. Because of that, she never saw the inside of a school. As a child, she was given to farmers to work for the family. Since she could not read and write, she kept every piece of paper because every written word was important to her. My grandfather spent a year at school before he, too, was given to the farmers to work for his family. The year in school allowed him to read basic sentences, and he could at least write his name and surname. My grandmother could not.

My grandmother always yearned to be able to read and write, but the household responsibilities never fully allowed her to give it her all. Over the years, she tried, but she could never fully commit because of her duty to her family. For this reason, I have dedicated this book to them in honour of their teaching. Their teaching and guidance allowed me to complete my education. My first education and my Western education many times do not see eye-to-eye. It is this contestation that the reader will experience in this book. I know my story is not exceptional, and many people of different backgrounds on the continent have similar stories to mine. Therefore, I hope this book will inspire many others to embed them in their research and "write back" and "research back". With this said, this book is not entirely an autoethnographic account. I draw on elements of autoethnography to share an insider's perspective on issues regarding the "coloured", Khoekhoe, and San identities.

There are several practices and purposes of autoethnography. Firstly, auto-ethnography offers "accounts of personal experience to complement, or fill gaps in, existing research" (Adams et al., 2017, p. 3). In this book, I am sharing my personal experience to fill the gaps that I come across regarding the Khoekhoe, San, and "coloured" identities in South Africa. I am also sharing my experience as a person whose ancestral identity was stripped of him and the pain and shame that come with reading how the university and research portray your community.

Secondly, autoethnography helps articulate insider knowledge (Adams et al., 2017, p. 3). I have insider knowledge as a person of Nama and Griqua descent raised and educated in the culture. I was also subjected to the "Coloured" identity and have resisted that classification for much of my life. Therefore, it is fair to say I have the insider's knowledge to provide a more nuanced understanding regarding the "Coloured," Khoekhoe and San identities.

Thirdly, autoethnography allows writing against other outside accounts that are harmful or lack the insider's understanding (Adams et al., 2017, p. 4). This is the practice of "writing back" and "researching back". Much of the earlier research on the "Coloured", Khoekhoe and San identities was written from an outsider's perspective. The situation has improved over the last 40 years, and many Khoekhoe, San, and "Coloured" researchers are "writing back". Their work forms a large part of this book. However, their work is not without limitations. In the same manner, this book would not be without limitations. The most significant limitation for me in engaging the works of these scholars is that it is written from urban and metropolitan perspectives. Sometimes, assertions such as "Khoisan revivalism" do not reflect the resistance of Khoekhoe and San people against the "Coloured" classification. Many people in the Kalahari, Bushmanland, and Namaqualand continued to live their Khoekhoe and San identities. Therefore, from an urban perspective, they might have experienced a revival since 1994, but in Kalahari, the Bushmanland, and Namaqualand, the Khoekhoe and San cultures and identities were alive. Since I grew up in Namaqualand, I am offering an insider's look at the community I grew up in.

Fourth, since autoethnography is about personal experiences, traditional research methods sometimes find it challenging to capture them (Adams et al., 2017, p. 4). In this book, I am drawing on my experience in the university, as a documentary filmmaker, and as a colonised and racialised person. I am sharing key moments in my life that profoundly shaped my thinking and interaction with the university and the "coloured" identity. It is for this reason that this book does not follow the classic or traditional structure of an academic text.

Finally, autoethnography creates "texts that are accessible to larger audiences, primarily audiences outside of academic setting" (Adams et al., 2017, p. 4). I wrote this book in a creative and easy-to-follow manner. I tried to keep the language simple to reach people outside the university. However, in a recent conversation with my *mikis* (aunt), she told me that I had to translate the book into Afrikaans so she could read it. When she said that, I realised that if I wanted to reach a large part of the people this book was meant for, I had to translate it into Afrikaans. Therefore, for me, accessibility goes hand in hand with accountability. They must be able to read the book and keep me accountable for what I am writing.

Discourse Analysis

I also used discourse analysis because much of this book deals with power. Hence, I used the Foucauldian approach to discourse analysis. A Foucauldian approach to discourse analysis consists of three dimensions.

> Firstly, the analysis of discourse entails historical inquiry, otherwise known as 'genealogy'. Secondly, analysis attends to mechanisms of power and offers a description of their functioning. And lastly, analysis is directed to subjectification – material/signifying practices in which subjects are made up (Arribas-Ayllon & Walkerdine, 2008, p. 91).

Regarding the first dimension, "Genealogy is gray, meticulous, and patiently documentary. It operates on a field of entangled and confused parchments, on documents that have been scratched over and recopied many times" (Foucault, 1977, p. 139). The scholarly works I have consulted in writing this book have been repeatedly scratched over and recopied. These works have been featured in many other scholarly works too. And yet, as Foucault suggests, I will not be the last.

Regarding the second dimension, this book gives attention to power. It will also use a Foucauldian approach to power. In *Discipline and Punish: The Birth of the Prison*, Michel Foucault argues that knowledge and power are always entangled. In *Discipline and Punish,* Foucault shows how knowledge and power converge to form disciplinary power. Hence, Foucault conceptualises power as discursive and dispersed (Cloete, 2019).

Regarding the third dimension, in *The Psychic Life of Power,* Butler reflected on Foucault's notion of subjection and subjectivation (subjectification). She extended this notion of power to the psyche of the subject. Butler argues that if power is discursive, it has a psychic life and continues to live in the psyche of the oppressed after the power source (the colonial power in its variants) is removed. In line with this argument, it is possible to argue that power (colonial) recognised itself when it returned in the form of neo-colonialism. This power maintains the boundaries of identities and informs the postcolonial subject's sense of belonging (Cloete, 2019). Through subjectivation (subjectification), Khoekhoe and San people became "Coloured." This process was particularly violent and stripped the Khoekhoe and San people of their humanity and sense of self-worth. They were taught to combat their self-image. Chapter 3 provides a detailed discussion of this.

Main Argument

Two central questions guide this book. First, how do we unmask structural violence in post-apartheid South Africa? Second, how did the Khoekhoe and San resist their erasure in South Africa? Let me explain how I will answer the first question.

To unmask the long history of structural violence in South Africa, I am drawing on Walter Benjamin's essay Critique of Violence to support my argument. In Critique of Violence, Benjamin argues that law is essentially violence. It is the law that institutes and preserves violence (Benjamin, 1996). Throughout this book, I am using a Benjaminian approach to violence, and this is complemented by the works of Frantz Fanon, Steve Biko, Michel Foucault, and Judith Butler. However, before the law can institutionalise and preserve violence through discourses. In the state, the law becomes the primary mechanism of subjection. Discourses thus inform the viewpoints in law. Hence, this book will give attention to colonial, apartheid and post-apartheid laws.

In addition, I am extending the work of Butler and Foucault regarding the discursive and psychic dimensions of power. I have developed the three limit-ations framework for this because three dimensions perpetuate structural violence in South Africa. Therefore, from a theoretical point of view, I will draw on the work of Benjamin, Fanon, Biko, Foucault, and Butler. Their works inform how I read laws, policies, and various texts. Moreover, from a practical point of view, I will use the three limitations approach. The three limitations approach in this book is the "how to" unmask structural violence in various disciplines in post-apartheid South Africa. In this book, I dedicated a chapter to a limitation to help answer this question: Chapter 3 – First Limitation (selectiveness of the frame), Chapter 4 – Second Limitation (subjectivity of the audience) and Chapter 5 – Third Limitation (invisibility of the researcher).

Firstly, in academia and research, discourses and disciplines select and frame the subject. And through this, research objectifies and masks the historical process of dehumanisation. Tuhiwai Smith (2012, p. 41) explains, "Research has not been neutral in its objectification of the Other. Objectification is a process of dehumanisation." In this book, I will show that the Khoekhoe and San people were objectified (framed) and systematically and bureaucratically erased.

In Chapter 2, I will show that structural violence in South Africa formally started in 1652 and was institutionalised over a long time. However, in Chapter 3, I will show that there is a much longer tradition to this violence, which scholars often ignore. This tradition can be located in the Spanish conquest of America.

Through the "civilising" discourse, various institutional apparatuses such as the state, religion, and the university constantly shaped and reshaped this violence. Colonial, apartheid, and post-apartheid laws institutionalised this violence to elevate some and subjugate and marginalise others. For example, in Chapter 3, I will show that colonial and apartheid laws attempted to subjugate and erase the Khoekhoe and San people in South Africa. They were trapped in a problematic "coloured" identity, making them strangers in South Africa. Post-apartheid laws did not help much because the problematic "Coloured" classification continued. Thus, the structural violence continues.

In addition, this book looks at the university in South Africa's contribution to the colonial and apartheid projects with specific reference to the attempted erasure of the Khoekhoe and San people. The book argues that the university is also responsible for framing and institutionalising colonial subject identities such as' "Hottentot", "Bushman," "'Khoikhoi", "San", and "Coloured". This framing led to their forceful inclusion in the "coloured" identity. As a result, a bureaucratic erasure occurred, and the state institutionalised this erasure.

Therefore, the university in South Africa is complicit in the violence against the Khoekhoe and San people in South Africa. During colonialism, universities collected and became the custodians of indigenous archival artefacts. They did not become the custodians of these artefacts ethically. It was taken by force. The artefacts contain the spirit and philosophy of indigenous people in South Africa. These artefacts and knowledge systems have become the property of certain South African universities. They appropriated the indigenous knowledge systems of the Khoekhoe and the San as their own.

Secondly, audiences are implicit in the violence. For example, early texts that form the bedrock of many discourses and disciplines are from the travel accounts of European explorers. According to Tuhiwai Smith (2012, pp. 8-9), the stories of travellers were generally the experiences and observations of white men whose interactions with indigenous "societies" or "people" were constructed around their own cultural views. It reflects the imperial power rather than an accurate account of indigenous people. Their tales also had wide coverage in the empire. For example, their "dissemination occurred through the popular press, from the pulpit, in travel brochures which advertised for immigrants, and through oral discourse. They appealed to the voyeur, the soldier, the romantic, the missionary, the crusader, the adventurer, the entrepreneur, the imperial public servant and the Enlightenment scholar" (Tuhiwai Smith, 2012, p. 9). In Chapters 2 and 3, I discuss several of these texts to show how the imperial audience was complicit and participated in the violence against indigenous people.

If I learned a lesson from the *Strike a Rock* incident, it would be this: not everyone is aware of the continuation of structural violence against black people in post-apartheid South Africa. In Chapters 4 and 5, I pay attention to this phenomenon. Here I draw on Fanon's work on the collective consciousness and collective unconsciousness. It seems as if society is unaware of this violence. It seems as if society and the state are in a trance. There were fleeting moments, such as during the #RhodesMustFall (RMF) and #FeesMustFall (FMF) protests, when people became conscious of the violence. Both RMF and FMF were national events that received national and international attention. At first, universities in South Africa invited some of the most progressive and prolific intellectuals to speak and advise on decolonising the university. However, as the protests continued for a second, third, and fourth year, FMF became "normal", we became unconscious again, and the violence persisted.

In Chapter 4, I will also show how a particular audience in South Africa appropriated a Khoekhoe traditional dance and made it a spectacle of its former self. This is a result of the collective unconsciousness. It is the collective unconsciousness that fuels the expectations and perceptions of audiences. This audience expects a particular way the dance must be performed to satisfy their expectations. This organisation and its audience are implicated in the violence of the Khoekhoe and San.

Thirdly, the invisibility of the researcher masks a power relationship rather than it is an attempt to be objective or neutral. The act of objectifying (framing) in itself is violence. Tuhiwai Smith argues that "Indigenous peoples have been, in many ways, oppressed by theory" (2012, p. 39). It is a theory that helps the researcher to objectify certain subjects. We cannot look past the interpretative nature of social sciences, and this brings its subjective nature to the fore. Thus, certain theories created a caricature and an archetypical Khoekhoe and San person or group. The Khoekhoe and San people are rarely liberated from this image because it is frozen in museums, textbooks, films, and disciplines.

In addition, universities have designed academic courses and disciplines around Khoekhoe and San's knowledge systems. Some universities in South Africa now presume a level of authority over these knowledge systems and present themselves as the custodian and vanguard of a people's way of living. This relationship is the same paternalistic attitude the colonial state had towards the Khoekhoe and the San. It masks the subliminal colonial power relationship the postcolonial university has over their knowledge. The postcolonial university is implicated and complicit in appropriating and reproducing Khoekhoe and San's knowledge to their benefit.

Hence, the invisibility of the researcher is only possible through institutional-isation. The university presents itself as an objective and impartial player in society. It is built on values of intellectual freedom and helps society progress to a more just and equal society. However, this is not the case, as FMF and RMF have shown us in recent years. In Chapter 5, I will show how the university is not objective in the structural violence against black students. On the contrary, they are implicit in the violence.

This brings me to the second question: How did the Khoekhoe and San resist their erasure in South Africa? The Khoekhoe and San resisted their erase since Van Riebeeck sat his feet on the shores of *||Hui !Gais*[10] They resisted their erasure in various spheres of colonial, apartheid and post-apartheid society. In Chapter 2, we will see that they openly went to war against colonial forces. We will also see in Chapter 3 that they resisted religious (Christian), social ("Bastard"), and state (Coloured) subject categories. In Chapter 4, we encounter their resistance in the cultural sphere – through the *|khâba ra*. Preserving the *|khâba ra* was possible because the oppressed subject resisted the oppressors' collective consciousness. Even though the oppressor class wanted to shape the oppressed to their will, they failed. Any person from the oppressed class knows what it is like to be in a constant state of resistance. One's whole outlook on life, being, and relationships are shaped by resistance. Finally, in Chapter 6, we discuss the Khoekhoe and San's resistance in post-apartheid South Africa.

Structure and Style

In the spirit of a decolonised text, this book does not follow the structure of a classic academic text. The book instead follows the narrative structure of a documentary film. Since documentary films are rarely scripted, a large part of the film's story structure comes together in the editing phase. During this phase, the filmmakers develop a story and most documentary films I have watched follow a three-act structure. Aristotle introduced the three-act story structure, which we have used for over 2300 years. The three-act structure has a beginning, middle, and end (Yanno, 2006). Act 1 introduces the reader to the protagonist and the antagonist. The protagonist wants something, and the antagonist stops them from achieving it. The antagonist can be a person or something. The story ends when the protagonist finally gets or does not get what they want (Allen, 2013).

---

[10]   *||Hui !Gais* means "veiled in clouds", and this was the name the Nama gave what we know today as Cape Town (Hahn, 1881, p. 34).

I can be viewed as the protagonist in this book, the university, the documentary film industry, and the South African state as the antagonists. The book is also divided into three acts. There are two chapters dedicated per act. The book starts in Chapter 1 with an inciting incident. This inciting incident is the screening of *Strike a Rock*. The screening eventually led to my quest. My quest in this book is to revisit some of the debates and literature that led to the inciting incident. It takes the reader on the road of rediscovering some of the debates in the distant past. In Chapter 4, the audience is hopeful that the protagonist will reach a satisfying resolution and will not end in a tragedy. However, Chapter 5 introduces a surprising twist. Since the debate on decolonization is only restricted to research and curriculum transformation with no attention given to the institution, it becomes clear to the protagonist that we will end in the same loop that sparked the protagonist's quest. Hence, Chapter 6 attempts to get us out of the ending and beginning loop. Thus, Chapter 6 is a continuation of Chapter 5 and tries to resolve the loop.

Outline of the Book

I am less interested in rewriting the history of the Khoekhoe and San. Instead, I am interested in the frame that created the Khoekhoe, San, and "coloured" identities. It is against this frame that I am writing. Some scholars would call this frame coloniality. I will simply refer to this European gaze as the frame. Hence, in Chapter 3, I identify the frame and show how the university is complicit in the violence against the Khoekhoe and San. Some scholars have a shorter historical gaze that forms their argument. I found many scholars over the 40 years starting at 1652 (Adhikari, 2002, 2004, 2014; Abrahams, 1994, 2000; Besten, 2006; Bredenkamp, 1980, 1981). They tend to speak of the arrival of the Khoekhoe and "Bantu-speaking" people in Southern Africa. Some also frame the Khoekhoe as "pastoralists" and the San as "hunters-and-gatherers". Some use the migration theory derived from Richard Elphick's *Khoikhoi and the founding of White South Africa*. This theory is primarily reconstructed using archaeology and linguistics.

However, there is a long tradition of European relations with the indigenous people of South Africa. One of the few accounts with a longer historical gaze is that of Patric Mellet's *The Lie of 1652: A decolonised history of land*. Mellet's work shows the complex pre-colonial encounters with Europeans at the Cape. Mellet (2020) has a historical gaze from millennia before 1652. Mellet starts with the evolution of *Homo sapiens* and *Homo sapiens sapiens* and systematically works his way to 1652, establishing an alternative migration theory. He also vividly illustrates what was happening at the Cape before the arrival of Van Riebeeck. He explains the impact of these European visitors on the Khoekhoe society and how the "ownership" of the port changed from indigenous to colonial powers with the arrival of Van Riebeeck. However, Mellet's gaze is towards the East. Mine is towards the West. Starting at the Valladolid Debate in Spain.

Chapter 2 is my diagnosis of the frame (problem). Hence, in Chapter 2, *Unmasking Colonial Epistemologies*, I revisit various colonial texts and archives and use rock art as a pre-colonial medium to critique the sites of colonial and postcolonial archives. I believe that the South African university is the most prominent postcolonial archival site maintained by colonial epistemologies. It is in these epistemologies that the so-called post-apartheid coloured subject is discursively produced. Hence, the section on rock art is about the European frame through which we encounter rock art. I am using the works of Lewis-Williams (1990), Parkington (2013), and Bleek and Lloyd as the frame through which one encounters rock art and its interpretation in Southern Africa. I offer an alternative view of rock art: to approach rock art as an archive. The critique in this chapter attempts to decolonise the postcolonial archive. This chapter also shows the reader what is at stake and why it is necessary to revisit some older texts.

In Chapter 3, *Erasing the Khoekhoe and the San,* I introduce and operationalise the first limitation: the selectiveness of the frame. Chapter 3 shows how the Khoekhoe and San were framed as "Hottentot", "Boesman", and "Coloured". This chapter is about how a frame was developed to erase and classify a group of people as "Coloured" with the help of universities and missionaries. In this chapter, I argue that the colonial university was complicit in creating and institutionalising the "uncivilised" frame. Many university disciplines adopted this framing of the Khoekhoe and San, which was embedded in the curriculum. The archive was built around this frame. Hence, it is difficult to dislodge this problematic frame. To dislodge it, one must engage the archive's guardians (academics, scholars and researchers). However, the guardians of the archive "do not only ensure the physical security of what is deposited and of the substrate. They are also accorded the hermeneutic right and competence. They have the power to interpret the archives" (Derrida, 1995, pp. 9-10). Clearly, institutional power, in its complex discursive nature, is vested in the postcolonial university. Many disciplines draw from this archive to construct various disciplines, such as Anthropology, Archaeology, History, Film, Television, and Media Studies.

The point I am making in Chapter 2, which I returned to in Chapter 5, is that the university in South Africa shapes a significant part of society. They framed and created subject categories later institutionalised in law (Chapter 3). However, the oppressed are not completely docile and are resisting their oppression. Sometimes, this resistance is not found in conventional spaces. The |khâba ra is a point in case.

In Chapter 4, *Resisting Coloured-ism*, I discuss the second limitation. The second limitation is the subjectivity of the audience. In this chapter, I turned to dance. For me, dance has the potential to show how this limitation operates. Since dance choreography is the written notation of dance moves and their meaning, in this sense, the |khâba ra can be considered an archive passed down generations that tell a story of a people. Therefore, Europe's quest to destroy Africa's past, present, and future was unsuccessful. Instead, the |khâba ra preserved the history of Khoekhoe and the San.

In Chapter 5, *Ending and Beginning*, I discuss the third limitation: the invisibility of the documentary filmmaker/researcher. In this chapter, I trace the long history of apartheid, from the plantations in the American South to a university such as the University of the Western Cape (UWC). After the bureaucratic erasure of the Khoekhoe and San with the Population Registration Act in 1950, UWC was destined to be a "coloured" university. The aim was to make them better servants in an apartheid society. However, this was not the destiny they chose.

I drew on the David Hlongwane statue at UWC titled "Ending and Beginning" in this chapter. This statue also inspired me to make a film about the institutional and subliminal nature of power in the university. Hence, the name of the documentary film is also *Ending and Beginning*. The film uses symbolism, music, photographs, and dance to connect the history and power relations in which the UWC was birthed. This film reveals the subliminal power relations between the university, people, and society. For example, the institution has control over how it is remembered. It deploys the archive to produce a particular institutional memory that masks the structural violence it reproduces.

In Chapter 6, I ponder whether there is a future beyond the "coloured" identity. This chapter is a continuation of Chapter 5, which tries to resolve the issues left unanswered in the previous chapter. Hence, I conclude with President Thabo Mbeki's speech, *I am an African*. His speech poetically recognises the genocide of Khoekhoe and San and yet fails to acknowledge their existence in post-apartheid South Africa. This final chapter examines the Khoekhoe and

San's struggle to gain recognition in post-apartheid South Africa. It looks at some of the gains made by the Khoekhoe and San against their classification as "Coloured". However, their struggle is far from over because there are still obstacles to overcome in the state and the university. Yet, the possibility of a future beyond the "coloured" identity does exist.

2

Hidden Away:
Unmasking Colonial
Epistemologies

While working on the documentary film project, "Wie se dans is dit?"[1] I decided to visit the "rieldans" group of Barrydale. I set up an interview for the documentary film with the group leader Oom Peter Takelo, in December 2018. During our interview, he kept talking about the Redfin Minnow. He was not much interested in the "rieldans". He explained that they annually have a giant puppet parade to raise awareness about certain topics, and this specific year it was about the Redfin Minnow. He explained that the Redfin Minnow is one of the oldest freshwater fishes and is on the brink of extinction. The biggest threat for the Redfin Minnow appears to be agriculture.

The next day I had another interview for the documentary film. This time it was with Lando Esau. He, too, was critical of the big agricultural projects along the Tradouw valley and their effects on the environment. He also spoke about the forced removals that took place in Barrydale. His family and many other families who lived in the valley were forcefully removed during apartheid. They had to make way for white people under the *Group Areas Act of 1950*. Lando Esau also spoke about the pain these forced removals caused his family, which they must relive daily. For Lando and Peter, the answer to dealing with this pain is to return to their traditional Khoekhoe roots, but this isn't easy because they do not have access to their ancestral land, where there is a cave full of rock art.

I returned in 2019 for their annual giant puppet parade. The day after the parade, two guides led me to the cave. Peter organised the guides. We drove to the hiking trail. We climbed through a fence and did a 20-minute hike to

---

[1]   "Wie se dans is dit?" translates to: Who can claim this dance? From my experiences in Barrydale and the Tradouw Valley, I changed it from "Wie se dans is dit?" to "Steek My Weg" (Hidden Away). Hence, the title of the chapter is inspired by the film.

the cave. We felt excitement and expectation as we hiked to the cave, but our voices immediately lowered once we entered the cave. It felt like we were walking on sacred ground. I did not expect the magnitude and beauty of the rock art in this cave, and this was not the first time I had visited a rock art site. The rock art at this particular cave told a story of the early inhabitants. How they lived and what they valued.

Unlike the previous rock art sites I have visited, the art in this cave covered the walls much more than the other sites I have visited. Some of the art was dispersed, and others were condensed. Some were well-preserved, and I could identify most of the figures. Others were not as well preserved as the others, and it was difficult to make out those figures painted on the cave wall. Some were painted next to each other, others on top and over each other. The painted figures also varied in size. Some figures were smaller, and others bigger. There were also abstract figures that I could not make out.

I realised that this site is an archive. The artists had to live in a specific cave for some time to draw a series of rock art. But, more importantly, the point of any archive is to preserve memory, and this site did just that. The people who lived in this cave over the ages wanted to preserve memory. There was a story they wanted us to find. The question it left me was: What memories were the artists trying to preserve? Are those paintings for someone? How were they able to preserve it for so long? After returning from the Barrydale rock art site, I realised a story in the Khoekhoe and San history is missing. From the scholarly work I have read on the Khoekhoe and San, they are presented without an archive and history. They are presented as "hunters and gatherers" and "pastoralists". The presupposition is that they are unable to preserve memory because they are "pre-historic." However, here is an example of an archive. Thus, if they have an archive, they have a philosophy. A philosophy the university was unable to understand.

The Interpretation of Southern African Rock Art

On my return, I turned to the works of John Parkington and J.D. Lewis-Williams to make sense of the Barrydale rock art. They, after all, are regarded as the "authorities" on rock art in Southern Africa. I started with the John Parkington book *Cederberg Rock Paintings*. The Parkington book is an excellent piece of research. His research can guide any scholar who wants to research rock art. Parkington, for example, discusses the location, the composition, the age, and the artists of rock art, and even though the book focuses on the Cederberg, this research was helpful to me in making sense of the Barrydale rock art.

Firstly, Parkington explains the location's suitability for preserving rock art. According to Parkington (2013, p. 27):

> The painters of the Cederberg images were very careful to select suitable canvases. They clearly preferred smooth, firm rock faces, more or less vertical, usually protected from the elements and with fairly pale white, cream, yellow or orange colouring so that paintings would stand out.

The Barrydale rock art is located in the same geological formation as the Cederberg, which is part of the Table Mountain Group (De Beer, 2002, p. 10). The Barrydale rock artists thus picked a similar canvas. Thus, rock art location was not by accident; it was carefully selected.

Secondly, what do the images represent? Parkington suggests that "we should start by acknowledging that much of the imagery is very literal: human and animals have recognisable and fairly faithfully represented morphologies: bags, bows, breasts, buttocks and baby rhino are depicted in ways that aid their identification" (2013, p. 8). Hence, we can identify some images and what they represent. One can identify from the Barrydale rock art humans, animals, and objects.

Thirdly, rock art also consists of composition. According to Parkington (2013, p. 55), "Isolated images are quite common, but most painted images are found in groups of juxtaposed or superimposed "compositions"." The composition of rock art allows one to construct narratives. One can also make sense of directions and the movements of the animals and humans in the art. In this sense, rock art images also appear to be animated. In addition, Barrydale rock art consists of various compositions quite different from the Cederberg ones, or at least the ones I saw. It is quite dynamic, but I will return to this later in this chapter.

Fourthly, based on archaeological evidence, one can estimate the age of San rock art. According to Parkington (2013, p. 25):

> Some of them, such as the colonial farmers with feathery hats, high heeled boots and hands on the hips, are less than two hundred years old; others such as the many handprints across the landscape may be 1000 or 1500 years old; but the bulk of the beautifully rendered eland, hartebeest and lines of dancing humans are probably at least 1500 years and, in many cases, twice or three times in age. Although it is possible that some of the images are as much as 10 000 years old.

I did not find figures of colonial farmers, elands, or hartebeests among the Barrydale rock art. Using the Parkington scale, I estimate that most of these paintings are older than 1000 years. Some of the art must be older than others. For example, one notices that newer images were drawn over older ones. The period between the paintings of the two images is not known.

Finally, one can ask who these artists were. For Lewis-Williams (1990) and Parkington (2013), it was the work of the San people. This conclusion is based on Bleek and Lloyd's research on rock art among the /Xam prisoners at Break Water Bay during the San genocide. Parkington states, "The rock paintings of the Cederberg, and elsewhere in Southern Africa, are often known informally as 'Bushman paintings'" (2013, p. 47). Since the Dutch colonists were the first to ascribe the terms "Bushman" or "Bosjesmans" to the San people, Parkington states, "When the groups of Quena and Europeans encountered people living in the isolated mountains of what would later become the Cederberg, people without cattle or sheep, the name Sonqua was suggested by the Quena" (2013, p. 47). Parkington (2013) assume that Sonqua translates to San. However, as I explained in Chapter 1, Sonqua could also mean *San(khoe)* or *Sa(n)!haos?* Based on Bleek and Lloyd's research and an assertion by the Quena that the Sonqua lived in the Cederberg Mountains, Parkington concludes that the San were the artists of the rock art found in the Cederberg.

The San could have been the artists of rock art. I am not disputing that. However, I want to caution against the neatly colonial and postcolonial separation of what constitutes Khoekhoe and what constitutes San. I believe that the San was a political organisation separate from the Khoekhoe. Still I disagree with Parkington's distinction between the Khoekhoe and San is based on "pastoralism" and "hunting-and-gathering".

In early colonial accounts, the San are always painted and described as murdering thieves without livestock. However, this is the metanarrative. In this narrative, Van Riebeeck appears to be the saviour of the Khoekhoe from the San. If one digs deeper, one finds that a complex and integrated pre-colonial society existed below the metanarrative. As the colony expanded, this integrated society continued to operate in the cracks of the institution (colonial authority).

There were various intergroup relations. For example, there were interrelations between the Khoekhoe, San, Tswana, Xhosa, 'Bastards', and white people. This integration is also apparent from Burchell's travel account, and the case of the Griqua state is an excellent example of this. For example, while Burchell travelled through the "Boschman's Land", he wrote about how his Khoekhoe assistants integrated with the various San communities. They live with the San in their homes, speaking a similar language. The clear colonial and postcolonial distinctions between the Khoekhoe and the San were not visible. Hence, as scholars, when we say the San were the artists of rock art in the Cederberg, we need to be open to who the San could have been.[2]

Another excellent book regarding rock art is that of J.D. Lewis-Williams. His book *Discovering Southern African Rock Art* is older than the Parkington book and is about the various ways rock art is analysed. His book discusses the three approaches to making sense of rock art. The first approach is the aesthetic approach. According to Lewis-Williams (1990, pp. 12-13), "From an aesthetic point of view, it is the depictions of animals that have attracted the most comment and praise." San rock art is indeed beautiful, and Barrydale rock art is no different because there are many details in the art. One is often forced closer because of the fine lines and delicate figures. When one looks closer the art reveals more information. One notices the artists' style and composition. One sees the combination of fine lines, and different colours that bring the art to life and gives it meaning.

The second approach is the narrative approach. According to Lewis-Williams (1990, p. 22), "It is, after all, reasonable to suppose that the sort of life they lived would find its way in some measure into their pictures." Parkington, for example, uses a narrative approach to make sense of the Cederberg rock art. Parkington identifies specific compositions and uses these compositions to construct a narrative. Applying this approach to Barrydale rock art allows one to identify several compositions and create several narratives. However, the concern of Lewis-Williams is that the narrative approach tends to essentialise San culture and knowledge systems for the sake of constructing a narrative.

The third approach is the interpretive approach. For Lewis-Williams, San, rock art is more than animals, hunting, and dancing. For him, the San also had a religion and much of the rock art depicts this. Given this, Lewis-Williams is critical of the first two approaches and believes that San rock art was mainly the work of shamans. For him, San rock art is mostly about trance dancing. He believes that trance dancing is a religious practice. Here, the therianthropic figure becomes the foremost image in analysing San rock art. However, like the narrative approach, the interpretive approach also essentialises the therianthropic figure to construct the shamanistic narrative.

Furthermore, the narrative and interpretive approach uses the Wilhelm Bleek and Lucy Lloyd archives to understand San rock art. Bleek and Lloyd recorded the stories of ||Kabbo, |Han‡kass'o, Dia!kwain and others. Bleek and Lloyd

[2]   I am aware of the Khoekhoe or "herder" rock art theory. However, I am uncomfortable using this theory because those who support that theory position the so-called "herder" rock art as less sophisticated than San rock art.

were also responsible for developing the orthography of the /Xam language. According to Lewis-Williams (1990, p. 46):

> It is, moreover, important to remember that /Han≠kass'o was familiar with rock paintings as well as engravings and told Lloyd a story in which he mentioned haematite and specularite as substances used in red and black respectively. He, therefore, had some first-hand experience with rock-art, but he nevertheless admitted that he could not explain all the features of the 'mermaid' painting.

However, he identified some of "the figures as shamans of the rain who were protecting people from, curiously, 'the rain's navel' that was threatening to kill them" (Lewis-Williams, 1990, p. 46). The shamans in this painting and others Lewis-Williams discusses are depicted as therianthropic figures. Amongst the Barrydale rock art, there are some therianthropic figures. Therefore, if one follows the explanation of Lewis-Williams, then some of the Barrydale rock art is the work of shamans.

Nonetheless, the works of Parkington and Lewis-Williams have limitations. Their works' limitations result from the Bleek and Lloyd archives. One of my central concerns about the Bleek and Lloyd archive is the translation and interpretation of the voices of the aboriginal other. Since /Xam was not the only San language, one has to consider the Bleek and Lloyd archive as an incomplete archive to translate all the cultural nuances of the San. The informants of Bleek and Lloyd have indicated this several times (Bank, 2006). The English language is also incapable of translating these cultural nuances. //Kabbo and others translated and taught Bleek and Lloyd the /Xam language. Bleek and Lloyd, in turn, developed the orthography and a written language of the /Xam language. This orthography allowed them to capture not only the stories of //Kabbo, /Han≠kass'o and Dia!kwain, but also of many others. The other stories, like that of //Kabbo, /Han≠kass'o and Dia!kwain, are also full of cultural metaphors. Some cultural metaphors are not universal and need specific local and sometimes historical context to be understood. Without this context, translating and interpreting the meaning is nearly impossible. Finally, Mellet (2020) stresses that the ethics of the collection of stories by Bleek and Lloyd is often overlooked. I agree with it, and I suggest we follow Bam's (2021) example and rename it to the "Dia!Kwain, /Han≠kass'o, //Kabbo, et al. archive" or the "/Xam, !Kun, !Kora (Korana), et al. archive".

Limitations to Interpreting San Rock Art in South Africa

Bleek and Lloyd were not the first to develop an orthography of the indigenous Khoekhoe and San languages. Apart from the /Xam, there are also the G/wi and !Gõ San languages. These languages were "members of the Khoisan linguistic family, which comprises the languages spoken by the Khoekhoe (Hottentots) and the San (Bushman)" (Lewis-Williams, 1990, p. 43).[3] Mellet (2020) stresses that there are, in total, 35 different "Khoisan" languages that were borrowed from one another to construct a particular language. During his travels in the interior of Southern Africa, William John Burchell developed an orthography for the now-extinct !Kora dialect (Burchell, 1822, pp. 253-255).[4]

Burchell was among the first British explorers to travel the Southern African interior. He documented his travels in a two-volume book, *Travels in the interior of Southern Africa*. These two volumes are ethnographic accounts of his time among the Khoekhoe, San, and Tswana people of South Africa. He published the book in 1822, ten years after completing his journey. Burchell arrived in Cape Town on 13 November 1810, and his journey started in 1811. This was 47 years before Wilhelm Bleek arrived in Cape Town. Bleek arrived on 10 November 1857 in Cape Town.[5]

At the time of Burchell's journey, the Cape Colony entered another phase in the expansion of the colonial frontier border, and the San and !Kora people were under immense pressure from various fronts.[6] It was during his journey that Burchell developed an orthography of the !Kora dialect. Burchell believed that the !Kora was a dialect of the Khoekhoe language, forming part of the

---

[3] Also, see A.J.B. Humphreys. (1981). Before Van Riebeeck – Some Thoughts on the Later Prehistorical Inhabitants of the South-Western Cape. *Kronos*, Vol. 4.1-9.

[4] There are mainly four clicks in the Khoekhoe language. These clicks are: (I) the dental click; (II) the lateral click; (!) the alveolar click; and (ǂ) palatal click. For an explanation of these clicks, please see W.H.G. Haacke. (2010). *Khoekhoegowab is veral die taal van die Damara, Haiǁom en Nama*. Macmillan Education Namibia Publishers (Pty) Ltd. Burchell wrote !Kora without the alveolar click. He wrote it as Kóra. However, Theophilus Hahn, who also later became the Grey Collection's custodian, wrote it as !Kora. Hahn, in his book, *Tsuni-ǁGoam. The Supreme Being of the Khoi-Khoi* mentions Burchell's orthography and several other orthographies. From these orthographies, he developed a more standardised orthography for the language of the Khoekhoe.

[5] See Burchell, W.J. (1822). *Travels in the interior of Southern Africa. Volume 1*. Hurst, Rees, Orme & Brown for Burchell's arrival date, and see Bank, A. (2006). *Bushmen in a Victorian World. The remarkable story of the Bleek-Lloyd Collection of Bushman folklore*. Double Storey Books, for Bleek's arrival date.

[6] For a detailed analysis of the South African frontier during Burchell travels, please see Martin Legassick, M.C. (2010). *The Politics of a South African Frontier: The Griqua, the Sotho-Tswana, and the Missionaries, 1780-1840*. John Meinert (PTY) Ltd.

"Hottentot languages" (Burchell, 1822, p. 251).[7] Burchell struggled to develop the !Kora orthography because of the interpretation and translation of the language to Dutch. His interpreter and teacher were Muchùnka. However, he later found out that Muchùnka could not explain some of the expressions of the !Kora language fully. Some words had more than one meaning, and sometimes the pronunciation of these words differed. It was only until much later that another interpreter, Gert assisted him "to rectify several of Muchùnka's interpretation" (Burchell, 1822, p. 398). Burchell believed that the mistakes of his interpreter arose "both from heedlessness and from an insufficient acquaintance with the Dutch" (ibid.). Burchell was English and learned to speak Dutch in Cape Town. Even though Dutch was the most common communication medium for most farmers, Khoekhoe, and San people, not everyone spoke Dutch. During his journey, Burchell had to use several interpreters who could speak various Khoekhoe, San, and Tswana languages.

Burchell's biggest challenge in developing the !Kora orthography was a triple translation. Muchùnka, whose first language was Setswana, had to translate !Kora to Setswana (for his comprehension) and then to Dutch for Burchell's comprehension. Burchell then had to translate it from Dutch to English. In this triple translation, cultural nuances and expressions were bound to get lost. Even though orthography is primarily about developing a spelling system for a language, language is more than just spelling. Words and phrases are full of metaphors, expressions, and cultural nuances, and not everyone can access them. Access was only granted to visitors or newcomers when they lived a significant time in a specific community. Gert was that person for Burchell. Gert lived at Klaarwater (later Griquatown) for a substantial period, where he "acquired some proficiency in the Kora dialect, which was facilitated by his own knowledge of the Hottentot language" (Burchell, ibid.).

Klaarwater was a town that consisted of missionaries from the London Mission Society (LMS) and various Khoekhoe and San groups. Initially, the population was small, but as the population in and around Klaarwater grew, it became a dynamic cultural intersection where people from various cultural backgrounds lived. For example, John Campbell, the director of the LMS, estimated that by 1813, there were 1266 Griqua and 1341 !Kora at Klaarwater (Legassick, 2010, p. 96).[8] Campbell notes that 291 Griqua men were Dutch, Khoekhoe,

---

[7]   Hahn (1881) was also convinced that !Kora was a dialect of the Khoekhoe language. He was convinced that the Namaqua, the !Koras and the Griqua were Khoekhoe tribes because they all spoke the same language. However, the language had regional differences. Hence, !Kora is considered a dialect of the Khoekhoe language.

[8]   Campbell's census was during the time of Burchell's journey.

Koranas, and San descendants (Legassick, 2010, p. 97).[9] Burchell observes that the Griquas at Klaarwater mostly spoke Dutch, and Gert, who was Griqua learned to speak the *!Kora* dialect at Klaarwater. He certainly was exposed to more cultural nuances than Muchùnka, who was not a resident of Klaarwater. Hence, Gert's ability to better interpret the *!Kora* dialect for Burchell.

Apart from the misinterpretation, Burchell needed help in translation. He could not understand the various Khoekhoe and San languages. He was lost whenever the San and the Khoekhoe conversed in different languages. However, his lack of understanding did not stop him from interpreting and translating their actions. For example, when he gave the Khoekhoe at Klaarwater tobacco, he interpreted it as being pleasantly received from their animated reactions. It is also clear that Burchell and the San could only understand each other with an interpreter, which led to miscommunication. Burchell mentioned that the San found it very difficult to speak Dutch. They only tried speaking Dutch to impress him to receive some tobacco. The irony is that Burchell, too, was not Dutch.

Moreover, one of Burchell's assistants, Ruiter, was used as an interpreter to communicate with the San. Burchell mentioned that only Ruiter was able to speak the language of the San. He only found out later that Ruiter could interpret the San language because Ruiter's mother was San and his father was Tswana. Amongst the Griqua, his name was *Ruiter*. Amongst the Tswana, he was *Makhowta,* and amongst the San, his name was *Arreé* (Burchell, 1822, p. 51). Arreé, thus, had a fluid identity. Burchell regarded him as Bachapin (Tswana). Still, amongst the San, he was San.[10] The cases of Gert and Ruiter show a complex integrated frontier society that was out of the reach of the colonial authority.

Apart from the Khoekhoe, San, and Tswana, the Griqua also provided refuge to many escaped colonial enslaved people and were incorporated into the Griqua society. According to Besten (2006, p. 29), "the political dimension of Griqua identity, that is, identification based on allegiance to a Griqua captain or membership of a Griqua polity, facilitated the accommodation of 'outsiders' as Griqua. Many who were not Griqua would have been incorporated first as Griqua-dependents and later as full members." Thus, runaway slaves were accepted in Khoekhoe society. Klaarwater (Griquatown) and among the Griqua were not the only instance of fluid identities. According to Besten, a "number of Xhosa (or Xhosa-speakers) were varyingly incorporated into the society of the

---

9   Koranas is also spelt as *!Koras* in Hahn (1881, p. 4).
10   Bachapin is a mispronunciation and spelling of Batlhaping. The Batlhaping is a Tswana tribe.

most westerly located Khoekhoe, notably the Gonaqua. Some Khoekhoe also became incorporated into Xhosa society" (2006, p. 19). From these instances and many others, it is clear that pre-colonial identities were fluid and were not crystalised in race, nationality, or culture.

Besides being "lost in translation", Burchell's interpretation was often subjective and from a superior racial point of view. Burchell's sense of racial superiority resulted in an empathetic response.

> I lost no time, but desired my people to give these poor creatures some meat. The Hottentots represented to me the uncertainty of our own resources, and that present stock of provisions was already so much reduced, that prudently nothing could be spared. But feelings of humanity and commiseration rendered it impossible for me to quit this spot without affording some relief to their necessities (Burchell, 1822, p. 38).

Burchell's benevolent response exemplifies a "civiliser's" interpretation of humanity. He projected a sense of pity or empathy onto the San people from his benevolent position. The group of San people did not ask Burchell for food. They asked him to kill a rhino, and this was because Burchell had a gun. However, he did not want to. So this particular instance is not about humanity but a civilising discourse.[11] After giving them some of his food, Burchell translated it as follows:

> Their grateful voices, raised with one second to express their feelings, still sound in my ear; and though their words were unintelligible, their looks bespoke their meaning and conveyed to the heart sensations the most delightful, and repaid a thousand times the trifling sacrifices we made (Burchell, ibid.).

However, later on, in Burchell's journey to repay him for the hospitality, Kaabi, the Chief of this group of San, presented Burchell with a skinned goat. Thus, Burchell's early patronising depiction of the San as loafers was incorrect. The San had a sense of dignity. Burchell's patronising depiction of the San is because he placed himself in a superior racial position. For example, Burchell refers to him several times in his book as the "Master" of his Khoekhoe assistants. Also, in 1812, the word "baas" was already used to elevate white colonists to a position of superiority over the Khoekhoe and San people. However, he translates "Baas" as "Master" (Burchell, 1822, p. 95), which lost all the nuances of racial superiority and class in the Cape Colony and the frontier.

---

[11]   To read more about this civilising discourse, read Cloete, J. (2019). *The Politics of Belonging and a Contest for Survival: Rethinking the Conflict in North and South Kivu in the Democratic Republic of the Congo.* PhD Dissertation. University of the Western Cape. Print. This also relates to my discussion regarding the 'white saviour complex" in Chapter 1.

Furthermore, whenever Burchell's Khoekhoe helpers wanted to conceal something from the San, they spoke Dutch. The reason the Khoekhoe spoke Dutch when they wanted to conceal something from the San appears that the San could understand the various Khoekhoe dialects. An example of this concealment is Speelman's remark about the San boy's appearance. He described the San boy who travelled with them in Dutch to Burchell and the other Khoekhoe men as "net zo mager; net zo lelyk (just as lean; just as ugly)." It left the boy in the dark (Burchell, 1822, p. 102). Hence, they spoke in the Khoekhoe dialects whenever they wanted to conceal something from Burchell.

Therefore, one must consider these shortcomings translating and interpreting the |Xam and !Kora languages. One must also consider these shortcomings in developing the |Xam and !Kora orthographies. Therefore, the over-reliance on the Bleek and Lloyd orthography, which only focuses on the |Xam, !Kung and !Kora languages misrepresented the complex San and Khoekhoe societies. In addition, the over-reliance on the |Xam language for interpreting San rock art presupposes that rock artists were only |Xam speaking San. Other San groups spoke many other languages and could have also been responsible for rock art.[12]

Furthermore, anyone can have an essentialist reading of San rock. Suppose one considers Burchell's two volumes an ethnographic account of the Khoekhoe and the San societies during the 1800s. In that case, an essentialist reading of rock art is possible. For example, Burchell described several incidents where the San danced at night to entertain themselves. During such occasions, the audience would sit in a circle, and one person would perform (Burchell, 1822, pp. 64-66). One can use this account to make inferences about the circles one sees in rock art relating to this event. Burchell also describes the methods and the preferred animals the San hunted. The hunters were distinguished from the rest in the San communities Burchell visited. Not all San men were hunters. The San also used bows and arrows for hunting, as well as for protection (Burchell, 1822, p. 61). A hunter wore a *Bekruip-muts* (a headgear) of a springbok skin to confuse the animals (Burchell, 1822, p. 56).

However, the San were not the only indigenous hunters, and they were not the only ones who knew the behaviour of animals. The Khoekhoe hunted like the San, and seemed to share a knowledge system of animal behaviour. Given this, one needs to be careful. An essentialist reading of rock art and relating the compositions of animals and hunting to only the San community would be

---

[12] See Mellet, P.T. (2020). *The lie of 1652: A decolonised history of land.* Tafelberg for a more complex understanding of the linguistic diversity in South Africa.

misleading. An analysis like that would disregard the complex integrated pre-colonial and frontier society. We can also argue that when there is a bow and arrow image in rock art, that specific composition is about hunting. However, this would ignore that the San also carried a bow and arrow for protection. One can also argue that not all the therianthropic figures were shamans. Some could have been hunters who wore a *Bekruip-muts* (a hunter's headgear). *Dia!kwain* pointed this out to Lloyd (Bank, 2006, p. 315). A San man or woman also wear a "karos" and "uyentje-zak" (Burchell, 1822, p. 57). A karos was an animal skin coat, and an *uyentje-zak* or *knap sak* was a carry bag. If one, therefore, looks at Burchell's sketch in the opening of Volume Two, the figures in the sketch look like the images in many rock art compositions. Thus, an essentialist reading of rock art would be problematic because the Khoekhoe, too, wore karosses and lived in huts. The Khoekhoe also arranged their huts in circles.

VIEW OF A BUSHMAN KRAAL

Figure 1   A sketch of a 'Bushman kraal' by William Burchell in 1812
            (Burchell, 1822, p. 198)

Burchell also mentioned that the San also has extensive knowledge of the behaviour and the spoors of animals. Most of their survival and existence depended on it. One may interpret the images of animals in rock art to have something to do with the San's drive to survive. In addition, Burchell also mentions that the San also owned goats, sheep, and cattle. For example, at Kaabi's kraal, Burchell found oxen, sheep, and many goats. Individuals owned the livestock. Some San also owned dogs (Burchell, 1822, p. 56). Given this, one may also interpret the images that appear to be livestock as that of the San. Clearly, the Khoekhoe were not the only ones who owned livestock. Thus, the idea that the San were only "hunters-and-gatherers" is problematic.

These limitations raise a question about how one must read rock art, especially if the limitation to the *Dia!Kwain, |Han#kass'o, ||Kabbo,* et al. archive is the orthography. From Burchell's ethnographic account, one risks essentialising the complex San and Khoekhoe societies. So how is one going to make sense of the Barrydale rock art? What is the meaning of these images on the walls of the cave in Barrydale?

Here I am departing from the conventional way of making sense of rock art. I am not interested in reading only the images because there is always a context to consider in making sense of it. Parkington and Lewis-Williams are ignoring the politics that these images provoke. Politics are absent from their reading of rock art. If one regards rock art sites as pre-colonial archives, it brings forth the political in the Derridean sense. It enters the debate around land dispossession, forced migrations, the appropriation of indigenous knowledge systems, and the violence that San experienced. The violence they experienced was not only from colonists but also from the Khoekhoe and later the "Bastaards" (Griqua). Therefore, my reading is less about what rock art is saying and more about the politics rock art is invoking.

Movement, Forced Migrations, and Land Dispossession

Movement, community, and livestock are central themes in the Barrydale rock art. However, I realised that they are outside the colonial framing of rock art. This opens several neglected topics in the analysis of rock art, including land dispossession, violence, race, and class. To help me rethink these topics, I would like to highlight the works of Abrahams (2000) and Ellis (2018).

Abrahams (2000) makes two salient points regarding rock art's interpretation and analysis. Firstly, rock art was meant for all future generations. According to Abrahams (2000, p. 18), "As far as is known, the Khoekhoe had time to study, paint, and chip away at rock for the sheer pleasure of it. Certainly, rock art was art for posterity. Mortality must have been of less concern to an African whose art would last for millennia." They wanted to leave a message that would last for thousands of years; hence, they were so particular in sites they chose to leave their message. In addition, "It may not have been the work of one artist, but a collective work, often stretching over generations as new detail was added over old" (Abrahams, 2000, p. 21). Rock art was clearly a generational conversation taking place. Therefore, future generations were free to add and erase as they pleased. It was passed down from generation to generation, as we shall see in Chapter 4, the same as the *|khâba ra* did.

Secondly, rock art offers a different reading of time. Abrahams (1994, p. 20) argues, "Rock art expressed the circularity in Khoekhoe thinking." If the time for the Khoekhoe was circular and not linear, it offered a productive way to think of the migration patterns of the Khoekhoe. The Khoekhoe and San migrated with the season and animals; thus, their migration patterns were circular. Time brings forth movement and migrations. This circular migration opens up a dynamic pre-colonial society.

Furthermore, Ellis recently offered another productive reading of rock art. He employs a cinematic reading that draws on the works of Henri Bergson, Gilles Deleuze, and Souleymane Bachir Diagne. According to Ellis (2018, p. 218), "The figures are almost always pregnant with possibility, the replete motion of action. There is the ever-present availability of these figures as bearers of meaning, the potential tale and even maybe a history." If rock art is full of motion and action, then rock art as a cinematic movement opens up new possibilities for analysing San rock art. It breaks the conventional mode of interpretation. If one thinks of "movement" in a Bergsonian and Deleuzean sense, it brings to the fore the movement-image and the movement-image brings forth "movement." "Movement" in the Bergsonian sense is a thought-provoking way of looking at rock art in Southern Africa. Most Barrydale rock art images are "moving" or symbolise "movement". This "movement" is not only directional but also about executing actions and tasks. Directional movement in the Barrydale rock art is dynamic. It is from left to right and from right to left.

Figure 2   Rock art figures that are executing actions and tasks

Figure 3   Directional movements of rock art figures

The art indicates a dynamic pre-colonial movement. This directional movement is not only of humans but also of animals (Figure 2). Rock art, therefore, gives one a sense of the dynamic nature of the movement of the San. They were not sedentary people. The San migrated with animals, which is clear from many rock art sites. This movement could have been with their livestock, or it could have been with the game. Many scholars interpret this movement as 'hunter-and-gatherer' or 'pastoralist' (Adhikari, 2014; Barnabas & Miya, 2019; Besten, 2006). For me, the 'hunter-and-gather' and 'pastoralist' frames are problematic since they contribute to erasure. Even though many of my colleagues use this frame, many go to great lengths to avoid these frames. For example, Mellet (2020) does not describe the San as "hunter-and-gatherers" and the Khoekhoe as "pastoralists" or "herders". Instead, he refers to a "hunter-gatherer" and "herder-pastoralist" culture and economic system.

Abrahams (1994), on the other hand, explains that the "hunter-and-gather" and "pastoralist" frames are the results of Elphick's migration theory. Abrahams (1994) believes there is too little evidence for this. Abrahams notes that Elphick based his theory of pastoralist migration on archaeological evidence. According to Abrahams (1994, p. 23.), "He [Elphick] then argued for a theory of conflict by deduction – pastoralism as an economic system must necessarily conflict with hunting and gathering. However, the archaeological evidence showed a technological diffusion, not an ethnic one." Abrahams (1994) argues that cattle and iron implements could have been spread through gifts and sharing. Abraham's argument compliments Mellet's theory of a "hunter-gatherer" and "herder-pastoralist" culture and economic system.

This classification of people ("hunter-gatherer" and "herder-pastoralist") resulted from taxonomy, which was born in the colonial power. These classifications are disputing the Khoekhoe and San's rights to land. "Hunters-and-gatherers" and "pastoralists" presuppose they did not have a sense of belonging to specific geographic areas and, therefore, did not have a right to these lands. From the first occupation of Van Riebeeck at the Cape, the Khoekhoe and the San made it clear that the land on which colonialists were settling was theirs. The Dutch permanent settlement led to many conflicts over land dispossession (Mellet, 2020).

Conflict over land dispossession is intertwined with the colonists' need for livestock. Both early Dutch colonists and the Khoekhoe valued livestock. For the Khoekhoe, livestock determined the wealth and status of their society. The colonists' survival at the Cape depended on livestock (Coetzee, 2000; Leftwich, 1976; Schoeman, 2006). Hence, at first, the Dutch East Indian Company depended on the Khoekhoe's continuous livestock supply. However, the reluctance of the Peninsula Khoekhoe groups to trade with Van Riebeeck forced him to formulate an alternative strategy. The Company decided to pursue a two-pronged strategy.

Van Riebeeck's planned to first establish a trading network with the Cochoqua, Chainouqua, and the Namaqua (Bredenkamp, 1981; Coetzee, 2000; Leftwich, 1976; Schoeman, 2006). From the works of Bredenkamp (1981), Leftwich (1976), Coetzee (2000) and Schoeman (2006), it seems the Cochoqua, Chainouqua, and the Hessequa were more prone than the Namaqua to trade with the Company. However, even though livestock trading took place, it was not significant enough to ensure the Company's survival at the Cape. Only after the first Khoekhoe-Dutch war was a permanent trading network between the Company and the Chainouqua established (Bredenkamp, 1981; Coetzee, 2000; Leftwich, 1976; Schoeman, 2006).

Before the war, the livestock numbers of the Company were quite low. According to Leftwich (1976, p. 275), "There was, for instance, a modest supply of about 130 cattle and 350 sheep in January 1653, which plummeted to a desperate low of 1 cow, 1 ox, 4 calves and 60 sheep in October 1653." So why was the company's livestock so low?

From Mellet's reading of the colonisation of the Cape, he explains the central leadership role Autshumao played in the Khoe-Dutch relations. Mellet also believes that Autshumao and Oedasoa deployed a containment strategy since Autshumao was exposed to Dutch and English slavery and colonialism in other parts of the world. Krotoa (Autshumao's niece) was instrumental in that strategy. The aim was to contain or keep the Dutch in the vicinity of Table Bay. Anticipating the devastating effects that slavery and colonialism would bring, the Khoekhoe at the Cape was pre-emptive in resisting Dutch colonialism.

The first was to negotiate a fair price for livestock trading. Since the Dutch were not interested in giving the Khoe a fair exchange for their livestock, Autshumao stepped in to urge the Khoe to up their prices. This was an attempt to demoralise the Dutch and give them second thoughts about permanently settling at the Cape (Mellet, 2020). Autshumao's interference greatly annoyed Van Riebeeck, and he saw Autshumao as a threat to their existence at the Cape. The second was to further weaken the Dutch by depleting their food supply. According to Mellet (2020), this led to the 20 October 1653, raid by Autshumao and the Goringhaiqua on the Dutch. Thus, the depleting food supply in Van Riebeeck's journal directly results from Autshumao and Oedasoa's containment policy. Knowing that the Dutch's existence depended on livestock, he devised a plan to get rid of Autshumao. According to Mellet (2020), Van Riebeeck initiated a different plan and collaborated with Nommoa (Doman). This situation also forced the Company to adopt another strategy: breed their own livestock. However, for that, they needed land.

On 21 February 1657, the Company released nine employees as *Free Burghers*. As Burghers, they were given farms in and around the Peninsula. However, these farms were the property of the Dutch East Indian Company (VOC). Mellet (2020) explains that the Dutch East Indian Company adhered to a communal feudal approach to "land ownership". In Europe at the time, private land ownership was emerging. However, that type of ownership was restricted to the feudal upper class or corporate ownership. Hence, land ownership remained with the VOC at the Cape and was leased to Free Burghers. Thus, the first Free Burghers had leasehold tenure on these "farms". However, the system later developed into the leningplaats (loan farm) leasehold system. The leningplaats system was based "on 'grazing licenses' that led to staking a claim, which was then translated into a leningplaats bond whereby the VOC benefitted from an annual 10% of farm produce as rental" (Mellet, 2020, p. 161). Individual freehold tenure was only introduced in 1814 by Governor Sir John Cradock.

Free Burghers only received these farms on the condition that they sell their produce directly to the Company. Cattle battery between the Khoekhoe and the Burghers was strictly forbidden. Instead, Burghers had to buy cattle from the Company (Coetzee, 2000; Leftwich, 1976). This historic moment marks the start of the systematic and often brutal dispossession of Khoekhoe and

San lands. The more Free Burghers attained livestock, the more they needed grazing lands. Since the Dutch demarcated and erected fences around these "farms", they limited the movement of the Khoekhoe and their livestock, and this led to the first Khoekhoe-Dutch war in 1659 (Coetzee, 2000; Schoeman, 2006).

The leading Khoekhoe figure in the war against the Company was Nommoa (Doman). From Mellet's reading of Van Riebeeck's Journal, the downfall of Autshumao and the rest of the Cape Peninsula Khoekhoe started when Nommoa entered the picture. Mellet (2020) points out that Nommoa was named by the Dutch "Doman" (translated to "simpleton") because they regarded him as a very simpleminded person. I believe this supposed "simplemindedness" could have been because Nommoa could not converse in Dutch as fluently as Autshumao and Krotoa. Mellet (2020) believes that Van Riebeeck sent him on a voyage to Batavia to develop the Dutch language and be employed when he returned from Batavia.

As I mentioned earlier, Van Riebeeck needed to get rid of Autshumao if the Dutch were to settle permanently. Thus, according to Mellet (2020), Van Riebeeck collaborated with Nommoa to betray Autshumo. To understand Nommoa's supposed betrayal, one needs an understanding of intra-Khoekhoe politics at the time. At the arrival of the Dutch Van Riebeeck, various groups were made up of the Cape Peninsula Khoekhoe.

The Cape Peninsula Khoekhoe group were made of the Cochoqua, Gorachouqua, Goringhaiqua, and Goringhaicona. Some scholars treat these various Khoekhoe groups as independent entities. I, however, see the Cape Peninsula Khoekhoe as an intra-Cochoqua system, and my argument is informed by my reading of Nienaber's *Khoekhoense stamname: 'n voorlopige verkenning*. Nienaber (1989) argues that Cape Peninsula Khoekhoe was related. If one follows the tribute system explained by Nienaber, the intra-Cochoqua system emerges.

Cochoqua [Leaders: Oedasoa & Gonnema] Oedasoa was married to Krotoa's Sister Namies	
Gorachouqua [Leader: Gogosoa]	
Goringhaiqua [Leader: Osingkhimma (the son of Gogosoa)] Nommoa (Doman) Krotoa's mom belong to this tribe.	
Goringhaicona Krotoa belong to this clan.	
ǁAmmaqua [Leader: Autshumao] Krotoa was the niece of Autshumao.	**Sonqua / Ubiqua**

Figure 4   This is my reconstruction of the available information from various texts

The leaders of the Cochoqua were Oedasoa and Gonnema. The leader of the Gorachouqua was Gogosoa, who paid tribute to the Cochoqua. Gogosoa's son Osingkhimma (Schacher) was the leader of the Goringhaiqua and paid tribute to Gorachouqua (Schoeman, 2006; Wilson, 1990). Mellet (2020, p. 96) argue that the Goringhaicona was made up of the *ǁAmmaqua* (Watermen), the Sonqua and the Ubiqua. Apparently, Goringhaicona translates to "our kin who left us."[13] From Mellet's reconstruction, it emerges that Autshumao was the leader of *ǁAmmaqua* (Watermen) and not the Sonqua (Strandlopers or beachcombers). From available texts, the Goringhaicona paid tribute, before the First Khoe-Dutch War, to the Cochoqua, Gorachouqua and the Goringhaiqua.

Mellet is of the view that the *ǁAmmaqua* was drifters. According to Mellet (2020, p. 108), "the Watermans (*ǁAmmaqua*), who were made up of Autshumao's entrepreneurial family and drifters and outcasts from all the social formations." I do not think the *ǁAmmaqua* were drifters or outcasts. If one follows the tribute system of the Cochoqua, as Nienaber (1989) explains, all the Peninsula

---

[13]   I have to note that Nienaber (1989) argues that the Sonqua was not part of the Goringhaicona. Nienaber also notes that certain texts use the Sonqua and the Ubiqua interchangeably.

Khoekhoe were related in some way or another. For example, Oedasoa was married to Krotoa's sister, Namies. Both Krotoa and Namies were the nieces of Autshumao. In addition, Gogosoa's son was the leader of the Goringhaiqua. Furthermore, families are rarely rejected in the Khoekhoe customs (Hahn, 1881). I believe that the bigger intra-Cocoqua system tasked the /Ammaqua (Goriginghaicona) with a different political role regarding the presence of Europeans on the shores of /Hui !Gais, especially since Autshumao had first-hand experience with the devastating effects of colonialism in the East. This political role became apparent with Krotoa's placement in the Van Riebeeck household. In addition, Mellet (2020) indicates that Autshumao found refuge among the Cochoqua near Saldanha Bay when he escaped Robben Island. This strengthens my theory that the /Ammaqua (Goringhaicona) was part of the Cochoqua. In addition, when the /Ammaqua were raided and the leaders were killed, many of the Gorachouqua and Goringhaiqua fled the Peninsula and took refuge among the Cochoqua (Mellet, 2020).

When the Dutch first arrived, the Khoekhoe did not expect them to settle permanently in the Cape. They never expected the Dutch to take over their land at the Cape. Hence, before the first Khoekhoe-Dutch war, there were no negotiations or treaties between the Khoekhoe, the San and the Dutch to build a fort at the Cape. Van Riebeeck, upon arrival and heavily armed, started building the fort. Since it was winter and most of the Cochoqua were away. Van Riebeeck succeeded in building the fort with significant resistance from Autshumao and the rest of the Khoekhoe at the Cape. Even though this resistance did not escalate into violence, Van Riebeeck used force to resettle Autshumao and the rest of the /Ammaqua. Van Riebeeck did this to secure the freshwater supply (Mellet, 2020). When the Cochoqua returned in the spring of 1652, Van Riebeeck was already settled in and had built a defence against any attacks from Khoekhoe groups.

Van Riebeeck developed an in-depth understanding of the Cape Peninsula Khoekhoe. Who their allies were and who were not. Ultimately, Van Riebeeck played the Khoekhoe groups against each other to gain the upper hand in political relations at the Cape (Mellet, 2020). For example, before the First Khoe-Dutch War, there was tension between Gogosoa and Autshumao. This largely stemmed from the Goringhaiqua's attack on Krotoa on a trip to her sister (Mellet, 2020; Schoeman, 2006). In addition, since Van Riebeeck's arrival and Autshumao's close relationship with the Cochoqua, he developed into a wealthy and respectable leader among the Khoekhoe. He was known to the Chariguriqua, Grigriqua, Chainouqua, and Namaqua. In stature, he was at the same level, if not more than Gogosoa. Van Riebeeck saw the tension between

Autshumao and Gogosoa and used it to his advantage. Nommoa, being part of the Goringhaiqua, led by Gogosoa's son Osingkhimma (Schacher), "collaborated" with Van Riebeeck to take Autshumao out.

During the slave escape saga in 1658, Nommoa assisted Van Riebeeck with the arrest of Autshumao. He insisted that Van Riebeeck arrest Autshumao because he suspected that Autshumao aided with the escape of the slaves at the Cape. Autshumao was invited to discuss the matter and was arrested for the shepherd's death in 1653 (Mellet, 2020, p. 150).

Did Nommoa, as Mellet (2020) suggests, work on behalf of Van Riebeeck and not the Goringhaiqua and the Gorachoqua? I believe that Nommoa acted in the interest of the Goringhaiqua and Gorachoqua. His negotiations with Van Riebeeck to release Osingkhimma and take Autshumao clearly indicates this. If he had acted in Van Riebeeck's or himself's interest, he could have consolidated power with Osingkhimma and Autshumao out of the way. If he had collaborated and acted in Van Riebeeck and his own interest, he would not have led the First Khoe-Dutch War the following year.

On Nommoa's voyage to the East, he had first-hand experience of the resistance against the Dutch's occupation of Batavia. Therefore, months after his return, the first Khoekhoe-Dutch war started. Three months into the war, Nommoa and two other Khoekhoe warriors were wounded in a battle. Nommoa managed to escape, but one of the warriors, Eykamma, was captured and brought to the fort for questioning. When asked why the Khoekhoe suddenly decided to wage war against the Company, Eykamma replied as follows:

Version 1: Olfertus Dapper

The reason for all their attacks, he continued, was nothing else than to revenge themselves for the harm and injustice done to them: since they not only were commanded to keep away from certain of their grazing grounds, which they had always possessed undisturbed and only allowed us at first to use as a refreshment station, but they also saw their lands divided out amongst us without their knowledge by the heads of the settlement, and boundaries put up within which they might not pasture. He asked finally what we would have done had the same thing happened to us. Moreover, he added, they observed how we were strengthening ourselves daily with fortifications and bulwarks, which according to their way of thinking could have no other object than to bring them and all that was there under our authority and domination (Dapper, 2011, p. 15).

Version 2: Schapera and Farrington 1933 translation

The prisoner, one of the Capemen, who could speak Dutch fairly well, having been asked there as on why they caused us this trouble, declared for no other reason than that they saw that we kept in possession the best lands, and grazed our cattle where theirs used to do so and that everywhere with houses and plantations we endeavoured to establish ourselves so permanently as if we intended never to leave again, but take permanent possession of this Cape land (which had belonged to them during all the centuries) for our sole use; yea! To such an extent that their cattle could not come and drink at the fresh water without going over the corn lands, which we did not like them to do (Van Riebeeck cited in Schapera & Farrington, 1933, p. 15).

Eykamma's response is quoted in several scholarly works, and some scholars debate the deviation between the Schapera and Farrington translated version from the Dapper version. A debate over the deviation in Eykamma's response obscures the fact that the first Khoekhoe-Dutch war was about land. This issue is evident in both versions.

After Nommoa's defeat in 1659, the colonialists strengthened their grip over the Peninsula, and the Dutch colonial expansion began. According to Schapera and Farrington Van Riebeeck said:

They pressed this point so hard that their lands should be evacuated by us, that we were finally compelled to say, that in consequence of the war made against us, they had completely forfeited their rights, and that we were not inclined to restore them, as the country had become the property of the Company by the sword and the rights of war (Schapera & Farrington, 1933, p. 17).

Van Riebeeck's line of reasoning suggests a never-ending cycle of violence. Van Riebeeck's interpretation of the outcome of the first Khoekhoe-Dutch war was that the Khoekhoe and those who later were dispossessed could only get their land back through violence. Violence sealed the contract, and only violence could break the contract. These words of Van Riebeeck are also a hint of his real intention. For example, in his journal, he contemplated seizing the Khoekhoe's cattle and enslaving them.

If one cannot get from them by friendly trading, why should one suffer their thieving without making any reprisal? This would only be necessary once: with 150 men, ten or twelve thousand cattle could be secured without danger of losing a single person. On the other hand many savages could be captured without a blow as they always come to us unarmed; they could then be sent to India as slaves (Van Riebeeck Journal I, p. 112, cited in Leftwich, 1976, pp. 268-269).

From a military point of view, he knew that the fight against the Khoekhoe and the San would never be fair. Van Riebeeck's intentions were always forcefully to seize the Khoekhoe's cattle and land. However, forceful land seizures were against the policy of the Directors of the Company. Hence, the first Khoekhoe-Dutch war was the excuse Van Riebeeck needed to establish a norm through which the Company could systematically seize the Khoekhoe's land. Notably, Van Riebeeck also refers to the Khoekhoe as "savages". To him, they were not humans.

After violently dispossessing the Gorachouqua, Goringhaiqua, and the Goringhaicona of their land in the Peninsula, the next step for the Dutch was to dispossess the Cochoqua, and this led to the second Khoekhoe-Dutch war in 1677. One saw another defeat of the Khoekhoe and another land grab. This time, the war was against the Cochoqua. The second Khoekhoe-Dutch war was a result of Dutch colonial expansion. To understand the outcome of the war, one has to consider the context in which it happened. The Dutch colonial expansion happened rapidly towards the East and was more difficult towards the North. The reason for a slower expansion to the North was the Namaqua's reluctance to trade with Dutch colonialists and the climate. The Namaqua also participated in many wars after the Second Khoe-Dutch War (see Mellet, 2020).

The expansion towards the East started from 1672 onwards. The Company armed and protected the Chainouqua against the Cochoqua. Since the Chainouqua traded with the Company, the Dutch also came to the aid of the Chainouqua in several instances. During these instances, the Cochoqua was raided by both the colonists and the Chainouqua. These raiding parties were aimed at impoverishing the Cochoqua. The Company also used *straf ekspedisies* (raiding parties) as a tactic during the second Khoekhoe-Dutch war to impoverish the Cochoqua. With the help of the Chainouqua, the Company could raid a large amount of livestock from the Cochoqua. The Cochoqua could not recover from this loss, and retreated further to the North. Ironically, the Chainouqua and the Hessequa were also, after the Cochoqua, systematically impoverished and driven off their lands. They, too, were forced to migrate northward. They found their refuge in the North amongst the Griqua, Little Namaqua, the Great Namaqua, the *!Kora* and the San (see Nienaber, 1989). According to Legassick (2010, p. 41):

> By the end of the century [1700], it was only the Khoi along the Orange, those generically known as Nama and Kora, many of whom had retracted before the advance of the colony frontier who could be said to have retained their economy and polity intact. Other fragmented Khoi groups sought refuge in less hospitable and less desirable areas, perhaps buttressing their claims to territory by the acquisition of a company "staff of office" for their Chief.

I have to note that the Khoekhoe and San did not "retracted before the advance of the colony frontier"; they were exterminated and driven off their lands (Adhikari, 2014; Van der Merwe, 1988). Some of them might have "retracted" in advance to escape the genocidal impulse of the colonists. Nienaber (1989) illustrates this forceful migration.[14]

However, a century later (1800), when Burchell reached the Khoekhoe and the San in the North, they were not in as good a position as before. During his travels, Burchell encountered a group of San who he thought were very poor. He was travelling to Graaff-Reinet, from Klaarwater (Griqua Town). According to Burchell (1822, p. 37), "Within these huts there was no property of any kind, except in one or two, a dirty furless skin, or the shell of an ostrich-egg. Never before had I beheld, or even imagined, so melancholy, so complete, a picture of *poverty*." Burchell interpreted the group of San he encountered lack of "property" as poverty. Given Burchell's interpretation of what constitutes "property", "property" becomes a critical vantage point through which one has to look at the land question in South Africa.

Did the Khoekhoe and the San see land as property? Yes. The Khoekhoe and San considered land property because they had a sense of belonging to the land they had occupied for centuries. According to Bredekamp (1980, pp. 9-10), land, water, and natural resources were inalienable common property. According to Khoekhoe's custom, land could be rented to a foreign group, but they had to pay tribute. Where the Khoekhoe and the San deviated from the European notion of land as "property" was that in European society, some land was considered to be "private property". Individuals, companies, and organisations could own property and erect borders and fences.

The colonial state played a critical role in developing this notion of private property. For example, the *Free Burgher* notion set off the vicious trek Boer phenomenon. Through this, the trek Boer could, on behalf of the Dutch East Indian Company, raid the Khoekhoe and San and seize their lands. In return, this seized land became the Company's property, leased back to the colonists. This particular phenomenon continuously expanded the colony, leading to "a series of 19 wars over 227 years lasting into the third decade of the 19th century against the Cape Khoe, Nama, San, Gqunukhwebe and Xhosa" (Mellet, 2020, p. 117).

---

[14] See, Van der Merwe, P.J. (2006). *Trek: Studies oor die Mobiliteit van die Pioniersbevolking aan die Kaap (1770-1842)*. African Sun Media for this practice.

As the *trek boere* migrated north and eastwards, the colonial state needed to extend its authority. District offices and magistrates were established where *trek boere* could access them. In this way, the colonial state could exercise its powers over its *Burghers* or Citizens.[15] New "farms" in the frontier zone had to be registered. If not, the colonial state could not intervene in land disputes. According to Bredekamp (1980), in contrast, there was no need to register land because it was communal and inalienable common property in the pre-colonial Khoekhoe and San societies.[16] In addition, Mellet argues that "traditional Khoe leaders on their own had no right to dictate to individuals regarding parting with land or livestock" (2020, p. 161). Therefore, the leaders could also not sell cattle to European powers on behalf of others.

More than a century and a half later, the San in the north still viewed the Cape Colony as their country. For example, the "Kraaikop" San "declared aloud, that I was the best man they had ever seen, for the boors, they said, never gave them either tobacco or meat, though they came into their country and killed their game" (Burchell, 1822, p. 86). The emphasis is on "their country" because it reveals the San's sense of belonging. Also, explorers like Burchell knew Europeans seized the Khoekhoe and San's land through force:

> I fear I must conclude that the present state of all the Hottentot race, is far less happy, far less peaceful, than it was before our discovery of the Cape of Good Hope. If *they* rob *us* of cattle, what is *that* crime to *ours!* Who has robbed so large a portion of these tribes, of their liberty and of the land of their fathers? If European policy requires our taking possession of the country, (and I do not dispute that policy,) let us in return, as the smallest boon, be kind to its aborigines; kind to men who may no longer thread the ground over which their forefathers have led their flocks; over which their ancestors were probably the first to imprint the human footstep (Burchell, 1822, p. 203).

---

[15] At first, only the Dutch in the colony had the title of Citizen (Burgher). This, however, changed with English colonialism. There was an incident where Burchell was summoned to see the acting magistrate. Even though the magistrate had considerable power in the colony, Burchell as a rights-bearing citizen (to the Crown), knew his rights and refused to go while he was sick (Burchell, 1822, pp. 134-135). His stance was respected, and they let him be. In this case, Burchell was subject to the British Crown, and it superseded colonial citizenship.

[16] There was no need for fences because of the Khoekhoe's ability to know their animals amongst those of their peers. For example, let us look at an incident Burchell encountered on his way to Graaff-Reinet. During his stay at Jan Bloem's kraal, one of the residents told Burchell that one of Burchell's oxen did not belong to Burchell and that he was the owner. This person explained that his ox had disappeared in Namaqualand seven years before Burchell's travels (Burchell, 1822, p. 8). This particular person at that time lived in Namaqualand, and the particular ox in question was his riding ox. Burchell was sceptical, but he was proved wrong because the previous owner informed Burchell that there was a mark he made inside the ox's nose, which proved to be the case. This amazed Burchell because the six oxen looked the same, all black.

Burchell believed that the land in the Cape Colony belonged to the Khoekhoe and the San and was aware of the injustice of colonisation. Colonisation impoverished and robbed the Khoekhoe and the San of their lands. Burchell considered colonisation the bigger crime if compared to cattle theft.

At the time of Burchell's journey, the San was raided and exterminated for apparently cattle theft. However, this was another excuse to seize more Khoekhoe and San lands. From Burchell's account, one can determine that farmers in the Colony intended to extend the colonial frontier zone and seize more San land. Several farmers questioned Burchell, for example, about the nature of the country of the San. According to Burchell (1822, p. 106), "... they began to put further questions merely to satisfy their curiosity respecting the nature of the country and the quantity of game beyond the borders." At the time, there was also a migration of Khoekhoe and slaves in the Colony to the north. For example, the *Hottentot Proclamation of 1809 (or the Hottentot Code)* forced the Khoekhoe to carry passes.[17] The *Hottentot Code* also established Hottentot Reserves for the Khoekhoe, and they had to carry a pass if they left the Reserve or visited or conducted business in or outside the Colony. They were also conscripted into the Hottentot Korps and participated in the genocide against the San (Legassick, 2010). Thus, as the Colonial border expanded, the Khoekhoe, without a pass, was trapped in the Colony. Those imprisoned for petty crimes had to stay there until their "masters" or "owners" claimed them (Burchell, 1822, pp. 158-159).

Civilisation, Colonial Class Attitudes, and Taxonomy

Europeans arriving, settling, travelling, and interacting with the Khoekhoe and the San believed that the Khoekhoe and the San were still mainly in an "uncivilised" state of human existence.[18] They held this belief because the Khoekhoe and the San societies did not mirror European customs and philosophies. According to Legassick (2010, p. 78), "civilisation" at the time "was broadly understood, implied the acceptance and practice of the customs and institutions of European, and specifically, British, society. It included the Protestant virtues of industry, regularity, thrift and cleanliness no less than the wearing of European clothes, the building of European-style houses, secure and square." "Civilisation" took various forms, and for the Khoekhoe and the San, it meant they had to be landless servants of colonialists.

---

[17]   The *Hottentot Proclamation of 1809* is also known as the *Hottentot Code of 1809.*
[18]   I will deal with the 'civilising' and 'civilisation' discourse in the next chapter.

Servitude started with Dutch colonialism, as they systematically impoverished the Khoekhoe. Colonialists seized the lands of the Khoekhoe and the San, and those who had not "retracted before the advance of the colonial frontier" were forced into servitude. However, British colonialism and the *Hottentot Proclamation of 1809* formalised servitude. The proclamation aimed to address the labour shortage in the Colony that was created by the abolishment of slavery in the British Empire. This law strengthened colonists authority over the Khoekhoe (Legassick, 2010, p. 81).

The Khoekhoe and San were forced to convert to Christianity. Conversion to Christianity promised the Khoekhoe in the Colony a move up the "civilisation ladder", and it also "opened the way to full incorporation in the Colony society" (Legassick, 2010, p. 91). Baptised and converted Khoekhoe received petty privileges in the Colony, including land ownership and the right to trade. As a result, they were regarded and treated as superior to the unbaptised Khoekhoe. However, the Khoekhoe who were more prone to religious conversion were of mix-descent (Legassick, 2010; Schoeman, 2006). According to Legassick (2010, p. 87), "The Bastards families, with their 'charter' of colonial descent, their guns, their horses, and in some cases wagons, regarded themselves as 'swarthy Hollanders'."[19] Burchell also observed this class difference during his travels in the interior:

> This meat [Zebra] though much eaten by Hottentots, is, as already noticed, rejected by the colonists; my two *baptised men*, therefore, informed me, that they were unable to it; as they declared that it always created a nausea, I suffered a sheep to be killed, as we had no other game to give them. I thus soon began to perceive, that I had with me, two men who were of a class superior to Hottentots (Burchell, 1822b, p. 238).

The Khoekhoe who converted to Christianity had to let go of their cultural practices and customs. Once converted, they regarded themselves superior to other Khoekhoe and the San. Colonists, colonial officials, and travellers also treated them that way. Burchell, for example, paid the baptised "mixed-Khoekhoe" who could read and write a full salary, whereas the unbaptised and not of mix-descent received only half (Burchell, 1822b, p. 155).

Present in the civilisation discourse were the naturalists' classifications of the world. Here, the European university played a central role in the taxonomical classification of plants, animals, humans, and things in Africa. This natural classification of South Africa and its people started as early as the first

---

[19] Burchell mentions that "Most of the mixed – Hottentots [mixed-Khoekhoe], in whom there is any Dutch blood, deriving it from the father, but very seldom from the mother" (Burchell, 1822, p. 155).

settlement at the Cape. Olfertus Dapper, in 1668, published *Naukeurige Beschrijvinge der Afrikaensche Gewesten* (Description of Africa). At a considerable length, this book deals with the topography, zoology, and ethnography of the whole continent and "was long regarded as one of the most authoritative accounts of Africa" (Schapera & Farrington, 2011, p. 1). A section titled "Kaffrarie of Lant der Kaffers, anders Hottentots Genaemt" follows a detailed description of the various Khoekhoe groups of Southern Africa.

However, George McCall Theal believes that George Frederick Wreede might have helped Dapper. Wreede was a runaway German student who joined the Dutch East Indian Company and came to the Cape in 1659 (Schapera & Farrington, 2011). Wreede devoted him to the study of the Khoekhoe and their language. He went as far as to develop an orthography of the Khoekhoe language. Presumably, the dialect that was spoken around the Cape Peninsula. Since it does not appear that Dapper ever travelled to the Cape and spent a significant time among the Khoekhoe, he most likely was in contact with Wreede to help him with the documentation of the Khoekhoe for his book. Dapper's attitude towards the Khoekhoe was one of belonging to a superior culture, and he wrote from that point of view. For Dapper, the Khoekhoe were "kafirs" and "savages."[20]

> The country or land of Kaffraria, or, according to Marmol, Quefrerie is so named after the Kafirs, its native inhabitants. They are commonly known to our countrymen as Hottentoos or Hottentots, because their language is so clumsy and difficult; and they live without any laws or religion (Dapper, 2011, p. 7).[21]

> Like other savages, they do not know how to prepare or dress their food, but fall on the dead beast like dogs, eating it raw, and seldom cooked, with entrails and guts as well, first however, pressing out the excrement backwards or squeezing it out with the teeth (Dapper, 2011, p. 57).

From Dapper's texts, "civilisation" was marked by religion and culture. If one's religion did mirror the "civiliser's", one was considered a "kafir", a heathen or non-believer. If one preferred eating raw food, one was regarded as "savage". I have to note that Khoekhoe had a religion, and they had laws. Hahn (1881), for example, deals in depth with the Khoekhoe religion. Dapper's observations in this text are racist and ill-informed.

---

[20] In South Africa, the word 'kafir' is very offensive. It was first used to describe the Khoekhoe. However, later, it was solely used as a derogatory term to subjugate Black people in South Africa.

[21] Dapper is referencing Luis del Marmol Caravajal. Marmol, for many years, lived in Northern Africa, where he learned to speak Arabic. It must have been here that he encountered the word 'kafir', which is an Arabic description of 'heathens' in Africa.

It is also clear that many Dutch colonialists also named and renamed the people, things, and animals. The Khoekhoe became "Hottentot," the San became "Bosjeman", and Krotoa became "Eva".[22] The exercise of naming and renaming is a demonstration of power, which continued as the Colony expanded. Hence, farmers also named and renamed the environment. For example, the mountain close to Jacob Van Wyk's farm was called "Groote Tafelberg" (Burchell, 1822b, p. 105). The Khoekhoe referred to the Orange River as the *Kai !Gariep*, and in the Colony, it was renamed the "Groote Rivier" (Burchell, 1822b, p. 114).[23] Interestingly *Kai !Gariep* means Great River or Groote Rivier. "Kai" means "Great", and *!Gariep* means "River" (Nienaber, 1989).

The institution that benefited the most from this classification of things, people, and animals was the colonial power. By the 1800s, the depictions of the Khoekhoe and San did not change much. Europe believed Africa was primarily still in an 'uncivilised state' and needed "civilisation." For Europe, this was a vastly "undiscovered continent" and provided the opportunity, through taxonomical classifications (languages, people, animals, plants, rocks), to show the evolution of "Man." This evolutionary scale made Europe "civilised" and Africa "uncivilised." It demonstrated Europe's "superiority" and Africa's "inferiority". It showed Africa's need for "civilisation" and Europe's need for paternalistic assistance. Taxonomical classification proved, and incorrectly so, that race is biological.

With these pretences, travellers like Burchell travelled to South Africa to document its people, animals, and insects. Before and after him, many Europeans saw the San as "savages" and were very adamant about explaining this 'savage life' in their books. Burchell deemed it his duty to civilise his "fellow-creatures" (Burchell, 1822b, p. 37). For example, "it was extremely interesting, because it gave an opportunity of observing *man in an uncivilised state*, and enabled me to distinguish some of those characters which may be regarded as common to all the human race" (Burchell, 1822b, p. 54). Burchell was specifically interested in the morphology of the San and how this deviated from that of Europeans. Hence, he encouraged the readers of his book to study the skeleton of the San because he noticed some form of deformity. He believed this was an innate deformity that, to a certain degree, proved the views of some European scholars (Burchell, 1822b, p. 60). Where they would

[22] I am aware of the debate around the word 'Hottentot.' Some scholars believe it to be an intra-Khoekhoe description of themselves, and others believe it to be a description the Dutch attributed to how the language of the Khoekhoe sounded to the Dutch. However, I must stress that this word subjugated the Khoekhoe people, and is very offensive.

[23] Burchell, in his book, writes it interchangeably as "Kygariep" (*Kai !Gariep* or Great River) and "Nugariep" (*≠Nu !Gariep* or Black River) (Nienaber & Raper, 1980; Haacke, 1999, p. 124).

find these skeletons, Burchell did not mention. However, after Burchell's travels, there was a racist scientific explosion, and the human remains of victims of the genocide ended up in European universities and museums (see Skotnes, 1996).

As a botanist and a scholar, Burchell had a great interest in the work of Carl Linnaeus. Linnaeus is regarded as the father of modern taxonomy. Burchell used Linnaeus' work as a guiding framework to name and rename the places, objects, animals, and insects in the South African interior. For example, some places Burchell travelled to and passed through had distinct indigenous names, but he sometimes disregarded them and renamed them. Other times, he neglected to write the indigenous name down in the renaming process. For example, Burchell mentioned that names were often "… distinguished by the natives, with a name correspondent import in their language, but which in our hurry, I neglected writing down" (Burchell, 1822b, p. 27). In cases like these, Burchell just renamed them. For example:

Example 1

The newly-discovered river, which we had hitherto wronged by the name of the 'Brackish river,' seemed as if kindly resolved to keep us Company and lend us its friendly assistance during the journey … (Burchell, 1822b, p. 28).

Example 2

We did not discover any fish in these waters; but observed a very pretty and new *species of frog* of a green color … (Burchell, 1822b, p. 32).

Example 3

A number of very small finches, (*Loxia Astrild*) frequented the bushes at this place, and I took advantage of the circumstances, to distinguish it by the name of *Astrild Station*. This little bird is not peculiar to Southern Africa; it is very common at St. Helena, and is said to be equally so at Madeira and the Canary Islands, in the tropical countries of Africa, and in India. It is known to the Dutch colonists by the appellation of *Rood-bekje* (Red-beak) (Burchell, 1822b, p. 41).

Example 4

Here we saw, with much pleasure, several herds of *kannas* (or elands) and quakkas grazing at a distance and appearing not much to heed the presence of our party (Burchell, 1822b, p. 42).

Example 5

The Hartebeest of the Cape Colony, called *Caama* (or *Kaama*) by the Hottentots, was considered by Linnaeus and many naturalists, to be same as the Bubalis of the ancients, which is an animal of Northern Africa (Burchell, 1822b, pp. 80-81).

Burchell classified the frog mentioned in Example 2 as *Rana Fasciata*. Example 3 sees the first colonialists versus the second colonialists' classification. In the fourth example, one sees the renaming of the *Kanna* to Eland and the *Kaama* to Hartebeest in the fifth. This naming and renaming formed part of the erasure.

The journals, maps, sketches, and classification of travellers like William Burchell and John Campbell informed the European university, which in turn informed a racial attitude towards the Khoekhoe and the San. For example, both Wilhelm Bleek and Theophilus Hahn received doctoral degrees based on the collections of travellers and missionaries who, for some time, lived amongst the Khoekhoe and San. In the works of Bleek and Hahn, the Khoekhoe and the San were regarded as subhuman or in a pre-human and pre-civilisation phase.[24] Thus, before Charles Darwin, John Buchan, and Bertford Mitford was the work of William Burchell. He not only held these racist ideas but also attempted to document and theorise them. For example, Burchell wrote: "One of the old Bushwomen was so characteristic a specimen of her nation at that age, that I made her sit for her portrait ... She scarcely, indeed, looked like a human being" (1822b, p. 195).

About 50 years after the published works of Burchell, the Anthropological Society of London was established. The same year, 1871, Charles Darwin published his book *The Descent of Man,* which argued that "man is descended from a hairy quadruped, furnished with a tail and pointed ears." Darwin believed that the ancestors of human beings are simian and based this theory on natural and sexual selection (Sloan, 2019). Therefore, by the time Bertram Mitford in 1891 wrote the "Bushman was no more than half ape, a descendant of the baboons" and John Buchan in 1909 wrote that the San was "one of the lowest created types" the racist views that the first colonialists held got progressively worst. It went from "savage" and "kafir" to "one of the lowest created types" and "half ape, a descendant of the baboons".

In Africa, the colonial university was born from these racist depictions of the Aboriginal other (Mamdani, 2019). The central function of the colonial university and its European counterparts was the renaming, reclassification, and erasing of indigenous names of things, places, insects, and animals. For example, the European university played a central role in the Herero and Nama genocide in Namibia. It provided the methodology and technology that was used in the genocide. Members of the European university had a close relationship with

---

[24] See Bank, A. (2006). *Bushmen in a Victorian World. The remarkable story of the Bleek-Lloyd Collection of Bushman folklore.* Double Storey Books for Bleek's racist views of the San. Also see Hahn, T. (1881). *Tsuni-//goam. The Supreme Being of the Khoi-Khoi.* Trübner & Co. for his racist views of the Khoekhoe and the San.

the *génocidaires* in Namibia. For example, German universities requested some of the skulls of the Nama and the Herero killed in the genocide (Olusoga & Erichsen, 2010). The reason for their request was to further the studies on race. Here, taxonomy informs, institutionalises, preserves, and reveals race. Thus, it erases the Aboriginal other.[25]

This racial attitude towards the Khoekhoe and the San contributed to a colonial class attitude. From Burchell's account, a class attitude among the English and the Dutch, between various Khoekhoe groups and between various Khoekhoe and San groups, was visible. For example, the farmers did not extend hospitality like the Khoekhoe and the San towards Burchell. On the other hand, the Khoekhoe and the San received Burchell in a friendly and hospital manner. For example, "A few of its inhabitants advanced to greet us as we rode by, and one or two of the men acknowledged us as old acquaintances, having met us before when we were hunting hippopotami on the banks of the Kygariep" (Burchell, 1822b, p. 6).

However, some farmers did not receive Burchell in the same manner. For example, Burchell was not welcome at Jacob Van Wyk's farm. He greeted Jacob and his wife, but they did not greet him (Burchell, 1822b, p. 106). Burchell's assistants explained to him that this was because he was English. Burchell believed that the English were better at enforcing the Dutch colonial laws:

> In various parts of the colony may be found men who, without any love for a Dutch government, hate that of the English, because it has enforced their own colonial laws, and put a check upon those persons who would rather live without any law at all (Burchell, 1822b, p. 107).

However, Burchell could not see that he elevated himself as an Englishman above the farmers. As an Englishman, he saw him as better, as "civilised", and in a different class than the Dutch farmers. For example, he condescendingly called them "boors" and described them "as wild and senseless" (Burchell, 1822b, p. 104). He also described the appearance of the colonist women as "fair" and that both the men and women had "a very ill-shaped and projecting nose" (Burchell, 1822b, p. 105). However, not all of the farmers' attitude was the same. They were different. Some were more hospital and friendly than others. For example, the people of *Krieger's Fontein* welcomed Burchell and his companion. However, they had to sleep in some outhouses and were not welcome into the main house.

---

[25]   I will speak more about this erasure, in the next chapter.

Some farmers were also wealthier than others. Some owned slaves, and some did not. Nevertheless, on all these farms were some Khoekhoe and San people in service of the farmer. The servant class that Burchell encountered in the 1800s was mainly Khoekhoe and San. For example, Burchell wrote: "Among the boors, the demand for Hottentot labor on their farms is everywhere so pressing, that all my search and inquiries for men, ended unsuccessfully" (Burchell, 1822b, p. 149). This labour shortage was clearly after the *Hottentot Proclamation of 1809*. Some Khoekhoe were also conscripted to military service and participated in the colonial wars against the Khoekhoe and Xhosa. They were "achter ryers" and carried rifles (Burchell, 1822b, p. 132).

However, these racial and class attitudes did not stop the trading system between Europeans, the Khoekhoe and the San groups. The trade of livestock, tobacco, guns, brandy, furs, gunpowder, and ivory continued between these parties. The value of these goods had different subjective values. Looking back from the present, the transactions between the Khoekhoe, the San, and the Europeans might seem ridiculous if one considers them in terms of commercial value and the technological advances of that era. However, the Khoekhoe, the San, and the Europeans traded rare things in their respective communities, thus of great value to them. Therefore, one cannot look at it as literal value or even think of this exchange as a kind of "backward" exchange. Instead, one must consider this exchange in the proper context of that era. Things that are rare in any society are of more value. For example, some "Kraaikop" San worked in the Colony for farmers as shepherds to earn a few sheepskins for karosses. These karosses were "more valued, on account of their greater warmth, than the skins of any of the wild animals, and nearly every person here wore cloaks of that kind" (Burchell, 1822b, p. 86).

After spending time with the San, Burchell realised that Europeans' judgment of the San was wrong or "perverted", as he put it. As mentioned before, Burchell had a superior racial attitude towards the San. He saw the San as "uncivilised" and his God-given duty to "civilise" them. However, his sentiments changed the more he spent with the Khoekhoe and San. Burchell, later on, reflected that these "features would not indeed, according to the judgement of a European, be thought of a prepossessing cast; but the judgement and prejudices, as that of the Bushman" (Burchell, 1822b, p. 101). Something he hoped to overcome through his travels. When he ceased to think and opened to feeling and being moved by the aesthetics of the San, he started to feel at home amongst the San. "... I sat as if the hut had been my home, and felt in the midst of this horde as though I had been one of them; for some few moments, ceasing to think of sciences of Europe, and forgetting that I was a lonely stranger in a land of wild untutored men" (Burchell, 1822b, p. 67). From Burchell's reflection, it seems European science informed his initial beliefs and was the problem.

Violence against the Khoekhoe and San

The colonial violence against the Khoekhoe and the San was fuelled by fear. Their taxonomical classifications as a sub-human race made extermination easier. Colonial violence was both structural, personal, and psychological. Explicit forms of violence, among others, included the killing, raiding, flogging, and imprisoning of the Khoekhoe and the San (Adhikari, 2014; Burchell, 1822; Heese, 1994; Legassick, 2010; Skotnes, 1996). During the 1700s and the 1800s, the commandos were primarily responsible for the violence against the Khoekhoe and the San. According to Van der Merwe (1988, p. 25), in 1715, the first Burgher commando was established to recover the livestock the San stole. However, by 1774, these commandos aimed not to recover stolen livestock but to wage war against the San (Van der Merwe, 1988, p. 28). Adhikari (2014, p. 39) explains that in 1676, a commando was organised against the Cochoqua. That was a year before the Second Khoe-Dutch War. The commando, therefore, was institutionalised early to aid with the dispossession of the Khoekhoe. Adhikari (2014) explains that they were initially organised by the VOC and comprised Company soldiers, servants, and colonists. However, from 1715, these commandos became district-bound and consisted of farmers, "Bastards," and Khoekhoe (Adhikari, 2014; Besten, 2006; Legassick, 2010; Van der Merwe, 1988).

Furthermore, many commando leaders occupied high-profile positions in the Colony, resulting in unregulated violence. For example, Jacob Cloete was a commando leader appointed as a Magistrate. This conflation of power saw the commandos operating with impunity, and people in the Colony revered them (Legassick, 2010; Van der Merwe, 1988). However, Burchell describes them as a militia:

> This *militia*, or *commando*, consists of boors drawn from the different districts of the Colony, by the immediate requisition of their proper *veldcornets*, who, on such occasions, call out the inhabitants, not by lot, but by routine. The men so called out, repair to the rendevouz, generally mounted on horseback and armed with a musket of their own; and most frequently attended by one of their Hottentot servants. They wear no uniform, but are divided into squadrons, under the command of a *veldcommandant*, who is also a boor, nominated by the government, and who at all times retains that title, and with it, a rank superior to that of *veldcornet*. This militia is never called into service, but in cases of necessity; and if the duty should

appear likely to continue for a considerable length of time, as in the present case, they are allowed, after serving a certain period, to return to their homes; and are replaced by other called out by the same authorities. (Burchell, 1822b, pp. 119-120).

In the commando, the veld cornet played an important role. According to Legassick (2010, p. 45), apart from its military function, "the veldkorporaal [veld cornet] could exercise a measure of judicial authority in setting local disputes over land, etc." The judicial role is important in understanding the unregulated violence towards the San because the veld cornet was not a government-appointed position, but it was kin-based and a member of the local farm community (Legassick, 2010, p. 45). Hence, any land dispute would always favour the white colonist.[26] Thus, the veld cornet played a critical role in expanding the colonial frontier. In short, the commando system was an extension of the Company and provided a "cheap form of frontier defence" (Adhikari, 2014, p. 41).

Moreover, cattle and livestock raiding was a constant in the Dutch colonial expansion, and the Commandoes and the Veldcornets supported it. According to Adhikari (2014, p. 43), commando raids were usually conducted with exterminatory intent. For example, San men were executed on the spot while many women and, especially children, were taken captive. However, women and children were also often massacred. Children's heads were smashed on rocks, and women's breasts were skinned to make tobacco pouches (Adhikari, 2014, p. 46). Burchell, during his journey, firsthand experienced the brutality of the commandoes. He mentioned that the violence could have been justified in some cases, but, there was no justification in most cases. On the other hand, the San said they only stole cattle because of the past injustices against them (Burchell, 1822b). It seemed as if the San yearned for retributive justice.

There were also intermediary raiding partners for the white colonists; some were the "Bastards", and others were white people who fled the Colony to escape criminal prosecution. In addition, the helpers of these white raiding parties were indigenous (Adhikari, 2014; Legassick, 2010;). An example of this type of relationship is that of Klaas Afrikaner and Pieter Pienaar. Afrikaner and Pienaar were part of the commandos that killed over 600 San in 1792 (Legassick, 2010, p. 70). It seems that the Khoekhoe's participation in these commandoes was not voluntary. They were the servants of farmers and were regarded as *achter ryers*. In many instances, the families of the indigenous participating in the genocide against the San families were held hostage, and they were forced into participating in the genocide (Abrahams, 2000).

---

[26] Also, read G. Tylden, 'The Development of the Commando System in South Africa, 1715-1922,' *Africana Notes and News*, XII, December 1959, 8, 303-313.

The outcome of this expansion was the impoverishment of the Khoekhoe and the San people. The Colony drove them further and further from the Cape and off their original inhabited lands. This was a forced migration; through these forced migrations, the colonists could seize the Khoekhoe and the San lands (Burchell, 1822b; Coetzee, 2000; Legassick, 2010; Van der Merwe, 1988). As the colonial government evolved, several laws were passed to justify the violence against the Khoekhoe and the San. For example, the *Hottentot Proclamation* was passed in 1809 after the British colonial occupation of the Cape Colony. This proclamation introduced a pass system for the Khoekhoe people in the Cape colony. It also established reserves and permanent places of residence for the Khoekhoe.

In 1812, the *Apprentice of Servants Proclamation* was passed, and that legislation further forced the Khoekhoe into "serfdom". It was through this proclamation that farmers were able to bond Khoekhoe children to serve them under the guise of apprenticeship.[27] This practice became the preferred way for farmers to obtain cheap labour before and after abolishing slavery in the Colony (Legassick, 2010, pp. 65-66, cites Burchell's Travels Vol I, pp. 258, 352). However, Burchell distinguished between the "slaves" and the Khoekhoe on the colonists' farms (Burchell, 1822b). It appears that the Khoekhoe bound to servitude were treated better than slaves in the Colony. They, unlike slaves, were not regarded as property and yet were treated like property.

Even though they were not regarded as property, one can make the following distinction. Many farmers "seized" young San and Khoekhoe children and forced them to work on their farms. For example, Burchell writes of a white colonist, Jacob Van Wyk, who seized San boys and detained them to work for him (Burchell, 1822b, p. 108). The best phrase I came across to describe the consciousness of the coloniser is "Makgemaak vir bewoning", which means "tamed for occupation" (Coetzee, 2000, p. 13). Thus, the San who rendered their services to the 'boors' needed to be "tamed" to serve colonists unconditionally. For example:

> She told me that *Oud Baas* had tied her up to one of the wheels of the waggon and flogged her for a long time. The other women all joined in the tale, and two or three at once were showing me the position in which she was tied, first imitating the act of *flogging*, and then that of crying and supplicating for mercy: but she implored in vain, for no mercy was in his heart, till he had vented his rage (Burchell, 1822b, p. 95).

---

[27] See Wayne Dooling, 2005, "The origins and aftermath of the Cape Colony's 'Hottentot Code' of 1809". *Kronos*, 31(1).

It is also clear that under colonialism and apartheid, only white children were children. Khoekhoe and San children did not have rights and were considered part of the labour force. If they dared resist this labour exploitation, they were labelled lazy and treated as a threat to the survival of the apartheid and colonial state.

Burchell was also told that this particular colonist did not hand the San the tobacco but threw it on the ground "as if they had been dogs". For Burchell, this remark by this group of San needed not to go without notice, so he documented it. He documented it because he could sense their indignity. The same farmer also seized one of the San women's sons. He refused to let them return to their kraal with the rest of the group (Burchell, 1822b, p. 108):

> Another of the Bushwomen complained that this *baas* had compelled her son to remain in his service against his wish; nor could they by any means obtain leave for him to return with them to their kraal. Whatever might have been the stipulated wages for these people's services, they certainly carried away with them none of the rewards of their labor, unless a cap of scarlet cloth, and a pair of old cloth trousers, are to be considered as such, or the sheep skins which the women wore over their shoulders and which were probably given to them by their kind-hearted *baas*" (Burchell, 1822b, p. 96).

However, not only the San experienced this kind of violence. The Khoekhoe was subjected to the same violence. Burchell shares the story of Juli. Juli was a Khoekhoe of mixed origin and travelled with Burchell. Juli told Burchell that after his father died, his mother looked for refuge in the Colony, but "a brutal colonist who resided on the river which runs through that tract, seized her children, they nearly grown up and strong enough to be made useful on his farm, and drove her away from the place as she herself appeared too old to render him much service by her labor" (Burchell, 1822b, p. 161). Since his mother kept coming back for them, the farmer later killed his mom, and Juli and his sister were registered in the veld cornet's books to serve him for 25 years. Juli later escaped.

The Khoekhoe and the San did not want to work on the farms. From Burchell's account, it is clear that many of them stayed on the farms against their will. For example, the Khoekhoe man Burchell spoke to on the Viljoen farm wanted to go "to a land where there were no boors" (Burchell, 1822b, p. 179). After several of these testimonies and what he witnessed, Burchell later had to admit that he could not defend the violence against the Khoekhoe and the San (Burchell, ibid.). Since the Khoekhoe were not citizens, there was no justice for them. There were no laws that protected them against violence. The *Hottentot Proclamation* and the *Apprentice Servants Proclamation* made them the recipients of unregulated violence or the subject of violence.

It is clear that the violence against the San was unwarranted. There are many accounts in which Burchell explains about the San robbing the colonists of their livestock. He, however, had to admit that this was done "in retaliation of past injuries" (Burchell, 1822b, p. 112). One sees that cattle theft started very early during the Dutch colonial settlement. The Khoekhoe and the San's primary weapon in warfare was cattle theft. They were not much in favour of killing people (Schoeman, 2006, p. 100). An example is the struggle between the Chainouqua captains Dorhá and Koopman and the Ubiqua. Dorhá and Koopman did not like each other much, which led to a protracted power struggle. Bredekamp believed this resulted from the Company's preference to trade with Dorhá. As a result, Koopman regularly raided the cattle of Dorhá. The Ubiqua, too, occasionally attacked and raided the cattle of Dorhá and his supporters (Bredekamp, 1981).

I am of the view that the main reason for cattle theft was to impoverish their enemy. It was a strategy during the first Khoekhoe-Dutch war, and it seemed common practice amongst the Khoekhoe and the San groups. The San also used this strategy to stop colonists from encroaching on their lands as they were pushed more towards the *Kai !Gariep*, and into the lands of the Namaqua, *!Koras* and the Tswana cattle and livestock theft against the colonists intensified. As a result, the San was boxed in with nowhere to go. I believe cattle and livestock theft was a strategy to impoverish the colonists. Cattle theft during colonial times was thus an attempt to regain control over their lands. However, colonists retaliated by raiding and killing the San.

Burchell realised this injustice and reflected on it in his book. He spent close to nine months with the Khoekhoe and San, and his reflection also came after Piet Vermeulen's wife was surprised that he escaped alive going through "Bushman country". He realised that there was an unwarranted fear towards the San. This fear resulted in a hostility that Burchell was sceptical of ever being resolved. According to Burchell (1822b, p. 112), "the recollection of injustice on both sides, still operates to produce an international enmity which nothing but great forbearance and good sense can ever convert into mutual confidence." The explicit violent acts only stopped after the decimation of the Khoekhoe and San.

Irrational fear fuelled the violence. According to Burchell, the "tribes who inhabit the banks of the Nugariep, or Groote river, as they called it, were considered so extremely savage, that the boors had never yet been able to bring about any friendly communications with them" (1822b, p. 126). The image that this fear created was that the San was "the most ferocious of savages" (Burchell, 1822b, p. 36), which to Burchell's surprise was not the case. According to Burchell (1822b, p. 50), "our reception by these natives, who had been represented to us formidable savages, proved so truly friendly and so different from that which, I confess, I had myself expected ..." It was this irrational fear by colonists in the Colony that led to the extermination of the San.

This fear in the Colony led to anticipatory violence from the "savage Other". For example, the colonial farmers feared Burchell and his men when they entered the Colony. It was reported that Burchell and "three hundred of the Klaarwater Hottentots ... were marching to attack the colony" (Burchell, 1822b, p. 97). They were reported to the Veld Cornet, who visited them. However, Burchell was an Englishman, they had to follow colonial procedure. Therefore, Burchell was not harassed or attacked by the District Commando.

Burchell's and later Thompson's travels proved this was an irrational fear. For example, in the letter the missionaries wrote to the magistrate in Graaff-Reinet, they mentioned that they were not expecting Burchell to make it through the San territory. In addition, the people in the Colony believed that outside the Colony, there was a land of man-eaters (Burchell, 1822b, p. 159). The Khoekhoe, who travelled with Burchell, considered it "a tale invented for the purpose of frightening" people in the Colony. Thus, the Colonial power possibly used fear to control the migration and the interaction of white people with the Khoekhoe and the San. This manipulation of fear led to anticipatory violence against the San and the Khoekhoe. Whether the San and the Khoekhoe outside the Colony had the same fear is unclear. However, the Khoekhoe, who lived in the Colony, was also afraid of the San. Burchell initially also anticipated violence from the San because he made sure he "cast an additional store of bullets, that we might be prudently prepared against any attack from the inhabitants of the country through which we were about to pass ..." (Burchell, 1822b, p. 4). However, his views changed the more time he spent in the Bushmanland.

Conservation and the Tradouw Redfin Minnow

In his return from the interior, Burchell took a different route. He travelled to Graaff-Reinet and from there to Knysna. After spending significant time in Knysna and George, Burchell took what today is known, as the Garden Route back to Cape Town. On his way to Cape Town, he stopped over at Swellendam. There he stayed for three weeks. This was the beginning of 1815. It must have been during this stayover that Burchell 'discovered' the *Pseudobarbus burchelli,* commonly known as the Tradouw Redfin Minnow or Burchell's Redfin (Buchanan, 2015, pp. 16 & 293). The now critically endangered Redfin Minnow was named after William Burchell. It is also a reminder of the "civilising" mission of colonial power. It is also a reminder that taxonomy erased most of the indigenous knowledge before Dutch and British colonialism.

This fish bearing the name of William Burchell was there before any humans roamed the plains, valleys, and mountains of South Africa. In 1985 it was reported that "negative human influences have led to a drastic decline in numbers of this medium size minnow, especially agricultural demand on the water resource and the introduction of exotic predatory fish" (Cambray & Stuart, 1985, p. 155). A 2013 conservation brochure of Cape Nature indicated that the Barrydale Redfin is listed as Critically Endangered, primarily because of minimal natural water distribution (Cape Nature, 2013). In a 2016 study, it was found that "the town's water extraction point is above the upper limit of this taxon's current distribution. Complete water abstraction has left much of the upper Huis [River] completely dry, with the exception of a few isolated pools below the waterfall" (Jordaan et al., 2016, n.p).

When farmers want to store water, they need a permit from the Regional Office of the Department of Water Affairs and Sanitation. However, farmers can only store up to 80 000 m³/year. For this, they need a licence. The licence also permits altering river beds and banks (SABI, n.d). The altering of the river bed and the construction of dams and storage units on the Huis and the Tradouw Rivers destroyed the habitat of the Barrydale Redfin Minnow (Cape Nature, 2013). Both Peter Takelo and Lando Esau explained that the excessive pumping along the Huis River is causing the decline of the Redfin Minnow in the Huis River and the Tradouw River. Takelo and Esau were also critical of the relationship between government officials and farmers. They believe the Government is not taking the conservation of the Redfin Minnow seriously. Instead, they believe that the government is favouring agriculture.

The Khoekhoe community of Barrydale might have a case. The favouritism for agriculture is a result of colonialism. According to Gewalf, Spierenburg and Wels (2019, p. 3), "Contemporary southern Africa was established through the extensive and relentless exploitation of both people and animals in the interests of capital, on the basis of a morality that appeared to be divinely sanctioned, and was enforced through brute force of arms." Colonialism and permanent settlement (farming) destroyed the environment. For example, from the Burchell account, Piet Vermeulen had about 4 thousand sheep and Jacob Van Wyk six thousand. It is true that the Khoekhoe had similar amounts of livestock before the dispossession. However, the difference between the Khoekhoe and the colonists is that they did not permanently settle on a piece of land. Instead, they move their sheep to different grazing regions annually. The vegetation thus had enough time to recover on an annual basis. The amount of damage that sedentary animals caused the environment during colonial times is now unimaginable. Sheep and cattle farming also resulted in the systematic killing of wildlife to provide more pasturing lands. Those who settled also killed jackals and other carnivores to protect their sheep.

The Khoekhoe and San preserved the environment for thousands of years before colonialism. They knew they could not erect permanent fences because it would kill the veld. Hence, they adopted a more fluid notion of land ownership. It was colonialism, with its permanent fences and settlement, that destroyed the natural environment of South Africa. The Khoekhoe moved their livestock from region to region to give the vegetation enough time to recover. Thus, the difference between the colonial and pre-colonial attitudes was that the Khoekhoe and San lived with and in their environments. The colonial settler imported a technology that attempted to exterminate and erase the Khoekhoe and San, the same way they are now attempting to exterminate the Tradouw Redfin Minnow.

Conclusion

The political reading of rock art in this chapter helped to unmask the nature of the violence against Khoekhoe and San. This violence is both physical and structural. If one uses alternative interpretations of rock that are outside the Parkington and Lewis-Williams frames, one realises that movement is a central feature in rock art, and it raises a historical question about migration and land dispossession. Colonialism and colonisation were about land, and it is a myth that the Khoekhoe and San exchanged their lands for next to nothing. On the contrary, the Khoekhoe and San were systematically impoverished to create the conditions for colonial expansion. At first, it was gradual, but as the Dutch colonial settlement grew, it became rapid and more brutal. The Khoekhoe and San resisted this land dispossession since 1652. Unfortunately, this resistance led to extreme violence against the San and the Khoekhoe.

Furthermore, with English colonialism came a tighter race consciousness. This race consciousness led to the first pass system with the introduction of the *Hottentot Proclamation of 1809* for an indigenous group in South Africa. The English tried to get rid of slavery but rendered the Khoekhoe to a role of serfdom in the Cape Colony. The Dutch settlement introduced segregation in

South Africa, but it was not as formalised and institutionalised as that of the English. Hence, segregation became more formalised as the Colony extended its borders through violence. In this sense, the *Hottentot Code* was the first in a series of laws passed to frame the Khoekhoe and San in South Africa. Moreover, people, animals, insects, and plants were classified and placed on a civilisation ladder on which the San was the lowest. Race and taxonomy not only informed the racial and class attitude in the Colony but also contributed to the violence and erasure of the San and Khoekhoe. Therefore, the *Hottentot Proclamation* laid the foundations for structural violence against the Khoekhoe, San and other indigenous groups in South Africa.

The violence against the San was unregulated and genocidal. It was fuelled by fear, and the taxonomical classification that rendered them sub-human, and the European university benefited from the classification and erasure of the Khoekhoe and San. They were also active participants in the appropriation and erasure of the Khoekhoe and San's knowledge systems. This contributed to a genocidal impulse to exterminate the San and Khoekhoe. Hence, the consciousness that best describes the consciousness of the coloniser was *"Makgemaak vir bewoning"* (tamed for occupation). They did not only try to tame the indigenous people but also the natural environment. They killed off the animals in their hordes to make way for the permanent European settlements, and this settlement led to the destruction of the natural environment in South Africa.

Act 2
The Confrontation

3

Erasing the Khoekhoe
and the San

I started as a still photographer before taking up documentary filmmaking. In 2015, I completed a photographic project titled *Rural Pornography* but later shelved it. Shelving the project came after I realised the danger when people do not read the photo's caption. For me, the danger for the photographic "subject" was the interpretation of the photo outside the caption. This was the first time I encountered the selectiveness of the photographic frame. I realised that the still photograph only offers a fraction of the complete or larger context of the world of the photograph.

With documentary filmmaking, I hoped that the movement-image would resolve this.[1] However, after watching Patricio Guzman's *Nostalgia for the Light*, I realised that the movement-image also could not escape this dilemma.[2] In Guzman's film, there is a particular scene of a train moving across the desert landscape. The train moved from left to right. The interesting part is that you only first see the head of the train and later the rest. Here the frame only allows you to see parts of the train as it moves through the frame. Even though you are only privy to parts of the train, you know the rest is still coming. Like the still image, the movement-image can only show particular frames of a particular reality. Out of the five human senses, the movement-image can only stimulate one: sight. When sound is added, it stimulates two. Thus, the selectiveness of the frame manipulates the audience into imagining the rest, the parts that happened outside the frame and that which one cannot taste, smell, or feel.

---

[1]   The movement-image here is a reference to Henri Bergson's movement-image in *Matter and Memory*.

[2]   Patricio Guzman, *Nostalgia for the Light* (USA, 2011).

In addition, there is also violence that accompanies the framing of certain photographic subjects. The photographs of /A!kunta, ||Kabbo, #Kasin, /Han#kass'o, Dia!kwain and others while imprisoned at Breakwater Prison in Cape Town are examples of the violence the camera inflicts.[3] Another example would be the photographs taken of the Nama and Herero prisoners at Shark Island during the Nama, Herero, and San genocide in Namibia is a demonstration of this violence.[4] This colonial framing of the Khoekhoe, San, Herero, and others produced a universal and problematic "black figure".[5] This figure is always a subject of suffering, pity and pain. It lacked agency. Hence, some documentary filmmakers use this "black figure" in a voyeuristic manner to invoke an empathic response from the audience.[6]

As I mentioned in the opening chapter, one can apply the three limitations as a conceptual method to unmask coloniality in various texts and scholarly debates. This chapter will focus on the first limitation, which is the framing of the colonial subject. Colonialism and apartheid created and *framed* the "coloured" subjectivity. Discussing the "coloured" identity is controversial and complex in post-apartheid South Africa. In this chapter, I hope to show that the first limitation, *the selectiveness of the frame*, is most prevalent in the formation of the "coloured" identity formation in South Africa.

In South Africa, the "coloured" identity started with the framing of Krotoa. In Van Riebeeck's Journal, the "civilisation" of the "Hottentot" and "Bushman" was one of the ultimate aims of the colonists who settled at ||Hui !Gais. As one saw in the previous chapter, the more the San resisted the "civilisation" attempts, the more the violence intensified to subject them to the European notions of "civilisation." I will primarily focus on the Khoekhoe in this chapter, starting with Krotoa. Various colonial records, show that Krotoa, who joined the Van Riebeeck household at a very young age, struggled with her colonial identity and resisted it. However, through colonial records and texts, we encounter Krotoa as Eva, the "civilised Hottentot" and interpreter.

Keeping Krotoa's struggle as a reference point in South Africa, this chapter investigates how the "coloured" colonial subject was framed and formed. All sorts of violence marked this formation. This violence affected their psyche and

---

3   See *Bushmen in a Victorian World* for a collection of these photographs.
4   According to Biwa (2006), after the decimation of the Nama and Herero population in German South West Africa (later Namibia). German forces also targeted the San. The genocide, therefore, did not stop with the Nama and Herero, and hence my inclusion of the San.
5   Here, I am using Biko's notion of black, which included "Coloured" and Indian people in his definition of Black Consciousness.
6   Also, see Skotnes. (1996). *Miscast: negotiating the presence of the Bushmen*. University of Cape Town Press.

still manifests ontologically in post-apartheid South Africa. Thus, power and the psychological effects of power are central to my discussion in this chapter. Colonialism was introduced not only as an economic and authoritarian project but also as a project that created fossilised subjectivities. European missionaries, colonial administrators, and early European explorers brought a "civilising" European epistemology to what became South Africa. They reduced the Khoekhoe and San to sub-humans with their sense of racial superiority. Colonialism used power to construct a frame through which the so-called coloured is identified and dealt with in the post-apartheid society.

This chapter does not attempt to write a history of the so-called coloured people in South Africa. There are many scholarly works on the history of the so-called coloured subject (Adhikari, 2002, 2004; Erasmus, 2017; Marais, 1939; Oakley, 2006; Patterson, 1953). However, these scholarly works do not focus on the sub-human colonial frame that created and institutionalised the "coloured" identity in South Africa. Part 1 of this chapter focuses on the sub-human colonial frame that brought the "coloured" identity into existence. Part 2 focuses on the Bureaucratic Erasure of the Khoekhoe and San and the institutionalisation of the "coloured" identity in South Africa.

Part 1: Framing the Colonial Subject

Before I discuss the formation of the "coloured" subject in South Africa, I will put that formation in a broader international context. I will start with the Valladolid debate of 1550 to 1551. The Valladolid debate resulted from Spain's "discovery" of the "new world", and it happened a hundred years before the Dutch East Indian Company's intention to start a settlement at the Cape.

The Valladolid debate

Before the "discovery" of the "new world", Europeans were under the impression that all the world's nations had been discovered. Hence, Europe's believed that they discovered a "new world" when Columbus reached the Americas in 1492. However, Europeans faced new philosophical and religious challenges with the "discovery" of this "new world". Thus, a debate ensued in Europe about whether they could consider the "newly discovered people" as rational beings with souls. The Roman Catholic Church was the first institution to recognise the rationality of Native Americans, and this was proclaimed with the papal bull of 1537. The publication of the 1537 papal bull meant that Native Americans could be Christianised. Although the Roman Catholic Church recognised the rationality of Native Americans, not everyone in Spain agreed to the Christianisation of Native Americans. This proclamation also legitimised the presence of Spain in the "new world", even though the Church questioned the legitimacy of the extermination and subjugation of Native Americans (Hernandez, 2001). This division led to the Valladolid debate between Las Casas and Sepúlveda.

Bartolomé de Las Casas opposed the violence against Native Americans and the *encomienda* system. His opposition came from his first-hand experience as a colonist, soldier, and slave owner. After an apparent "crisis of conscience", he converted to Catholicism and openly opposed the *encomienda* system (Castro-Klaren, 2008, p. 120). Scholars like Castro-Klaren (2008) and Mignolo (2008) believe that this crisis of conscience resulted from witnessing the Caribbean holocaust and coming from a family *conversos*. The *conversos* were Jewish people who were violently converted to Christianity during the Catholic monarchs of Ferdinand and Isabella (Mignolo, 2008; Castro-Klaren, 2008). Las Casas' documentation of the cruelty of the Spanish invasion or "conquest" of the Americas led to the Valladolid debate.

The principal question to be debated was the human status of Native Americans and whether the violence against the peoples of the Americas was just (Castro-Klaren, 2008, p. 123). Juan Ginés de Sepúlveda, a lawyer and a defender of the Spanish Crown, put four propositions in favour of a just war against the American natives: (1) the natives were barbarians; (2) they committed cruelty against natural law; (3) the natives oppressed and killed the innocent among themselves; and (4) they were infidels who need to be instructed in the Christian faith. The counter-argument of Las Casas was that even if the Native Americans were "backwards," they were no less rational beings than their European counterparts. For this reason, they must receive the Christian faith peacefully like the people of the "Old World." Thus, "since the [Native Americans] were rational and civilised human beings, Spaniards had no right to subject them neither to slavery nor to war" (Hernandez, 2001, p. 99). No one won the Valladolid debate, but it set a precedent for dealing with the indigenous people of any country that was not European.

Two problems arise when revisiting the Valladolid debate. The first is that one must be careful that it does not happen in "the logic of coloniality or [in] the colonial matrix of power" (Mignolo, 2008, p. 24). According to Mignolo (2008, p. 15), the colonial matrix of power has four sociohistorical domains: (1) control of the economy, (2) control of authority, (3) control of gender and sexuality, and (4) control of knowledge and subjectivity. If one re-reads the debate in the logic of coloniality (the colonial matrix of power), it will re-inscribe the fourth domain: the control of knowledge and subjectivity. Thus, a de-linking or de-colonial reading of the Las Casas and Sepúlveda debate recognises that they excluded other views contrary to the dominant imperial logic or knowledge system of the times. Notably absent were the indigenous people's beliefs, ideas, principles of knowledge, and subject formations. In addition, it excluded other marginalised groups in the imperial/colonial matrix of power (Mignolo, 2008, p. 24). The Valladolid debate changed history for Latin American indigenous people and, after that, for most of the colonised world. First, it instated subjectivity in the colonies that served domination. Second, it justified Europe's control over America, India, Australia, Africa, and their people.

The second problem with revisiting the Valladolid debate is justifying the violence against the natives. This justification took the form of a "civilising" discourse. In colonial texts, the control of the economy, the control of authority, and the control of gender and sexuality were justifiable means to "civilise" indigenous people. Thus, the significance of the Valladolid debate is that it laid the foundation for the justification of violence against indigenous people. This violence was theorised and justified as natural law.

Natural Law

John Locke's *Two Treaties* relies heavily on natural law to justify colonialism and the colonisation of America. Locke wrote the *Two Treaties* from his experience supporting slavery and colonialism in America. For Locke, every individual has political power in a state of nature, and people are naturally self-governing. Locke argues that individuals should give up this right to preserve mankind or the public good and form institutional forms of government. Institutional forms of government create laws in the interest of the public and society, which are regulated accordingly (Tully, 1993).

Locke argues that natural law applied to Native Americans. He advanced two reasons for this argument. Firstly, Native Americans did not have a political organisation (Institutional forms of government) and operated in a system of individual self-government. Secondly, Locke argued that Native Americans used a system of individualised labour-based property. Locke's concept of individualised labour-based property raised the question: Do Native Americans have a claim over all the lands? For Locke, the answer was no. Locke argued that since Native Americans were in a state of nature, they did not have "large tracts of land" but only "a few spots of enclosed and cultivated land" (Tully, 1993, p. 167). The lands that were not enclosed or cultivated were considered empty or wasteland, and colonists had a right to occupy, enclose, and cultivate these lands.

As with the Valladolid debate, the Native American political society was analysed through a European lens. It left out the voices of those who were to be affected by Locke's argument. Since Locke's argument happened in the colonial matrix of power, it used Europe as the prime example of "civilisation." Any society that did not resemble Europe and had different values, beliefs, and systems of government was regarded "uncivilised" and in a state of nature. Since it was argued that Native Americans were as "uncivilised" and in a state of nature, the principles of natural law applied to them. Hence, the principles of natural law were used to dispossess Native Americans of their lands. This method later had severe consequences for Africans.

Ian Glenn's reading of François le Vaillant, one of the earlier European explorers amongst the Khoekhoe and San, shows that Le Vaillant framed the San as "savages". Glenn (1996) points out that Le Valliant's view of the San was informed by his belief that the San was still trapped in a state of nature. Burchell also held the same views when he travelled the interior of South Africa. He, too, believed that the San was in a state of nature. Le Vaillant's travelled in the 1780s, and *Voyage* was first published in 1790. Burchell travelled the interior of South Africa in 1811, and his *Travels* were published in 1822. Therefore, more than 100 years after Locke published *Two Treaties*, European travellers like Le Valliant and Burchell still gazed at indigenous people through Locke's state of nature lens.

European colonialists also found the justification to colonise, exterminate, and "civilise" Africans in the philosophical works of Hegel and Gobineau.[7] In the *Philosophy of History*, Hegel justifies the enslavement of Africans. Hegel argues that freedom can only exist in the state and is the only place "the individual has and enjoys his freedom" (Wright, 2004, p. 33). If there is no state (institutional forms of government), "man" will revert to "his primary animal existence" (Wright, ibid.). To support this argument, Hegel draws on the "Negro" whom he believes is incapable of development or culture (Hegel, 2001, p. 116). For Hegel, the "Negro's" lack of development and culture results from the "Negro" lack of history. The only way for the "Negro" to achieve freedom, development, and culture is through the dialectic of *Aufhebung* (Hegel, 2001, p. 117). In the dialectic of *Aufhebung*, the African can only achieve freedom through slavery and colonialism. Thus, "the African will attain subjectivity

---

[7]   I want to highlight that Hegel and Gobineau's works were contemporary to the African chapter of Imperialism. For example, Hegel's *Philosophy of History* was published in 1824, and Gobineau's *Essay on the Inequality of the Human Races* was published in 1853. For the full argument, please see my dissertation: *The Politics of Belonging and/or a Contest for Survival: Rethinking the Conflict in North and South Kivu in the Democratic Republic of Congo.*

through the European" (Wright, 2004, p. 35). Later in this chapter we will see that the Khoekhoe and San could only attain subjectivity through the state, and for this, their Khoekhoe and San identities needed to be erased.

Furthermore, Gobineau constructed a theory of racial inferiority influenced by Hegel. Gobineau constructed three races: the Negroid, Caucasoid, and the Mongoloid (Wright, 2004, pp. 39-40). Of the "Negro", Gobineau writes:

> The Negro is the most humble and lags at the bottom of the scale. The animal character imprinted on his brow marks his destiny from the moment of conception. He will never evolve beyond his limited circle of intelligence. He is not, however, a pure and simple brute, for within the narrow confines of his cranium, there exist indications of grossly powerful energies (Gobineau, 1983, pp. 339-340 cited in Wright, 2004, pp. 43-44).

In this text, Hegel's influence on Gobineau's work is visible. Like Hegel in the *Philosophy of History,* he classifies Africans as Negro and renders them sub-human. Furthermore, he contributes history and the civilisation of Europe to an "Aryan race". Gobineau argues that all civilisations have one thing in common: they share the racial heritage of the dominant group, which is always Aryan (Wright, 2004, pp. 40-41). Thus, civilisations in Egypt and Ethiopia were credited with being influenced by a fictional Aryan race. Since they were the bastards of this Aryan race, they did not look Aryan. Hence, their culture, history, and intelligence are attributed to a fictional Aryan heritage. Hegel and Gonineau's texts justified colonialists from England, France, and Germany for Africa's political and economic exploitation. They saw it as their duty to "civilise" the nations of the world (Wright, 2004, p. 45).

Moreover, the scholarly works of Robert Knox and James Hunt were also influential in establishing the African as sub-human. According to Lindqvist (1996, p. 129), "In 1863, Knox's followers broke away and formed the Anthropological Society, which was more markedly racist." James Hunt, in his first lecture, "On the Negro's Place in Nature", emphasised the Negro's close relationship to the ape. This argument is clearly in the colonial matrix of power. Their justification for this type of violence rested on natural order or *natural law.* In the Anthropological Society, they argued that in nature, "the weak must be devoured by the strong" (Lindqvist, 1996, p. 131). Europeans saw themselves as the 'strong' or the "superior race"; hence, they believed that "The eradication of the lower races ... would gradually reduce the difference between races until the world would again be inhabited by one single, almost homogenous race in which no one was inferior to the noblest example of the humanity of the day" (Lindqvist, 1996, p. 136). Once Africans were rendered sub-human, it was easier for imperial powers and their settlers to exterminate them. Those who survived extermination were subjected to colonial rule, and as sub-humans, they did not have land or rights whatsoever.

Becoming the African Colonial Subject

The becoming of the African colonial subject was a particularly violent process. David Olusoga and Casper W. Erichsen in *The Kaiser's Holocaust* made one aware of the scientific experiments the Germans carried out in the concentration camps of Swakopmund and Lüderitz. These experiments were carried out on the Nama and Herero people. These experiments were an attempt to support their theories of racial inferiority.

> In the course of the war, an industry had developed around the supply of body parts. In the Swakopmund concentration camp in 1905, female prisoners were forced to boil the severed heads of their own people and scrape the flesh, sinews and ligaments off the skull with shards of broken glass. The victims may have been people they had known or even relatives. The skulls were then placed into crates by the German soldiers and shipped to museums, collections and universities in Germany.
>
> ...
>
> In June 1905, the German racial anthropologist Felix von Luschan had begun a correspondence with Ralph Zürn, the lieutenant in Okahandja whose aggression towards the Herero had helped sparked the outbreak of the war. Disappointed with the Herero skull Zürn had donated him following his removal from the colony in 1904, von Luscharn enquired about the possibility of acquiring further specimens. Zürn made some enquiries of his own before assuring von Luscharn that 'in the concentration camps taking and preserving the skulls of Herero prisoners of war will be readily possible than in the country ...'
>
> ...
>
> Towards the end of 1906, the bodies of seventeen Nama prisoners, including that of a one-year-old girl, were carefully decapitated by the camp physician at Shark Island, Dr Bofinger. After breaking open the skulls, Bofinger removed and weighed the brains before placing each in preserving alcohol and sealing them in tins for export to the Institute of Pathology at the University of Berlin. There they were used by the aspiring racial scientist Christian Fetzer, then still a medical student, in a series of experiments designed to demonstrate the anatomical similarities between the Nama and the anthropoid ape" (Olusoga and Erichsen, 2010, pp. 224-225).

These violent and inhuman practices were used to fuel a particular racial epistemology of inferiority. It was the task of the European university to prove this inferiority. Hence, in the name of science, racial scientists could commit these horrendous crimes against humanity. From these aforementioned passages, the university was implicit in the violence against the indigenous. They build racist disciplines and discourses based on this science (see Chapter 2). In addition, Mahmood Mamdani, in his book, *When Victims Become Killers*, shows how this epistemology of racial inferiority was codified in law and how African people were subjected to it. The aim was to set the colonisers apart from the colonised and fragment the colonised into different ethnic groups. It was believed that some of the ethnic groups were of "Aryan" ancestry and received an elevated status in the colonial state. This fragmentation allowed Western powers to rule Africa and subject African people to certain subject positions and others to ruling classes. For example, the Hutu and Tutsi in Rwanda and Burundi were ethnic groups that were destined to rule. Consequently, the Tutsi received ruling status, and the Hutu received subject status. Western law was thus used to create different political identities and set the basis for the becoming of the colonial subject.

Frederick Lugard, in *The Dual Mandate in British Tropical Africa*, developed a political system in which Europe was to rule Africa indirectly. Mamdani, reading Lugard, found that the colonial state used direct and indirect rule to govern the natives and the non-natives (Mamdani, 1996). The non-native being of "Aryan" origin and the native "backward African". In this regard, "Direct rule tended to generate race-based political identities: settler and native. Indirect rule, in contrast, tended to mitigate the settler-native dialectic by fracturing the race consciousness of natives into multiple and separate ethnic consciousnesses" (Mamdani, 2001, p. 23). Thus, as the non-native, the settler received only a racial identity within the colonial state. On the other hand, the native received both a racial and ethnic identity in the colonial state. The native was black and sub-human. The settler was white or various shades of white and "Aryan".

Furthermore, political identities were institutionalised through Western law and conceptualised in the colonial matrix of power. Firstly, the "language of the law tried to naturalise political differences in the colony by mapping these along a civilisational ladder" (Mamdani, 2001, p. 25). Thus, the first step was positioning the non-native as more "civilised" than the native. The second step was to use race to differentiate between the non-native and native. The objective was to create a racial hierarchy. Since the European non-natives were regarded as "civilised", it was placed at the top of the racial hierarchy.

The African native was placed at the bottom of this hierarchy since it was considered "uncivilised". This civilisational ladder served as the basis for racial discrimination in the colony and was embedded in colonial law.

Secondly, "the law separated the minority of civilised from the majority of those yet-to-be-civilised, incorporating the minority into a regime of rights while excluding the majority from that same regime" (Mamdani, ibid.). This regime of rights was called citizenship. Natives could only access citizenship once they were "civilised". "Civilised" meant being educated in Western norms and religious practices. In addition, some natives had to undergo a test to attain an *évolué* or civilised status. It was only then that natives were regarded as citizens, whilst the rest were regarded as members of an ethnic group and yet-to-be civilised (Mamdani, ibid.).

Like the Valladolid instance, the beliefs, ideas, principles of knowledge, and subject formations of the indigenous people and other marginalised groups within the colonial state were notably absent. It was in this colonial matrix of knowledge that citizenship was created. Colonial laws decided who belonged and did not belong to the colonial state and who was a citizen and subject. Thus, at the end of this violent process, one had various colonial subject identities with specific roles and manifested in particular ways.

We will see in Part 2 that the Khoekhoe and San were first regarded as the "uncivilised" natives and were placed at the bottom of the racial hierarchy. However, as they were stripped of their land, Christianised and Western-educated, they became "civilised". As "civilised" and Christianised subjects, they were not regarded as their former "savage" selves. Hence, they were stripped of their "native" status and systematically included in the "coloured" identity. In 1911, the "coloured" identity became the non-native of "Aryan" ancestry, and the "Bantu" became the only authentic African native. I have to note that many social categories in the pre-colonial era became mandatory ethnic identities. Those pre-colonial social categories also signify subordination. However, when they became codified in European epistemology, they became permanent, and no mobility was allowed. As a result, these identities lost their fluidity.

Forming the Psyche of the Colonial Subject

The colonial subject is a product of subjection. In *The psychic life of power: Theories in subjection*, Butler argues that subjection is a form of power and tells one there are two ways of thinking about power. The conventional way, where power is pressed onto the subject from outside or Foucault's way, where power is forming the subject. According to Butler (1997, p. 2), "power is not simply what we oppose but also, in a strong sense, what we depend on for our existence and what we harbour and preserve in the being that we are." This means that the oppressed class, to some degree, collaborated in their oppression. Since the desire to survive "is a pervasively exploitable desire" (Butler, 1997, p. 7), the individual will only give into subjection because of their desire to survive or "to be". Since the desire to survive is exploitable, the Khoekhoe and San had no choice but to accept colonial subjection. European education and identities were given in a position of mandatory submission. They did not have a choice. Contradictory as it might seem, the Khoekhoe and San also found safety in the assigned category. Their existence depended on it.

Furthermore, subjection raises a question regarding the agency of the colonised. Butler argues that power acts as the agency of the subject:

> Because power is not intact prior to the subject, the appearance of its priority disappears as power acts on the subject, and the subject is inaugurated (and derived) through this temporal reversal in the horizon of power. [Thus], as the agency of the subject, power assumes its present temporal dimension (Butler, 1997, pp. 13-14).

Butler's theorisation of agency, thus, gives power a psychic dimension. The implication is that whenever the power source is physically removed from the oppressed, the power still lives in the psyche of the oppressed. In this regard, Butler proposes to think of the theory of power alongside the theory of the psyche. The individual has to achieve and reproduce their subjectivation, which Foucault calls *assujetissement*.[8] Subjectivation entails becoming the subject. We will see in Part 2 that Khoekhoe and San people had to become "Coloured".

For me, there is little agency in the "coloured" identity. Being "Coloured" or being forced to be "Coloured" is the power of colonial and apartheid subjection at work. These powers have long-lasting effects on the Khoekhoe and San communities, especially since their group identities were erased, and the effects are detrimental to this group of people.

Moreover, Butler (1997) argues that subjection is only successful if the power taking hold of the psyche is reiterated. The Khoekhoe and San's subjection was reiterated through subject positions such as "Hottentot," "Boesman", "Bruinmens," and "Kleurling". In addition, they also encountered the "savage" and "backward", "Hottentot" and "Bushman" in several colonial and apartheid texts books. These books celebrated their extermination. Therefore, they could not but reject the idea of being "Hottentot" or "Boesman".

---

[8] Butler uses subjectivation instead of subjectification.

However, power loses priority without reiteration (Butler, 1997). This meant the Khoekhoe and San had to reiterate that they were "Hottentot," "Bushman," or "Coloured." If resisted, the reiteration was ensured by all sorts of violence. Therefore, the continuation of "colouredness" is only possible through reiterating one's "colouredness". The colonial and apartheid states have ensured this through racial classification. They structured a society that could only access services in the state through one's racial classification. Unfortunately, the post-apartheid state has continued with this classification system, forcing a group of people to reiterate their oppression. This post-apartheid reiteration creates the illusion of agency in the "coloured" identity.

If power is what we depend on power for our existence, we have to collaborate in our oppression to some degree. Hence, the Khoekhoe and San in the colony were relegated to serfdom because their survival depended on it. Those who had the opportunity to escape the expansion of the colony joined other Khoekhoe and San groups where they were not oppressed. However, collaboration in our oppression is not in the absence of resistance. For the oppressed class, resistance is a constant. Hence, as Abrahams (1994) pointed out, resistance and collaboration are two sides of the same coin.

Autshumao, Goab Hendrik Witbooi (Biwa, 2006), the Griqua (Besten, 2006) and Nommoa (Mellet, 2020) are often made out as collaborators. I think there is an important aspect of collaboration that these scholars are missing. If one applies a psychological reading to "collaboration", one would have a more nuanced understanding of "collaboration". I think Abrahams' argument helps us to unpack the complexity of collaboration. Abrahams (1994) argues that some of the Khoekhoe who participated in the commandoes were not wilful participants. Their wives and children were, in most cases, kept hostage. For example, "one Willem Haasbek was regarded as one of the most trusted guides in the war of 1793 in the eastern Cape, yet in 1794, he complained of the continued detention of his wife and children by Coenraad de Buys, who had ignored repeated requests to set them free" (Abrahams, 1994, p. 44). In 1793, the Khoekhoe men at Genadendal received an order from the Commander of the Dutch East Indian Company to come and defend the Cape against the French. This happened after the French declared war against the Dutch after the French Revolution. In this instance, these Khoekhoe men barely had a choice. They barely had any rights. They had to go. Later that same year, they were sent to the Zuurveld to help the colony fight against the Xhosa (The Genadendal Diaries, 1992). What made it difficult for these Khoekhoe men was that they left the women and children behind at the mercy of the colony. It will be difficult for any person to refuse any order if they know the lives of their loved ones hang in the balance because of their choice. However, this is no excuse for the role some Khoekhoe played in the extermination of their kinsmen (Besten, 2006; Legassick, 2010).

Abraham (1994) highlights various strategies to survive oppression. According to Abrahams (1994, p. 41), "in negotiating the contradictions created by colonialism, one learns that collaborations and resistance are both two sides of the same coin. Survival, physical and spiritual, is the coin". This, therefore, raises the question: what would the oppressed do to survive, since to live is an innate human desire? Abrahams states:

> as a member of a colonised people, I know the difference between resistance and collaboration. The latter is what you do [to] survive. Still, beyond the necessities of daily life there are islands where you can just be yourself without question. Resistance is what you do to protect those islands, while war is what you wage to enlarge them. Then of course there is 'selling out', an act which is contrasurvival, both as an individual and as a people (1994, p. 41).

I think this reflection of Abrahams captures the spirit and the psychic operation of the colonised. Did any of the previously mentioned leaders sell out? I do not think so. Instead, I think they were caught up in the dilemma Abrahams so aptly explained: they had to collaborate for their and their people's survival. Notably, they all resisted once they felt strong enough to resist the colonial power.

Going forward, one must recognise the role that the colonial civilisation project played in crafting the "Hottentot", "Bushman", and "coloured" identities. The "coloured" identity erased the indigeneity of the Khoekhoe and San. They become a people with no history, no present, or future.

As Mellet poignantly pointed out, we must remember that the "first step in controlling communities is the obliteration of memory and the deconstruction of culture, replacing it with void, and then creating a new construct" (Mellet, 2020, p. 18). Memory has an important psychological dimension in controlling the oppressed. The memories of oppressed bodies are often associated with pain, and this leads to preventing future painful events or situations. Thus, whoever controls the memory of the oppressed controls the psyche of the oppressed. This is the act of subjectification, where an external power takes hold over the psyche of the oppressed. However, Butler explains that subjection also leads to resistance since the psyche knows an oppressive foreign power has taken hold of it. Resistance is born in this instance. Hence, the oppressed always resist. I will deal with the resistance in the next chapter. In the rest of this chapter, I will focus on how the Khoekhoe and San were subjected to the "coloured" identity.

Part 2: From "Hottentot" and "Bushman" to "Coloured"

The "coloured" identity is complex. It is generally believed that this group of people assimilated into the Cape colonial society by the late nineteenth century. This group comprises of other phenotypically diverse groups of people descended from the Khoekhoe, the San, slaves, and other black people in South Africa. However, it is also commonly thought that this group is partly descended from European settlers and is regarded as a distinct racial group (Adhikari, 2002). It is also believed that the "coloured" identity was a stable construct throughout the era of white rule and operated as a social identity (Adhikari, 2002, 2004). I am not convinced of Adhikari's argument. Oakley (2006) in Steinkop, Namaqualand, shows it was not a stable social construct. Various other identities existed before 1950. It was only after 1950 that the so-called coloured identity took root in Steinkopf. I will show that it was not a "social construct" but a bureaucratic construct. The colonial state invented the "coloured identity" at the end of slavery. The colonial state at first grouped everyone who was not considered European (White) into the "Coloured" category. These, amongst others, include: "Hottentot" (Khoekhoe), Bushman (San), Malay, Fingo, "mixed-Hottentot" (mixed-Khoekhoe), "Bantu", Griqua, Nama, etc., until 1911. After 1911 the law only created three racial categories: "Bantu" (Native in 1950), "Coloured", and White. The notable difference was the separation of those regarded as "Bantu" from the "Coloured" category.

Furthermore, it seems Adhikari's (2002, 2004) views are from an urban perspective if one compares them to Oakley's (2006). If this is the case, Adhikari's analysis excludes Afrikaans-speaking "coloured" people living in rural areas such as Steinkopf. For example, I had never encountered the English racist abbreviation "JACK" until reading Adhikari's paper.[9] This particular racist abbreviation must have originated from an English-speaking urban centre. In addition, Adhikari accepted the translation in a Cape Argus article of "bruin" (brown) to "coloured" (Adhikari, 2004, p. 172). If he had had a closer look, he would have noticed that "coloureds" were inserted in brackets in the original article because it was not part of the actor's (Anthony Wilson) actual words. Adhikari also fails to mention that Wilson attended a lecture titled: "Bruin?". It was the journalist Murray Williams who translated "Bruin?" as "Coloured?". If one reads the whole article, it becomes clear that Wilson equated "Bruin" to a "Khoi and San" ancestry and did not use it as "Coloured". Thus, in this instance, "Bruin" cannot be translated to "Coloured." Many "Coloured" people outside the urban centres and in more sparsely populated areas prefer the "Bruin"

---

[9] Please see Adhikari (2004, p. 170) for the meaning of the abbreviation. It is too offensive to mention it here.

category, which does not translate to "Kleurling". At times, the "Bruin" or Brown category was a more stable and acceptable "social construct" than the "Kleurling" (Coloured) construct.

Later in this chapter, we will see that not all "Coloured" people in South Africa are of "mixed race" and somehow of European descent. Likewise, not all "Coloured" people in South Africa are descendants of Cape slaves and other black people. The "coloured" identity in South Africa is the result of the colonial and apartheid racial classification. Over time, different groups of people were grouped into and excluded from the "Coloured" racial category. The Khoekhoe and San were the most affected by colonial and apartheid classification. Unlike black people, who were classified racially and ethnically (which gave them indigeneity), the Khoekhoe and the San were stripped of their ethnicity and thus their indigeneity and were only racially classified. We will see apartheid laws positioned them as mixed and descended from European settlers. Apartheid's classification was, thus, intended to be the final erasure of the Khoekhoe in South Africa. The San was, however, recognised by the university and became an entity worth "preserving". As a result, the San were placed in several reserves as an entity that needed "preservation". However, they still had to live with the state's racial classification. They were only allowed to be San in these reserves where they could be observed and studied, far removed from colonial and apartheid society.

From Krotoa[10] to Eva, the "civilised" *Hottentot*

Apartheid was a racist project based on the discourse of racial purity. It was to keep the Afrikaner pure from miscegenation. Miscegenation was believed to be the original sin that threatened the disintegration of the "Afrikaner race", whom they thought to be God's newly chosen race. The union of Krotoa and Pieter van Meerhof is one of the most well-known cases of miscegenation between the colonists and the Khoekhoe. However, before marrying Pieter van Meerhof, she had to become "Eva", the Christianised *Hottentot*.

---

[10]   Mellet (2020, p. 119) mentions that Krotoa's name is actually pronounced as (*!Goa/Gōas*) and apparently means "girl cared for by others." In the Khoekhoegowab dictionary, I found *!Goa* which can mean small consciousness, but I could not find /*Gōas*. However, I did find /*gôas* which means daughter. The *-ō* in /*gōas* is an extended vowel (oo), and the *-ô* is a nasalised vowel (Frederick, 2013). Therefore, I think it is /*gôas* instead of /*gōas*. Also, note "/" represents the dental click, which is the same click as "|". The latest Khoekhoegowab orthography "|" is the accepted indication of the dental click (Frederick, 2013). However, Mellet (2020) indicated that he consulted a *!Kora* language expert. Unfortunately, *!Kora* is not part of the Khoekhoegowab dictionary. Fredericks (2013) indicated the tonality difference in vowels in various Khoekhoe dialects. This could be one such incident.

As a result, a lot has been written about Krotoa's colonial and Khoekhoe identity (Landman, 1996; McKinnon, 2004; Mellet, 2020; Schoeman, 2006; Scully, 2005). Thus, the narrative of Krotoa that one commonly encounter is the following. Her uncle was Autshumao, or Harry, as the colonists knew him. At the age of ten or twelve, she was taken in by Van Riebeeck and his wife and was renamed Eva. While living with the Van Riebeecks, she dressed in European clothes and learned to speak and master Dutch and Portuguese. She later acted as the official interpreter of the Dutch East India Company at the Cape.

From colonial records, it seems that she was not much liked by Nommoa (Doman). Nommoa, like Krotoa, was at first an interpreter but later led the First Khoe-Dutch War against the Dutch in ||Hui !Gais. Krotoa was also the first indigenous person baptised as a Christian and believed in having helped with the conversion of several other Khoekhoe. She married Pieter van Meerhof in 1664, and they moved to Robben Island, where Van Meerhof was appointed overseer. When Van Meerhof died on a voyage to Madagascar, Krotoa and the children moved back to the mainland. She supposedly fell into prostitution and alcoholism to the extent that her children were taken away from her. She was banished to Robben Island as a prisoner, where she died in 1674, ten years after she got married and 22 years after the Dutch settled in ||Hui !Gais. She was buried on the mainland.

This particular metanarrative does not attempt to shed light on the psychological effect of colonisation on Krotoa. For the Khoekhoe ||Hui !Gais (the Cape) was changing, and colonialism disrupted the centuries-old socio-political structure of the Khoekhoe. Colonialism introduced a new value system, religion, technology, and customs. Khoekhoe leaders like Autshumao and Oedasoa must have seen this coming and decided they needed a Dutch representative. Given Krotoa's social standing among the Khoekhoe in and around the Peninsula, this task fell on her.

I believe that her role could have been that of a diplomat. It is generally believed that Van Riebeeck and his wife took in Krotoa as a servant (Landman, 1996; McKinnon, 2004; Schoeman, 2006). However, this was unlikely the situation. Krotoa was the niece of Autshumao, the chief of the ǀAmmaquas (Watermen) of the Goringhaiconas (see Figure 4 in Chapter 2). The Goringhaiconas was a clan of the mighty Cochoqua Khoekhoe tribe. Krotoa's sister Namies was married to Oedasoa, the chief of the Cochoqua. Considering Krotoa's social standing in the Khoekhoe, she can be regarded as royalty. Understanding her position in the Khoekhoe society warrants a different look at Krotoa's role in the European society at the Cape.

It is also unlikely that Krotoa was sent to Van Riebeeck to play a subservient role. Khoekhoe women did not hold subservient roles in their society. From the account of Hahn (1881), who studied the Khoekhoe language and lived with the Khoekhoe for nine years, one notices that Khoekhoe women fulfil an influential role in their society.

> All the Khoikhoi tribes use the expression *Taras* for a woman. We still have the name of *Tradouw* – i.e. *Taradaob* – for a mountain-pass not far from Swellendam. *Taras* is the woman, as ruler of the house, the mistress; it is exactly the Middle-High-German *vrouwe*. The root -da or -ta means to conquer, to rule, to master, and the suffix -ra expresses a custom or an intrinsic peculiarity. *Taras* is also a woman of rank, a lady. In every Khoikhoi's house, the woman, or *taras*, is the supreme ruler; the husband has nothing at all to say. While in public, the men take the prominent part, at home, they have not so much power even as to take a mouthful of sour milk out of the tub without the wife's permission. If a man ever should try to do it, his nearest female relations will put a fine on him, consisting in cows and sheep, which is to be added to the stock of the wife. In the house, the wife always occupies the right side of the husband and the right side of the house.

> If a chief died, it often happened that his energetic wife became the *gau-tās* (contracted from *gautaras*), the ruling woman – i.e. the queen of the tribe – in place of the son who was not of age (Hahn, 1881, p. 19).

> ...

> The eldest daughter was highly respected; to her was entirely left the milking of the cows. This was in accordance with the respect shown to the female sex in general (Hahn, 1881, p. 20).

> ...

> The uncle always calls his niece, the brother's or sister's daughter, "*Ti χamse*," my lioness.

> The highest oath a man could take and still takes was to swear by his eldest sister, and if he should abuse this name, the sister will walk into his flock and take his finest cows and sheep, and no law could prevent her from doing so. A man never can address his own sister personally; he must speak to another person to address the sister in his name, or in the absence of anybody, he says so that his sister can hear, "I wish that somebody will tell my sister that I wish to have a drink of milk," &c., &c. The eldest sister can inflict even punishment on a grown-up brother if he omits the established traditional rules of courtesy and the code of etiquette (Hahn, 1881, p. 21).

Hahn's account persuades one to reconsider the relationship between Autshumao and Krotoa. Since Krotoa was the niece of Autshumao, he probably referred to her as "*Ti χamse*" (my lioness). It is also clear from the customary practices of the Khoekhoe that it prevented Autshumao from giving Krotoa away as a servant. Khoekhoe women held important and powerful roles in the Khoekhoe society. This places a different perspective on the role Krotoa was intended to play in the Khoekhoe-Dutch relationship. This supports Scully's theory that Krotoa's intended role may have been that of a representative of the Khoekhoe amongst the Dutch colonialists (Scully, 2005). In this sense, Krotoa played a diplomatic role between Cochoqua and the Dutch, not as a servant or interpreter.

At first, Van Riebeeck did not take notice of Krotoa, but this changed when he realised who Krotoa was. As Van Riebeeck became aware of Krotoa's social standing, he used her diplomatically. First as an interpreter, and later, she was sent on various trading expeditions (Landman, 1996, p. 22). In addition, Van Riebeeck's treatment of Krotoa, Krotoa's niece Namies and her "brother-in-law" Oedasoa contradicts the servant narrative. For example, Van Riebeeck honoured Oedasoa and his daughter as guests at his main table before he departed from ||Hui !Gais.

It is also clear that everyone in the Dutch East Indian Company at the Cape knew of Krotoa's socio-political standing and honoured her with that kind of respect until her death. Hence, Krotoa's social standing continued with the departure of Van Riebeeck. For example, when she married Van Meerhof, the wedding feast was at the Commander House, and she was given a wedding present of 50 rix dollars which was more than her husband's salary (McKinnon, 2004, p. 48). Thus, Van Riebeeck and other colonialists at the Cape might at first perceive Krotoa as a servant, but it changed when they realised who she was.

However, based on Khoekhoe's custom, it is possible that they did not perceive Krotoa as a Dutch servant. This is evident from the Goringhaiqua and ǀAmmaqua relationship at the Cape. There was tension between the Goringhaiqua and ǀAmmaqua after the Goringhaiqua attacked and robbed Krotoa on her way to her sister. Since Gorachouqua and the Goringhaiqua wanted to increase their standing in the Khoe-Dutch relationship, they had to get rid of Autshumao. Therefore, Nommoa had to play the role Krotoa played for the ǀAmmaqua and the Cochoqua for the Gorachouqua and the Goringhaiqua.

Scholars wrote about Nommoa's mistrust of Krotoa, and to understand this mistrust, one must understand the intra-Khoekhoe politics at the time. There were three main clans in and around the Peninsula. The Goringhaicona (ǀAmmaqua and Sonqua / Ubiqua), the Goringhaiqua, and the Gorachouqua. These clans paid tribute to the Cochoqua and are considered smaller clans of the Cochoqua. Nienaber argues that Goringhaiqua means "high kraal people", and the Goringhaicona means "children of the high kraal people" (1989, p. 413). Since Krotoa's mother was of the Goringhaiqua, these two clans were related (Schoeman, 2006, p. 38). Krotoa belonged to the Goringhaicona and Nommoa to the Goringhaiqua. I believe that since Krotoa's sister was married to Oedasoa, who was the chief of the Cochoqua, Krotoa had a more prominent standing in Khoekhoe diplomatic relations than Nommoa. Nommoa's mistrust could have arisen from the Khoekhoe's custom. As we saw from Hahn's explanation, diplomacy customary fell in the domain of men.

Furthermore, as I have mentioned in the previous chapter, Van Riebeeck was aware that Cochoqua and the Chainouqua were opposing tribes and used this to his advantage in trading relations. Krotoa must also have in-depth knowledge of other tribes, such as the Namaqua and the Hessequa, which Van Riebeeck also used to his advantage. Hence, as the relationship between tribes intensified, she was cast to the side. When her sister passed in 1660, her influence in the Cochoqua also dwindled.

So where were Krotoa's loyalties? Krotoa's loyalties were with the Khoekhoe. According to Mellet (2020, p. 124), "In looking at the information available, one is indeed sometimes left wondering whether Krotoa worked for Oedasoa rather than Van Riebeeck. Her information from Oedasoa conveyed to the Dutch during the first Khoe-Dutch war was nuanced in favour of the Cochoqua's stance." Van Riebeeck suspected Krotoa of aiding the Khoekhoe with information during the first Khoe-Dutch war. He warned the VOC leaders against her when Van Riebeeck departed the Cape. In addition, in 1662, when Van Riebeeck departed, Oedasoa cut kinship with Krotoa (McKinnon, 2004). The reasons why Oedasoa did this are unclear, but we know he did that after Krotoa's sister Namies passed on. To make matters worse, her uncle Autshumao passed in 1663, leaving Krotoa alone and isolated at the Cape.

Sara, the other Khoekhoe Woman

To understand Krotoa's eventual "decline" and later her death is to understand the discrimination Khoekhoe women faced in colonial society. Not every Khoekhoe woman was treated as Krotoa or held in the same esteem as Krotoa. Sara (Zara) is a well-documented case often used to contrast Krotoa's life during early Dutch settlement. Sara is estimated to be the same age as Krotoa, and they were contemporaries in the Cape colonial societies. However, from colonial texts, it is clear that Krotoa and Sara moved into two very different social classes. Krotoa moved in with the Governor whilst Sara was in the "service" of Lydia de Pape. Lydia de Pape arrived in *||Hui !Gais*, on 3 October 1662 and, later that month, married to Hendrik Lacus. Around this time, Sara joined the de Pape and Lacus household. Lydia attended the baptism of Krotoa's youngest child, Solomon van Meerhof, on 12 September 1666 and was named his godmother. Clearly, Krotoa and Lydia were friends and were deemed equals.

Approximately a year after the baptism (5 September 1667), Lacus was accused of theft and embezzlement and was suspended by Commander Cornelis van Quaelberg, and his property was confiscated. A year later, Pieter van Meerhof was killed on an expedition to Madagascar in February 1668, leaving Krotoa a widow. A month after Van Meerhof's death, the trial of Lacus began. During this trial, it becomes clear that Sara could not testify under oath because she was considered a "heathen". Lacus' imprisonment started in May 1668 on Robben Island. Even though Lydia did not stand trial, she was banished with her husband to Robben Island. Lydia and Krotoa reunited on Robben Island while she (Krotoa) awaited her return to the mainland (Upham, 2013).

Thus, before the trial of Lacus started and before they were banished to Robben Island, Sara joined the household of *Maaji* Ansela and Arnoldus Willemsz Basson in January 1668. However, when Lydia returned from Robben Island in 1669, Sara did not return to her (Lydia's) service and stayed with the Ansela household. Two years later, on 18 December 1671, Sara's body was found hanging from the sheep pen of the freed-burgher Arnoldus Willemsz Basson. It appeared Sara had committed suicide.

There are two points to emphasise from this incident. The first relates to why Sara committed suicide. The reason why Sara took her life is open to speculation. Willem ten Rhyne, a Dutch East India Company physician, in his book *An Account of the Cape of Good Hope and the Hottentotes*, gives an account of Sara's suicide. However, Upham (2013) pointed out that his account is questionable and is considered hearsay. In his book, he claims that he met Sara and Krotoa, but this could not be true because he only visited the Cape in 1673, two years after Sara's death. Upham (2013) believed he had a source: the company surgeon (Johann Schreyer) who performed the autopsy on Sara's body. According to the ten Rhyne account, Sara committed suicide because she was pregnant, and the European man who promised to marry her did not commit to his word.

The second is how Sara's body was treated. The Colonial government appropriated Sara's body, and her corpse was put on trial. On the same day that her body was discovered, the Council of Justice was convened. Below is an extract from the trial.

> It was therefore concluded-as the said female Hottentot, known by Sara, and about 24 years of age, had (verkeert) from her childhood with Company's servants or free men; and that not merely for bare food, but also with some persons for wages, by which she had thus long maintained herself, and had thus acquired the full use of our language and of the Portuguese, and become habituated to our manners and mode of dress; and as she had also frequently attended divine service, and had furthermore, (as is presumed) lived in concubinage with our, or other German people (natien) not having any particular familiarity with her kindred or countrymen; which is the case also with her mother who also maintains herself by earning daily wages amongst our inhabitants - That, from the said allegations and reasons, it is concluded that the said Hottentot cannot be any longer considered as having led the usual heathenish or savage Hottentot mode of life, but to have entirely relinquished the same, and adopted our manners and customs and that accordingly, she had enjoyed, like other inhabitants, our protection, under the favour of which she had lived; as this *animal* then, has not only - actuated by a diabolical inspiration - transgressed against the laws of nature, which are common to all created beings; but also - as a consequence of her said education - through her Dutch mode of life - against the law of nations, and the civil law, having enjoyed the good of our kind favour and protection, she must consequently be subject to the rigorous punishment of evil ... (Moodie, 1838, pp. 315-316).

The interesting part of this judgement is Sara's colonial subject status. With the trial of Lacus, Sara was considered a "heathen" and was not allowed to testify under oath. Thus, she was not granted colonial subject status in the Lacus trial. However, after she took her life, she was given subject status. Sara's corpse was trialled using natural law and referred to as an "animal". She was denied burial, and her corpse was impaled and left in public to rot. Upham (2013) argues that Sara is the only known case handled this way, so she served as an example for the rest of the Khoekhoe. It could have been revenge for the two burghers Gonnema killed before the second Khoekhoe-Dutch War.

Even though Sara received the colonial subject status after her death, it was never a status she could enjoy. It also demonstrates that Krotoa and Lydia, in the colonial society at the Cape, were in a class higher than Sara. Krotoa and Lydia were equals in colonial society. According to McKinnon (2004, p. 48), "the Dutch held Krotoa up as a role model to other Khoekhoe women, an example of how successful they could be if they were baptised, 'educated' and 'civilised'." During the trial of Sara's corpse, other criteria for colonial subject status were added: speaking a European language and adopting European customs. It, therefore, seems as if baptism, speaking a European language, and adopting European customs moved the Khoekhoe and slaves up a ladder in the Cape colonial society.

Even though Krotoa and Lydia were treated as equals, it is clear that Krotoa did not readily accept her initial role in the Cape colonial society and frequently returned to her people. After her sister died, Oedasoa broke kinship with her. When her uncle Autshumao passed away, she was completely isolated. Only then was she forced to make herself home in the Cape colonial society. When she married to Van Meerhof, they moved to Robben Island, further isolating her. It seemed she finally broke after receiving the news of her husband's passing. Krotoa passed away on 29 July 1674.

Krotoa left a remarkable legacy. According to McKinnon (2004, p. 51), "Krotoa's genes flow through branches of the Bruyns, Botma, Buys, De Vries, Oosthuizen, De Witt, Redelinghuys, Van der Vyver, Theron, Opperman, Erasmus, Smit, Botha, Van der Heever, Huisamen, and Engelbrecht families." These are some of the most common Afrikaner surnames. The irony is that the Afrikaners believed in a pure "Afrikaner race" and were strongly against miscegenation. Apartheid was later institutionalised to keep the "Afrikaner race" pure and "European." They passed several laws that institutionalised this ideology. Some Afrikaners seemingly forgot about their "impure" origin. Those who were aware of it made sure they hid it or forgot about it. Like many others, they tend to forget about their "non-white" brother and sisters. They ensured they severed all relationships with their "non-white" family because they did not want to be polluted. Purity is, thus, one of the most problematic discourses in the Afrikaner identity. As a matter of fact, there is no pure race or ethnic group in South Africa. Colonial subject identities, such as ethnicity and race, were constructed in the colonial matrix of power and became crystalised in law. It is here that identity has lost its fluidity.

'Bastards' and Miscegenation

The colonial matrix of power established a frame through which one encounters Krotoa and Sara. In some of the earliest colonial texts, the Khoekhoe were described and indexed like animals, which rendered them sub-human. For example:

> In build and shape of the body, the Hottentots, such as the Goringhaiquas, Goringhaikonas and Gorachouquas (Watermen, Capemen and Tobacco Thieves) living at and near the Cape, are on the average people of medium stature, but

slender, with ill-formed bodies and insignificant appearance, and yellowish in colour, like mulattos or yellowish Javanese (Dapper, 2011, p. 43).

The hair on the head is, among all those at the Cape, short and curly, like the wool of lambs, but thicker in the women than in the men, especially among the Kobona women. The forehead is reasonably broad, but wrinkled; the eyes beautifully black, and as clear and pure as those of the hawk (Dapper, ibid.).

In addition, the Khoekhoe were not only described in racist ways; their bodies were also appropriated for a damaging racist science. For example, Wilhelm Ten Rhyne, in his book, describes how Sara's body was appropriated and dissected by his friend Johann Schreyer. Based on Schreyer's account, Ten Rhyne describes Sara's genitalia as follows:

A surgeon of my acquaintance lately dissected a Hottentot woman who had been strangled. He observed these finger-shaped prolongations of the *Nymphae* falling down from the private parts, two nipples in one breast, and various stones in the pancreas (Ten Rhyne, 2011, p. 115)

Dapper also shared Ten Rhyne's perverted fascination with the genitalia of Khoekhoe women.

The women are small in build, especially among the Kochoquas or Saldanhars. Some are found with features so regular (due in no small measure to the fact that they are not subject to measles or smallpox) that they could have been drawn with a pencil, except that they are somewhat flat in the nose. The married women, however, have exceedingly big bosoms, so big that their breasts, which hang loose and uncovered, can be passed back over the shoulders to suckle the children whom, as a rule, they carry there. But this does not hold for the unmarried ones. *The lining of the body appears to be loose so that in certain places, part of it dangles out* (Dapper, 2011, p. 45).

Schapera, in *The early Cape Hottentots*, explains what Dapper meant by the last italicised sentence in the paragraph quoted above (see footnote 62).

This very discreetly worded sentence refers to the well-established fact that among Hottentot women, the *labia minora* are sometimes considerably elongated and may project as much as 60mm. beyond the *rima pudendi*. This hypertrophy, the so-called 'Hottentot apron', has been regarded by some writers as artificially produced by manipulation, but Schultze, who has studied it carefully, maintains that it is a natural physiological characteristic (Schapera, 2011, p. 45)

This description, the dissection, and the display of Sara's body are early indicators of coloniality in South Africa. It also shows how the world participated in framing the Khoekhoe and San. Olfertus Dapper, a Dutch physician, never set foot in the Cape. Yet, he became an authoritative figure in the history of the Khoekhoe and San. He is believed to have received letters from the Cape describing the Khoekhoe and San. These works frame Khoekhoe women as ugly prostitutes with strange genitalia. In addition, as you will notice from Schapera's explanation, he quotes Leonhard Schultze, who participated in conducting "scientific" experiments on the Khoekhoe in concentration camps in German South West Africa. Schapera refers to Leonhard Schultze, the racial scientist who conducted experiments on the Khoekhkoe during the Nama and Herero genocide. Schultze must have dissected and studied the victims of the genocide at Shark Island. Like Ten Rhyne before Schultze, the bodies of the Khoekhoe were appropriated and used for pseudo-scientific endeavours. These pseudo-scientific endeavours rendered the Khoekhoe and San into a sub-human frame.

The solution was to import European women to the Cape (McKinnon, 2004). This step can be seen as the first attempt to keep the "European race" pure and safe from miscegenation. The bastard children of European colonists were not "pure" enough to be white and not "savage" enough to be entirely abandoned by European society. They were regarded as "mix-Hottentot". These "mix-Hottentots" were also referred to as "Bastards". As we will see later in this chapter, they grew up in a class above the Khoekhoe and San in the Cape colonial society.

The contempt with which J.S. Marais, in his book, *The Cape Coloured 1652-1937*, wrote about Krotoa and other Khoekhoe women is skewed. For example, he wrote: "Eva had few successors since it soon came to be considered a disgrace for Christians (i.e. Europeans) to marry people of colour even if they were free" (Marais, 1939, p. 10). Marais footnotes the contempt "the ordinary European" had for the Khoekhoe and mentions that they had been looked down upon since the establishment of the colonial society. He regards the marriages between the Khoekhoe and the colonists as "irregular" or not recognised by the colonial state and the church. Marais argues that:

> A Boer who took a Hottentot wife lost caste among his own people, nor could his children hope to join Boer society. By the second half of the eighteenth century, the Bastards were becoming a people apart from both Boers and Hottentots. They were already tending to intermarry only among themselves, and since they had large families, they were rapidly increasing in number. Thus did the Boers keep their own race pure and bring into existence a nation of half-breeds (Marais, 1939, p. 11).

The "Bastard" (also written as "Bastaard" in some colonial texts) is a problematic frame that was operationalised to first describe the so-called mix-Hottentots and later the Griqua people. For me, "Bastard" is the early form of a racialised "coloured" identity. However, as we will see later in this chapter, the "coloured" identity was not operational until *Ordinance 50 of 1828*. By then, in the Griqua states, the "bastard" identity was replaced with the ancestral Griqua identity. However, in the colony, the "bastard" identity was still operational. The "bastard" identity is colonialism's attempt to strip identity in South Africa of its fluidity. Establishing the "Hottentot" and the "Bushman" through pseudo-scientific endeavours as racial categories allowed colonialists to invent the "mix-Hottentot"; as a result, identity in South Africa lost its fluidity.

In addition, a cultural difference exists between "baster" and "bastard". I believe scholars lost a critical difference when translating "Baster" to "Bastard." From a cultural perspective, I know there is a difference between "Baster" and "half naaitjie". "Half naaitjie" was closely associated with the racialised framing of the Khoekhoe as "Bastard". "Half naaitjie" greatly offended my grandmother. "Baster", on the other hand, referred to her Khoekhoe ancestry, and she always said it with pride.

Hence, for me, reading these colonial texts, it is not surprising that these so-called "bastards" later chose their Griqua ancestry as their identity. Many of them were, after all, of Griqua descent. According to Besten (2006), "the 19th century Griqua derived their name comprised two groups referred to by the Dutch in the 1650s and 1660s as the 'Great Chariguriqua' and the 'Little Chariguriqua' or by some other variation of these words." Nienaber (1989, p. 57) explains that colonists did not realise that Chari (ǂkhari) already meant "little" and assumed that Chariguriqua was the name of the tribe. According to Besten (2006) the territory of the Little Griqua was "south of the Great Berg River, that is, in the vicinity of (what became) Moorreesburg and Malmesbury. The Great Griqua dwelled in the region between the northern side of the Great Berg River, the Olifants River further north and the Kouebokkeveld and the Cederberg in the east, that is, in the vicinity of Piketberg and Ebenhaeser". Since colonisation systematically dispossessed the Khoekhoe tribes of their lands and livestock, it forced the Khoekhoe (Cochoqua and Charigriqua) and the Griqua to migrate north into Namaqualand and Bushmanland.[11] The most famous of these migrations is the one of Adam Kok. Hence, notably, it was outside the colony's boundaries that the Griqua rejected the "bastard" identity. When they once again were in control of the state-building exercise (Besten, 2006; Legassick, 2010).

---

[11]   The forced migrations of the Khoekhoe are illustrated in Nienaber (1989).

Therefore, at a conceptual level, "Coloured people" means impure or dirty. "Coloured," thus, is a derogatory term. Martin Legassick, in *The Politics of a South African Frontier*, and Michael Besten, in *Transformation and reconstitution of Khoe-San identities*, troubles the metanarrative of J.S. Marais. For example, the "Bastards" rejected their "half-breed" status and formed the Griqua State at Klaarwater (Griquatown). This in itself is a testimony that they regard themselves as Khoekhoe. The Griqua State was an affiliation of various Khoekhoe and San groups. The state also gave refuge to slaves and anyone who escaped the colony's boundaries. In Volume 2 of *Travels in the Interior of Southern Africa*, William Burchell also painted a picture of an integrated Griqua State. The Griqua State comprised of people with various ethnic and racial affiliations. Since pre-colonial identity was fluid, anyone could become Griqua. Identity in the various Griqua states maintained most of its fluidity. However, a racialised notion of Griqua identity crept into its fold as the Griqua state-building exercise unfolded in Phillipollis, Kokstad, and later the apartheid state (Besten, 2006).

This racialised notion of the Griqua identity resulted from its relationship with the colonial state. Reading the works of Besten (2006) and Legassick (2010), it becomes apparent to me that the Griqua "state" had no true independence and was an early form of the "Homeland system". Firstly, the Griqua chiefs had to be appointed and recognised by the colonial state. Secondly, even though they saw themselves as independent states, the British colonial state did not treat them as such. According to Besten (2006, p. 42), "Just as it was with Griqua captaincies in Griqualand West, the Griqua stood in an ambiguous relation to the colonial government, treated at times as if they were independent and at other times as if they were British subjects." Thirdly, missionaries eroded the cohesion that existed among the Griqua. For example, the missionaries influenced the political structures of the Griqua. Missionary interference eventually led to Cornelius Kok I, Cornelius Kok II, and Berend Barendse moving away from Griquatown because they disagreed with the rule of Andries Waterboer (Besten, 2006; Legassick, 2010). Waterboer strictly followed the rules set by the London Mission Society (LMS). These influences of the colonial state and the church influenced how and when "Griqua citizenship" was given. This "Griqua citizenship" translated into being Griqua, and this identity was not racialised. However, this identity could be seen as ethnic, and this ethnic identity largely contained its fluidity.[12] Only when the Griqua state was absorbed into the colony were they formally classified as "Coloured".

---

[12] I am aware that in other parts of the world and Africa, ethnic identities were racialised and lost their fluidity.

This brief historical account of the Griqua raises the obvious question: What happened to the Cochoqua, Chainouqua, and Hessequa, among others? I believe two things happened. Firstly, some were absorbed into the colonial state. Others migrated northwards to escape the settler's violence and joined the Namaqua, Griqua, the San, and the !Kora. These are the lesser-known migrations. Nienaber (1989), in *Khoekhoense stamname: 'n voorlopige verkenning,* uses linguistic evidence to show the migration patterns of these Khoekhoe groups. Nienaber's (1989) migration charts show how these groups joined the Griqua, Namaqua, Hessequa, Chainouqua, etc. From Mellet's (2020) *The Lie of 1652,* one notices that this colonial expansion led to 19 wars over 227 years. For example, the third major war the Dutch wage was against the Chainouqua and the Hessequa from 1701 to 1705. In Nienaber's migration model, the Cochoqua migrated into Chainouqa, Hessequa, Attaqua, and other territories. Since these Khoekhoe Groups were linked through clans, I believe they were incorporated into one another.

Therefore, those who remained in the colony and at the frontier were branded "Hottentot" or "*Hotnot*" and "Bastards" (*half naaitjie*). We will see the colonial state absorbed the Khoekhoe and the San, erased their ancestry, and they were classified as the "Cape Coloured People". This colonial classification rendered them extinct in the colony. They no longer existed.

Nevertheless, they did exist. They were just bureaucratically erased. Hence, when Marais analysed the culture of the Cape Coloured People, he indicated that the Khoekhoe's pre-colonial way of living is "extinct" or "nearly extinct". However, it was just hidden and marginalised. In the next chapter, we will examine one such case: the /khâba ra. Words like Marais' (1939) further erased the Khoekhoe (Hottentot or *Hotnot*) and the San (Bushman or *Boesman*) who lived in the Union of South Africa. Those who still identified as Khoekhoe were systematically erased by bureaucratic classification. The Nama, the Griqua, Koranna, and the *Boesman* are good examples of this. They still identify as Khoekhoe and San even though they were classified otherwise.

Violence against the Khoekhoe and San

Bulhan (1985, p. 135) defines violence as follows: "Violence is any relation, process, or condition by which an individual or group violates the physical, social, and/or psychological integrity of another person or group." The definition allows one to uncover all hidden forms of violence. Generally, when one thinks of violence, one thinks of a physical act. For example, someone was beaten, shot or stabbed by someone else. However, Fanon broadened the scope of violence by "boldly analysing violence in its structural, institutional, and personal dimensions'" (Bulhan, 1985, p. 138).

The reason for the narrow scope before Fanon was that "Personal violence is the easiest to discern and control and its effects are easiest to assess" (Bulhan, 1985, p. 136). Thus, what one in most cases considers violence is only one form of violence (personal violence), whereas "Structural violence is a feature of social structures. This form of violence is inherent in the established modes of social relations, distribution of goods and services, and legal practices of dispensing justice" (Bulhan, ibid.). The laws and institutions are used to legalise and normalise this kind of violence. Thus, "structural violence leads to hidden but lethal inequities, which can lead to the death of those who lack power or influence in the society" (Bulhan, ibid.).

Apartheid, colonialism, and slavery, as systems of oppression, are all forms of structural violence. To explain this in more detail, let one consider the following:

> In a situation in which oppression spans generations, the violence to which it owes its origin and sustenance is masked and obfuscated. The law, the media, education, religion, work relations, the environment – the whole ensemble of cultural and material arrangements of society remain infused with violence, which becomes harder to discern the longer one lives under this condition of oppression (Bulhan, 1985, p. 137).

The majority of Africa was colonised after abolishing the transatlantic slave trade. Scott (1999, p. 86) makes an important observation in this regard: "Reform, therefore, depends upon a 'norm of civilisation' and a division between those who are ready for citizenship and those who have to be made ready for it (blacks, women, the colonised, and the working class)." In colonial Africa, those branded "savages" and "natives" first had to be "civilised" before they could qualify for citizenship. This happened to the Khoekhoe and San.

Europeans attempted to "tame" or "civilise" the Khoekhoe and San people from the first European settlement. Violence was structurally and physically imposed. The structural violence started with how they were written in colonial text. These colonial texts were written from a prejudiced Western ideological frame (Burchell, 1822a, 1822b; Dapper, 2011; Hahn, 1881; Moodie, 1838; Tachard, 1688; Ten Thyne, 2011). Western philosophical texts positioned Europeans as Man (human) and placed the rest of the world's population on a civilisation hierarchy. Since the Europeans were at the top, the indigenous Africans had to be at the bottom of this hierarchy. Thus, when Europeans encountered the Khoekhoe and San, they, too, were placed on this civilisation hierarchy. As mentioned, texts written on the Khoekhoe and San established them as sub-human.

> All the Kafirs or Hottentots are people bereft of all science and literature, very uncouth, and in intellect more like beasts than men. Some, however, through steady intercourse with our countrymen, gradually let the sparks of their human nature come to light, just as several at the Fort are also beginning to grasp the Dutch language (Dapper, 2011, p. 45).

Thus, miscegenation was identified very early as one of the key ways to "civilise" the "Khoekhoe race". This "civilising" responsibility fell onto European males, who required to have "steady intercourse" with Khoekhoe women to breed a more intelligent being. As mentioned earlier, command of a European language was also used as a "civilisation" marker. For example, Dapper positions Dutch as a more "civilised" language than the Khoekhoe language. Thus, the Khoekhoe's "civilising" potential also rested with Europeans.

Land dispossession played an important role in "civilising" the Khoekhoe and the San. The colonists (trek Boer) and their children saw it beneath them to work on the land taken from the Khoekhoe (Van der Merwe, 2006). As a result, slaves, Khoekhoe, and San, were forced to work on these farms. This also contributed to the rapid expansion of the colony and the dispossession of Khoekhoe lands. With the help of the Boer Commandoes, the children of frontier colonists drove the Khoekhoe and San off their lands to ensure that they, too, could have farms. The sub-human colonial frame made land dispossession and the extermination of the San and Khoekhoe easier.

The systematic land dispossession of the Khoekhoe and San rapidly expanded the boundaries of the colonial state. This colonial expansion resulted in an ever-expanding colonial frontier.[13] Laws implemented in the colonial state excluded the Khoekhoe and the San from accessing land. However, the "Bastards" were given some access. Some Khoekhoe also adopted colonial farming methods and established farms on the frontier. Since the "trek Boer" phenomenon resulted in an ever-expanding colonial state, the "Bastards" and Khoekhoe farmers, too, were dispossessed of their farms (Legassick, 2010).

The forced migration of the Khoekhoe, "Bastards", and the "trek Boers" also led to the clash with the San people and, subsequently, their genocide. The San genocide happened at the colonial frontier as the colonial state expanded into San territory. The sub-human colonial frame of the San made the extermination easier.

---

[13] See Martin C. Legassick. (2010). *The Politics of a South African Frontier: The Griqua, the Sotho-Tswana and Missionaries, 1780-1840.* Basler Afrika Bibliographien.

> The tradition early took root among the men on the frontier that the Bushmen were no better than wild animals and that it was justifiable to exterminate them like so much vermin. On their side, the Bushmen became fiercer and more predatory as their means of subsistence disappeared before their eyes (Marais, 1939, p. 15).

> But if the little hunters were shot down in their tens and twenties during the first half of the eighteenth century, during the next fifty years, they perished in their hundreds. That was the period of maximum extermination, and it effectually broke the back of Bushman resistance (Marais, ibid.).

The "Bushman" was framed as a wild animal, making their extermination possible. In addition, from Marais' text, it is apparent that the "Bushman resistance" presupposes a resistance against European colonists' attempts to dispossess the San of their lands and force (or tame) them into working as servants on the farms of these colonists. Moreover, scholars like P.J. van der Merwe justified the genocide of the San because they plundered the cattle of frontier colonialists. In the *Die Noordwaartse Beweging van die Boere Voor die Groot Trek* and *Trek: Studies oor die Mobiliteit van die Pioniersbevolking aan die Kaap (1770-1842)*, the San is labelled as thieves who liked to plunder the cattle of the frontier colonialist. In Van der Merwe's account, Frontier colonists only defended themselves. The colonists were treated as the actual victims and had to take it upon themselves to punish the "Bushman".[14]

However, Burchell (1822b) and Marais (1939) had to admit that the San only started to plunder because they were systematically driven off their lands, forcing them into the desert. Only when they faced starvation did they begin to plunder. According to Findlay:

> [Louis] Anything stressed that the San had not only suffered decimation from being shot, but that, in many cases the hunters were starving to death. He not only called the colonists "intruders and usurpers of the Native lands", he also recognised that "because of their encroachment, wild game had become scarce and almost inaccessible; so had honey, grass-seed, roots and ostrich eggs (Findlay, 1977, p. 36).

Louis Anything, a magistrate appointed by the British colonial government, was sent to investigate the genocide of the San. This investigation came after Anything wrote a letter to Attorney-General William Porter about possible atrocities against the San. The Louis Anything report details the San's starvation and that cattle theft was an attempt not to starve. However, as the report indicated, many died of starvation (Marais, 1939, pp. 28-29)

---

[14] See P. J. Van der Merwe. (2016). *Die Noordwaartse Beweging van die Boere Voor die Groot Trek (1770-1842)*. African Sun Media, 2016 and Van der Merwe, P.J. (2006). *Trek: studies oor die mobiliteit van die pioniersbevolking aan die Kaap (1770-1842)* (Spesiale herdruk.). African Sun Media.

The colonists' intention was extermination. According to Anything, "parties were in the habit of going out to hunt and shoot any Bushmen they might find" (Anything in Marais, 1939, p. 28). Marais (1939, pp. 16-17) argues that the Boer Commandoes were responsible for the San genocide. However, Legassick (2010) highlights that frontier colonists often had the help of "Bastards Commandoes". The "Khoi/Coloureds, Khoi and Xhosa from Schietfontein, Namaqualand, the Bokkeveld, Hantarn, Roggeveld, the districts of Calvinia, Fraserburg, and Hope Town had all shared in the San's destruction" (Findlay, 1977, p. 36). Thus, it seems that the colonists, the Khoekhoe, the Xhosa, and the "Bastards" all participated in the extermination of the San. In 1774, colonial records indicate that 503 San were killed, and 239 San were captured. From 1786 to 1795, colonial records show 2,504 San were killed and 669 were taken to prison. In addition, San children were generally imprisoned and signed-up for "apprenticeship" (Marais, 1939, p. 17). This practice continued well in the 19th Century. Thus, a century later, the photos Bleek took of /A!kunta, //Kabbo, ‡Kasin, /Han‡kass'o, and Dia!kwain give us a face to the victims of the ongoing genocide.

The 18th Century San genocide took place outside the legal boundaries of the Cape Colony.[15] Given this, those responsible for the genocide were never prosecuted. However, in 1847 Sir Harry Smith, then Governor of the Cape Colony, extended the colony's borders to the Orange River. Moreover, in August 1868, the Cape Government passed the *Northern Border Protection Act* to restore order at the border (Bank, 2006, pp. 77-78). From then onwards, the genocide took place inside the legal boundaries of the Cape Colony, but this time, the state spearheaded the genocide, not the colonists. Therefore, this violence was not seen as genocidal but merely as a means to protect the state. Given this, the extermination of the San is well-documented, but the Dutch and British states never recognised it as a genocide.

Missionary Societies

Since I discussed the land dispossession of the Khoekhoe and the San in the previous chapter, in this section, I am only responding to Marais' assertions regarding the land dispossession of the Khoekhoe. Marais states, "By 1809,

---

[15] Adhikari's *The Anatomy of a South African Genocide: The extermination of the Cape San people* is a curated work on the genocide and will give readers an easy-to-follow version of the genocide. Adhikari, at the end of his book, gives a list of further reading on the genocide, and to that list, I would like to add: Skotnes, P. (1996). *Miscast: negotiating the presence of the Bushmen.* University of Cape Town Press, and Bank, A. (2006). *Bushmen in a Victorian world: the remarkable story of the Bleek-Lloyd collection of Bushmen folklore.* Double Storey.

it is necessary to repeat, most of the Hottentots were already in the farmers' service. They had lost their land over which they had been thinly scattered as nomads" (1939, p. 123). There are two issues I would like to point out here. The first is the date 1809. This was the year the *Hottentot Proclamation* came into effect. The second is Marais' word choice. It does not recognise the violent manner in which the Khoekhoe "lost their lands." His word choice also situates the Khoekhoe as nomads with no fixed sense of home or belonging. They are depicted as wanderers over a vast, empty South Africa. In Chapter 2, I established that land tenure among the Khoekhoe was based on inalienable common property.

Access and ownership were outside the philosophical frame of European colonialists – outside the Lockean notion of land ownership. Hence, the underlying premise of Marais' argument is Lockean. Early colonialists applied Natural Law to dispossess the Khoekhoe and San of their lands. They also applied natural law to exterminate the San. Mellet (2020) makes a compelling argument regarding the land ownership model the VOC applied in South Africa. Mellet (2020) explains that from 1657 until 1814, a communal feudal approach to "land ownership" was applied. During that time, the Dutch East Indian Company owned all the property the frontier colonists violently took from the Khoekhoe and San. These lands were leased back to colonists in the form of *leningplaats*. Thus, the trek Boer phenomenon, constantly dispossessed the Khoekhoe and San of their lands, which were then transferred to the VOC as private property.

As a result, colonists continuously and forcefully occupied the lands of the Khoekhoe and San. In addition, Mellet also argues that "The VOC corporate ownership under of land was not very different from the community land ownership under trust or custodianship of indigenous African leaders, who were highly conscious of their role" (Mellet, 2020, p. 161). In contrast, a Khoekhoe leader had no absolute say over who could have livestock or land. Also, despite no fences, there were boundaries between various Khoekhoe tribes. For example, Khoekhoe groups knew where the Cochoqua's started, and the territory of the Chainouqua's began. Grazing rights within these territorial groups were shared. The same practices were visible among various San groups.[16]

---

[16] See Bank, A. (2006). *Bushmen in a Victorian World. The remarkable story of the Bleek-Lloyd Collection of Bushman folklore.* Double Storey Books, for an in-depth discussion.

The Khoekhoe were not allowed to own land within the colony's boundaries, and the *Hottentot Proclamation* forced them to carry passes and, ironically, work on the *leningplaats* of colonists. This proclamation trapped them within the colony's borders and made it difficult for them to leave. In addition, the only land that was made available to the Khoekhoe was through missionaries. According to Marais (1939, p. 123):

> The only practicable way of giving the Hottentots "a stake in land" was to utilise the assistance of the missionaries, who were prepared to try and convert the nomadic Hottentot pastoralists into agriculturists on the limited lands which were all that a poverty-stricken Government could make available as 'institutions'.

Thus, there was little room for being Khoekhoe in the colony. They could not live in the villages or towns. Their only option (provided in law) was to work for colonists or join missionary societies.

Moravian Mission Society

George Schmidt attempted to establish the first mission in 1737 at Baviaans Kloof. According to Marais (1939, p. 135), "Within a few months of his arrival at Capetown (July 1737), Schmidt had taken up his abode at a Hottentot kraal situated not far from where Genadendal now stands. Seven months later, he moved to Genadendal itself, then known by the name of Baviaans Kloof." The purpose of Schmidt's move to Baviaans Kloof was to Christianise the Khoekhoe. This was because the Khoekhoe in the area "still lived in the manner of their ancestors ... They still possessed some cattle, still spoke their own language, and could not understand Dutch" (Marais, 1939, p. 135). However, the colonists around the Baviaans Kloof area were against the Christianisation of the Khoekhoe. With Christianisation came Western education, which meant that more and more Khoekhoe children went to school, which created a labour shortage. Since Schmidt felt constrained and had differences with the local clergy members, he left in 1743.

Fifty years after George Schmidt, another attempt was made attempt to establish a mission amongst the Khoekhoe in the Cape Colony. 1792 saw the arrival of missionaries Hendrik Marsveld, Daniel Schwinn, and Christian Kühnel at Genadendal to pick up where Schmidt had left. Genadendal quickly grew. By 1806, it was the second-biggest town in South Africa. Cape Town was the only other town bigger than Genadendal. According to Balie (1988, pp. 36-40), the population of Genadendal grew from 705 in 1798 to 1457 in 1836. Since the mission at Genadendal enjoyed the protection of the Commander of the Dutch East Indian Company, the mission became a safe haven for Khoekhoe,

"Bastards", and black people. And later, they were protected by the Governor of the Cape Colony under British rule. In addition, locally, the mission also enjoyed the protection of Marthinus Theunissen (who the missionaries referred to in their dairy as "Baas Theunissen"). He was a soldier turned wealthy farmer in Baviaanskloof.

In 1992 H.C. Bredenkamp, & H.E.F. Plüddermann translated and published the diaries of the missionaries as *The Genadendal Diaries: Diaries of the Herrnhut Missionaries H. Marsveld, D. Schwinn and J.C. Kühnel.* I am reading "Volume I (1792-1794)" in the section below. Herein after this text will be referred to as *The Genadendal Diaries.*

A Safe Haven for the Khoekhoe

From the diary, it is clear that the Khoekhoe anticipated the return of missionaries to Baviaanskloof. They also knew they would have some level of protection in the missionary society. Below are just three of the many examples of Khoekhoe seeking refuge in the mission.

> On the 12th a young Hottentot woman came to us and said that the farmer for whom she had worked for two years had beaten her when she told him that she wanted to learn. We told her that if she had done nothing wrong she should stay in one of the kraals here, the farmer would probably not come and get her. This is something that they have done (in the past), they came to the kraals, got the Hottentots and beat them terribly. She is staying here (The Genadendal Diaries, Volume I, 1992, p. 79).

> On the 14th. A farmer had kept back the 2 month old baby of a Hottentot woman who had wanted to come to be taught, because he did not want her to go (The Genadendal Diaries, Volume I, 1992, p. 80).

> On the 18th yet another Hottentot arrived. He has a son. The father and the son worked for a farmer. Their time was up and the son asked the farmer, how much longer he had to go on working. Because of this question the farmer beat him up terribly with a sjambok (The Genadendal Diaries, ibid.).

Even a Khoekhoe Captain came to the Genadendal missionary to complain about the colonists. The Captain travelled four weeks to get to Genadendal. "He complained bitterly about the farmers. He said that the farmers take away the Hottentots' livestock, use their women sinfully and enslave their children" (The Genadendal Diaries, Volume I, 1992, p. 91). The violence Khoekhoe women reported to the missionaries indicates that the sex with Khoekhoe women could not have been consensual. In addition, the Captain reporting these crimes to the Landdrosts did not help much because the Landdrosts and the farmers were friends. In a footnote in the diaries Bredenkamp et al. (1992, p. 70), explain that the Landdrost was the chief police officer and Commander of the local Commando. The field cornet reported to the Landdrost. Nevertheless, often, the Landdrost and the field cornet were friends or related (Leggasick, 2010; Van der Merwe, 1988). Hence, no justice could be expected for the Khoekhoe from a system skewed toward the coloniser.

The Khoekhoe and San lived in a colony where their rights were minimal, and the colonists were a law unto themselves. As a result, the Khoekhoe were constantly in danger. Take, for example, the case of an unnamed Khoekhoe who travelled ten days seeking refuge for himself and his family at Genadendal.

> On the 14th a Hottentot arrived from ten days' journey away. He had been at the Cape and asked the Commander for permission to come here to us and learn. The Commander had sent him here to Baas Theunissen, assuming that he would still meet us here. He ran away from his master whom he had served for seven years. He has five children whom he wants to fetch and have taught here. But they are with that farmer and if he goes there now he is in danger of being shot (The Genadendal Diaries, Volume I, 1992, p. 70).

> Several Hottentots came to visit us. A few of them told us that on the other side of the mountains there lived many Hottentots who wanted to move to us to learn. Many of them are still employed by the farmers who do not want to let them go. There seems to be quite a rebellious atmosphere on the other side of the mountains. The Hottentots no longer want to stay (The Genadendal Diaries, Volume I, 1992, p. 78).

These accounts tell of the threat of ever-present violence against the Khoekhoe. In the first account, the Khoekhoe knew he could be killed if he returned to the farmer, yet his family was stuck on the farm. More striking is the practice of keeping Khoekhoe children captive and at ransom during this period. This is another example that Khoekhoe children were not considered children but part of the colonist's workforce. These accounts indicate that the Khoekhoe realised early on that Western and missionary education might rescue them and their children from serfdom. Hence, the Khoekhoe came from far and wide to give their children an opportunity to survive oppression.

Colonists, seeing the mission as a threat appeared to be friendly when the missionaries visited them. However, they soon found out that the colonists resented them for the work they were doing and what they were representing.

> But one cannot be surprised that they are cross. Many Hottentots are already saying that they don't want to continue working for the farmers but want to come to us and learn. Who is supposed to do the work on the farms if not the Hottentots? They cannot buy so many slaves, because sometimes they need many workers and at other times only a few. They hire the Hottentots for a few days or weeks. When the work is done they send them away. But that is impossible with slaves;

and many farmers are not allowed to buy slaves because they have maltreated them in the past. They have to rely on Hottentots. Further inland there are said to be farmers who employ 20 to 30 Hottentots (The Genadendal Diaries, Volume I, p. 70).

There are several interesting points to note from this passage. Firstly, colonial officials were aware of the cruelty of some colonists. Many colonists were so cruel that they were not allowed to own slaves. Hence, they relied on Khoekhoe labour for their work on farms. Secondly, since it was before machinery, much labour was needed for farming activities. As a result, some colonists needed up to 20 to 30 Khoekhoe to work on the farms. The Khoekhoe at Genadendal attended school five days a week. Most of the Khoekhoe helped the missionaries with various activities for the remaining two days. Thus, the settlement at Genadendal was a threat to the existence of the local economy and the colonists' existence. The colonists needed the Khoekhoe for their existence.

Moreover, some white people like Marthinus Theunissen admitted that white colonists were the true aggressors. "[Theunissen] said that the Christians had deserved it ten times over because the Christians had treated them without pity. They dispossessed them and took their land and hunted them like game. He said if a farmer shot a kaffir it meant as little as if he had shot a buck" (The Genadendal Diaries, Volume I, 1992, p. 113). In addition, since the Khoekhoe knew how cruel the colonists were, those who settled at Genadendal rarely took their wives and children with them when they did seasonal work. Burchell (1822a, p. 114) also mentions that Khoekhoe women and children were not paid for their labour on the colonists' farms.

The Christianisation of the Khoekhoe

With Christian education came Western norms, values, and religion. The belief among missionaries was "Decent Hottentot men and women also wear clothes. Many of (the Hottentots) don't want to work but lie in their huts all day long. Their clothing consists of nothing but a sheep skin which they call a karos. They hang it over their shoulders. In front they have a small bit of fur to cover their private parts" (The Genadendal Diaries, Volume I, 1992, p. 68). Firstly, the Khoekhoe knew they were exploited. Consequently, they did not want to work. Secondly, the measure of "decent" was set by Europeans. Hence, European clothing was one such measure. The Khoekhoe were actively encouraged by the missionaries to change to European clothing. Thus, when Burchell visited Genadendal in 1811, many Khoekhoe inhabitants already wore European clothing, especially the women. However, most Khoekhoe men at the time still mixed their clothes. Many wore trousers with a karos over their shoulders (Burchell, 1822a, p. 109).

Moreover, missionary education aimed to convert the Khoekhoe into Christians. "[T]hose who attended school have to be quiet and diligent and their purpose had to be to get to know the dear Saviour as their Creator and Redeemer and to live in this world in a manner pleasing to Him" (The Genadendal Diaries, Volume I, p. 104). However, these Christian standards set by the missionaries were different applied to the Khoekhoe than to Europeans. For example, Europeans, including the missionaries, could drink alcohol, but the Khoekhoe was discouraged and ridiculed for drinking alcohol. In addition, the Europeans could celebrate weddings, but the Khoekhoe were not allowed to dance or do their customary celebration when a child was born. The baptised Khoekhoe were also not allowed to continue their age-old burial rituals. Those found guilty of dancing and singing a Khoekhoe song were banished from the missionary and valley. They had to atone for their sins and were only accepted back into the missionary after the missionaries were convinced they had repented (Balie, 1988).

The condition staying on at the Genadendal missionary was baptism. Once a Khoekhoe person was baptised, they had to renounce their Khoekhoe culture, religion, and customs. If not, they had to leave the missionary.

> On the 12[th.] a sad thing happened with Dorothea, the last woman we baptised. She went to the hills to fetch firewood. There she started to sing a Hottentot song and danced. Soon some who heard and saw this came to tell us about it. We had her called straight away. She was quite calm and said: Yes, I did it. We reminded her of what she had promised us at her baptism. She said very often that she renounced the devil and all his works. This had now proved to have been a lie and she wanted to continue to serve the devil. For this reason she should leave us, for we could not recognise her as our sister (The Genadendal Diaries, Volume I, 1992, p. 215).

From this passage, the missionaries at Genadendal considered the Khoekhoe language and culture the devil's work. Therefore, to the missionaries being Khoekhoe was the work of the devil. The Khoekhoe had to renounce who they were to be educated at the Genadendal missionary.

Furthermore, when the missionaries met the Khoekhoe in and around Baviaanskloof, they could speak Dutch (The Genadendal Diaries, Volume I, p. 68). This did not mean that the Khoekhoe no longer spoke their language. They did, but were not allowed to continue speaking or performing songs once they were baptised. As mentioned earlier, it was considered the devil's work. Therefore, Western education and Christianisation contributed to the disappearance of the Khoekhoe language in Genadendal. In addition, missionary education in Genadendal was only in Dutch. However, when the Cape became a British colony in 1806, the Cape Governor Cradock in 1813 started to formalise the education system in the colony. In 1813, after a visit to Genadendal, Governor Cradock sent *The British System of Education* to the missionary at Genadendal to formalise their education system (Balie, 1988, p. 47).

Cradock and Somerset also went as far as to fundraise to improve the schooling system at Genadendal. In 1833, after acting Governor Wade visited, a concerted effort was made to introduce English in the school and the missionary station. From then on, Sunday services were in English. English was also formally introduced into the schooling curriculum at Genadendal. Hence, by 1838, many of the pupils at Genadendal could read well in English (Balie, 1988, p. 48). Thus, in 1850 Leefregt Ari was one of the last remaining Khoekhoe in Genadendal who could speak the Khoekhoe language (Balie, 1988, p. 103). The concerted effort in the missionary society to instruct in Dutch and English contributed to the systematic erasure of the Khoekhoe language in Genadendal.

Furthermore, the Khoekhoe preferred their traditional Khoekhoe home (*|haru oms*). However, the missionaries actively discouraged them and they were funded to build permanent structures. Moreover, a new type of traditional Khoekhoe home emerged. One built with clay. One of the colonists had to admit that only the Khoekhoe were able to build (Balie, 1988; The Genadendal Diaries, Volume I, 1992). Therefore, missionaries played an active role in "civilising" the Khoekhoe to Western standards. Sometimes, they used the carrot approach, and other times, they used the stick approach. However, the reality remained the same. The Khoekhoe were stuck between a rock and a hard place. They could either embrace Western "civilisation" efforts or perish at the hands of colonists. The "civilisation" option for them was the better option. Thus, the rapid population growth of Genadendal.

Apart from the labour shortage, the mission at Genadendal created colonists who were jealous of the education the Khoekhoe received from the mission. The colonists and Dutch clerics were against the education and Christianisation of the Khoekhoe. In their diary, Marsveld, Schwinn, and Kühnel, reflected on this jealousy.

> We have heard many rumours about what the farmers, coming into town from the interior have been saying about us. Some say: if the Hottentots are to be taught we would like to become Hottentots. Others: if the Moravians come to the country to teach the Hottentots we will kill them right away. These first-mentioned were telling the truth, according to Baas Theunissen. He assures us that many of the farmers cannot read a single word (The Genadendal Diaries, Volume I, 1992, p. 53).

Marsveld, Schwinn, and Kühnel were aware of these sentiments because they knew what happened to Schmidt. In 1795 with the Swellendam Nationalists' rebellion, colonists attacked the mission and burned down the school to break up the missionary society (Balie, 1988; Marais, 1939).

London Mission Society (LMS)

When Brittan occupied the Cape in 1795 and permanently colonised it in 1806, it changed how the government operated. One of the first missionaries to enjoy the support of the colonial government at the Cape was the London Mission Society (LMS). The LMS started operation in the Cape in 1799 (Marais, 1939, p. 141). Also, in 1799, the British recruited and sent Khoekhoe troops to Graaff-Reinet to assist in quelling the colonists' insurrection. Some of these soldiers were in the service of farmers who enlisted in the regiment. After quelling the insurrection, the British attempted to disarm the Khoekhoe. For the Khoekhoe, this was a sign that they would be sent back to farmers' service. Hence, they fled and joined the Xhosa insurrection on the Eastern frontier. Fearing that this alliance with the Xhosa would threaten the existence of the colonists at the Eastern frontier, it was decided to give the Khoekhoe "rebels" land since they could not be persuaded to return to the service of the colonists. Eventually, they settled at Bethelsdorp near Algoa Bay (Marais, 1939, pp. 114-115).

The land at Bethelsdorp was "entrusted to the care of the missionary Van der Kemp", employed by the LMS. Bethelsdorp is, therefore, one of the oldest LMS settlements. The second LMS missionary was established in 1811 in Zuurbraak and the third in 1813 in Pacaltsdorp (Marais, 1939, p. 143). During this time, a second Moravian mission was established at Mamre around 1807 to 1811. By then, land to the Khoekhoe was only available through "missionary societies". The missionary, thus, was earmarked for the rapid "civilisation" of the Khoekhoe.

The Hottentot Identity before Ordinance 28 of 1828

What constituted a "Hottentot'" and a "Baster" were unclear in missions and colonial society. For example, the missionaries at Genadendal learned that looks could be deceiving.

> Also, two women came who have a Christian father and a Hottentot mother. They wanted to have a look whether they liked it here, and if so, to move here. They were from a place two days' journey from here. They were dressed very neatly. If they had not said so we would not have thought them to be Hottentots (The Genadendal Diaries, Volume I, 1992, p. 103).

This is an example of "mixed-Khoekhoe" who identified as "Hottentot" and not "Baster". Thus, appearance alone was deceiving. In Chapter 2, I showed that precolonial identity was not codified in race and was fluid. Hence, one's appearance did not make one Khoekhoe, San, or Xhosa. There were different customary practices that welcomed someone into a family, clan, or nation. It was certainly not based on morphology.

Missionaries generally used morphology to differentiate between "Basters" and "Hottentots". As a rule of thumb, the missionaries look at the hair of the Khoekhoe to distinguish between "Hottentot" and "Baster". "One can recognise them by their hair. The real Hottentots have short and woolly hair, but the Basters have longer hair" (The Genadendal Diaries, Volume I, 1992, p. 94). Thus, a European notion of purity was applied to determine between true and "mixed" Hottentot. These European notions of race also crept into the colonial psyche of the oppressed. Hence, clear class tensions between "Basters" and "Hottentots" were visible. The "Basters" considered themselves to be better than the Khoekhoe. "These Basters believe that they are better than the others and thought that they would be the first (to be baptised) (The Genadendal Diaries, Volume I, 1992, p. 120). However, the official state documents in 1824 referred to these "Bastards" as Hottentot (Balie, 1988, p. 41).

Furthermore, in *The Genadendal Diaries*, Bredenkamp et al. (1992, p. 66) pointed out that "Christian" in the Cape Colony always meant (European). Hence, the "Hottentot" and "Kaffir" were the "uncivilised Other". If one contrasts the missionary experience at Genadendal with that of the Griqua states, there was a more evident race and class consciousness in the colony than at the frontier.

The Griqua in the Griqua states opted to use the missionary societies to their benefit as a new way of survival against the onslaught of colonialism. Firstly, Besten (2006) explains that missionaries found converting the Griqua to Christianity challenging. Those who converted did not play an active role in the missionary society. I believe this conversion was difficult because the Khoekhoe, San, Tswana, Xhosa, and Sotho had the freedom of movement, religion, and identity. They were free to be themselves. In the colony, they were not given the same privileges. In the colony, they were in bondage. Secondly, many Griqua opted for a Christian identity because it gave them access to Western education. Like the Khoekhoe and San in the colony, the Griqua understood they would need a Western education to survive the onslaught of colonialism. Western education allowed them to read and write, which became crucial to securing a future for generations to come.

Bureaucratic Erasure

The "coloured" identity was not a stable social construct throughout the era of white rule. As illustrated above, the Khoekhoe and San lifestyles were systematically erased to create a "civilised" and "Christianised" version of the "Hottentot" (Khoekhoe). At first, they were framed as "savages" and rendered sub-human. Then, some were even labelled as the "bastards" or "mix-Hottentot". They were also dispossessed of their lands and bonded to farms and missionary societies. The next phase was their bureaucratic erasure. The Khoekhoe's bureaucratic erasure happened systematically from 1828 onwards in various colonial and apartheid laws. It started with the *Ordinance 50 of 1828*, and more and more laws and government processes added to this erasure. The move was from referring to the Khoekhoe and San as "Hottentot" and "Bushman" to "Coloured." Thus, the final bureaucratic erasure was the *Population Registration Act of 1950*. This section will briefly discuss these laws and processes.

Slavery and Pass Laws Until 1809

South Africa institutionalised a pass system for slaves. For example, from 1760 onwards, slaves in the colony had to carry a pass, and any European passer-by could ask to see it. This system was later extended to the Khoekhoe people. Marais (1939, p. 117) states, "In 1797 the Swellendam Board of Landdrost and Heemraden ordained that all Hottentots moving about the country for any purpose should carry passes." These early pass laws trapped the Khoekhoe inside the colony.

The Khoekhoe were similarly bonded as slaves to supplement the colony's labour deficit as it expanded into the interior of South Africa. Marais (1939, p. 112) states, "It was natural that in a colony where slavery flourished, the European should regard all coloured labour from the slave-owner's point of view." I have to disagree with Marais. There was nothing "natural" about slavery and how colonists treated the Khoekhoe. I am aware that Marais is trying to emphasise that not every non-European was automatically reduced to a servant position, but every European was elevated to a "master" position in the colony. Even the missionaries at Genadendal elevated themselves above the Khoekhoe to a master position. For example, Marsvled, Schwinn, and Kühnel make the following entry. "On the 10th we sent our Hottentot to Baas Theunissen to fetch six sheep for us" (The Genadendal Diaries, Volume I, 1992, p. 123). Their master sentiments are expressed with "our Hottentot." In addition, it was demanded by the Swellendam "Nationals" during the 1795 revolt that the Company must force the Khoekhoe and the San to call white people "lord and master" (Marais, 1939, p. 113). The Swellendam "Nationals" also asked "that all Bushmen captured by commandos or by private individuals might be retained in perpetual slavery by the Boers – they and their children after them" (Marais, ibid.). Clearly, the colonists had a slave-owner mentality and enforced the master-slave relationship in South Africa. The global practice of slavery had influenced them to the extent that they were no different from the plantation owners in the South of the United States of America.[17] Caledon, in 1809, supposedly passed the *Hottentot Proclamation* to protect the Khoekhoe and San from slavery. However, the *Hottentot Proclamation* revamped the colony's pass laws and put the practices of colonists into law.

Hottentot Proclamation of 1809

The *Hottentot Proclamation* was passed by Du Pré Alexander, the 2nd Earl of Caledon (also referred to as Lord Caledon). Caledon served as Governor of the Cape Colony from 1807 to 1811. The Proclamation was to address the labour scarcity in the Colony. This labour scarcity resulted from abolishing the slave trade in 1807 in the entire British Empire. Theal (cited in Marias, 1939) argued that the *Proclamation* saved the Khoekhoe from utter destruction. However, by the time of Caledon and the passing of the *Hottentot Proclamation,* many Khoekhoe groups had been erased from the Colony. Caledon's law did not amend this destruction or attempt to do something about the erasure. It just redefined the bondage of the Khoekhoe in the Colony.

The law stated that Khoekhoe needed "a fixed place of abode, registered at the landdrost's office, from which he was not to move without a pass" (Marais, 1939, p. 116). Marais (1939) explained that not all inhabitants had a fixed abode. The "trek boers" were nomads and were exempted from this. In contrast, the Khoekhoe needed a signed pass to travel anywhere. This could be obtained from the farmer where they were "employed" or from a missionary. They needed a pass from the field cornet if they wanted to leave the district. This made the missionary and farmers the masters of the Khoekhoe. Under the Proclamation, every Khoekhoe person could be detained and imprisoned if they did not present a pass. They had to stay in prison until their "master" claimed them. If the person did not have a "master", they had to remain in jail until a "master" was found (Marais, 1939, p. 126). The *Hottentot Proclamation* trapped them in the colony, and they were treated as the property of the colonists, the missionaries and the Colonial Government.

---

[17] In Chapter 5, I will discuss how slavery in the American South informed apartheid in South Africa.

In addition, the *Hottentot Proclamation* also created Mission Stations that were strictly reserved for the "Hottentot". The pass system ensured they were "civilised" at these Mission Stations. They could not leave without the permission of the missionary in charge. Since the missions became sites of refuge, the number of Khoekhoe who entered missionary societies increased rapidly. Moreover, the missionary societies allowed them to escape the devastating effects of the Hottentot laws that bound them to farms. Thus, more and more Khoekhoe fled the violence of the colonists and joined the missionaries. Through the missionaries, they were introduced to Western education and converted to Christianity.

Marais (1939) argues the law introduced some "positive" measures like the nonpayment of alcohol, wages needed to be paid as agreed on, and the Khoekhoe could not be detained for longer than they were contracted. In addition, the *Proclamation* stipulated that they had to be informed, and a representative must have a copy of it (Marais, 1939, p. 117). However, it is unclear whether the Khoekhoe knew about these conditions and whether they were informed about the *Proclamation*. However, given the power relations between farmers and the Khoekhoe, it is doubtful that they knew about these revamped labour conditions.

Sir John Cradock, 1st Baron Howden, was appointed governor after Caledon's departure in 1811. Craddock passed the 1812 amendment to the *Proclamation*. The amendment saw the introduction of the "apprenticeship" principle. According to Dooling (2005, p. 50), "The 'Hottentot Code' of 1809, as Caledon's proclamation became known in settler discourse, was bolstered by a law passed in 1812 that made provision for those Khoikhoi children who had been maintained by settlers in their first eight years, to be 'apprenticed' for ten further years." Under the apprenticeship clause, the "masters" of their Khoekhoe servants had "to instruct his apprentice in agriculture and other useful employment, to find and allow him sufficient food and clothing, and to instruct or cause him to be instructed in the principles of the Christian religion" (Theal cited in Marais, 1939, p. 128). Hence, artisans were introduced via the missionaries. As a result, the missions received an influx of "apprentices" (Marais, 1939, pp. 148-151). However, the "apprentice" principle was a smoke screen to address the labour shortage in the colony. The "apprentice" principle ensured sufficient cheap labour was available to colonists. In this sense, the *Proclamation* and "apprenticeship" principle replaced slavery. They prevented the labour shortage after abolishing slavery in the British Empire and stopped the Khoekhoe and the San from leaving the colony.

I must note that the *Proclamation* and the amendment also applied to the San. The San were also apprenticed under these laws. In these early laws, they were considered to be Hottentot. However, where the San could leave the colony after their "apprenticeship", the Khoekhoe could not (Marais, 1939, p. 24). Marais (1939) argues that here, one sees the merger of the Khoekhoe, the San and the slaves into a single category that became known as the "Cape Coloured", He argues that it was the result of social construction. However, the "coloured" identity is not a social construct. It came into existence with Ordinance 50 of 1828.

From Ordinance 50 of 1828 to the Population Registration Act of 1950

Ordinance 50 of 1828 scrapped the *Hottentot Proclamation* and the 1812 amendment. Patterson (1953, p. 26) states, "The instrument of this reform was the famous Ordinance 50 of 1828. As it referred specifically to 'Hottentots and other free persons of colour' and contained improved provisions for apprenticeship and relations between masters and coloured servants." Firstly, the Ordinance freed the Khoekhoe from forced labour. Contracts were once again "improved." At least this time they were limited to one year. Secondly, Landdrosts were not able to use "corporal punishment on misbehaving servants" (Marais, 1939, p. 156). Thirdly, "Ordinance 50 decreed that the children of Coloured People could only be apprenticed with their parents' consent" (Marais, 1939, p. 156). In this instance, the law described "apprenticed" children as "Hottentot", "Bushman", "Mantatee", "Caffre", and "Fitcani" (Malherbe, 1997, p. 129). Thus, *Ordinance 50 of 1828* gave birth to what became the "coloured" identity. At first, "Coloured People" included the "Hottentot", "Bushman", "Mantatee", "Caffre", and "Fitcani".

Needless to say, the colonists did not welcome this law. According to Patterson, the ordinance "evoked resentment and opposition amongst the majority of colonists" (ibid.). This law was responsible for an exodus of Khoekhoe from the farms and an influx of Khoekhoe "to the towns and villages" (Patterson, ibid.). This once again created a labour shortage in the colony.

Marais (1939) argues that *Ordinance 50* instituted "colour-blindness" in the law in Cape Colony. However, I cannot entirely agree with Marais. This law and the laws that followed discriminated on the basis of race. And race in South Africa was a "colour project". After *Ordinance 50*, several other laws followed that attempted to do away with bondage and to improve the labour conditions of Khoekhoe, the San and slaves in the Colony. For example, in 1833, the

Abolition of Slavery Act was passed, abolishing slavery in British colonies. In 1841, a revamped version of *Ordinance 50* saw the light, called the *Masters and Servants Ordinance of 1841*. In 1856 this ordinance was replaced with the *Masters and Servants Act no. 15*.

The Cape Colony took its first major Census in 1865. During this particular Census, there were three racial categories. They were "Hottentot", "Kafir", "European", and "other". The 1865 report does not explain what is meant by "Hottentot", "European", or 'Kafir'; who these categories included and excluded. The second official Census occurred in 1875. During this particular Census, the "Coloured" racial category appeared, including five classes of people regarded as "Coloured" in the Cape Colony. They were the "Hottentot", "Kafir proper", "Fingoes", "Malay", and "other". The 1875 report indicates that the "Hottentot" race consisted of the Namaqua, Hill Damaras, Korannas, and Bushmen. Here, it is apparent that the colonial state's deployment of the "Hottentot" erased the San.

The 1891 Census continued with the five classes that comprised the colonial state's "Coloured" racial category. In addition, the report also explains how a "Hottentot" was determined.

> Please note that there are comparatively few purebred individuals of the Hottentot Race extant, and that it is not intended that persons should be classed as Hottentots unless the distinctive characteristics of that Race predominate. Where the Hottentot characteristics predominate, then, although the individual is of a mixed race, he should be classed as a Hottentot, otherwise, it would be safer to enter him simply as a mixed race (Census Report, 1891, pp. xix-xx).

In this passage, one observes that Census workers, appointed by the state, were given the power to decide who were Khoekhoe and who were not. If the Census worker believed someone did not look like a "Hottentot", the authority vested with the Census worker to decide what racial class the person belonged to. Clearly, the state framed who was to be Khoekhoe and who was "mixed".

After the South African War and before the forming of the Union of South Africa, the *Mission Stations and Communal Reserves Act of 1909* was passed. This particular Act speaks of "natives or coloured persons." From this law, it is evident that it was before the term 'native' was attached to "black African". This law recognised the Khoekhoe as "native" and thus indigenous.

After the Union of South Africa was formed, the first Census in the modern era was conducted in 1911. The racial categories used for the 1911 census were the same as the 1865, 1875, and 1891 censuses. The difference in the 1911 Census is the "Bantu" racial category. The Census of 1865, 1875, and 1891 did not have a "Bantu" category. After the 1911 Census onwards, the racial profile for South Africa was set. It now consisted of the three racial categories forming the basis for the *Population Registration Act of 1950*. These three racial groups were "Bantu", "Coloured", and "European". These three racial categories, therefore, became instrumental in designing the apartheid state and society. One notices that the "Bantu" racial category in 1911 consisted of the "Fingoes", Tswana, Sotho, Xhosa, etc. who were previously included in the "Coloured" racial category. The "Coloured" racial category now consisted of the "Hottentot", the Griqua, the Nama, the Malay, the Bushmen, the American coloured, the Arabian, Creole, etc. (See the table in Khalfani & Zuberi, 2001, p. 165).

For me, this also marks a departure from the English notion of "Coloured". The "Coloured" frame, developed and institutionalised post-1911, was heavily influenced by the Afrikaners' thinking regarding the purity of races. Khalfani & Zuberi (2001) argue that after the 1911 Census, four facets of government were involved in the racial classification of people in South Africa. These institutions were "the legislature, the judiciary, the Secretary of Internal Affairs and the Classification Board" (Khalfani & Zuberi, 2001, p. 163). Khalfani & Zuberi (2001) point out that racial classification leads to social stratification, which in turn leads to the discrimination of certain racially classified groups. The Afrikaners' thoughts on race introduced a regime of rights that systematically, over time, reshaped South African society. Therefore, the racial composition of South Africa building up to 1948 was designed by racist ideologues to ensure their political and economic power. These racist ideologues will be discussed in Chapter 5.

In 1948 the National Party won the election and institutionalised apartheid.[18] The National Party government passed several laws that institutionalised apartheid in South Africa. Notable amongst these was the *Prohibition of Mixed Marriages Act, Act No 55 of 1949*, the *Immorality Amendment Act, Act No 21 of 1950*, amended in 1957 (Act 23), the *Population Registration Act, Act No 30 of 1950*, the *Group Areas Act, No 41 of 1950* and in 1961 the *Coloured Persons Communal Reserves* replaced the *Mission Stations and Communal Reserves Act*. It also repeals the *Coloured Persons Settlement Areas Act*.

Of these laws, the *Population Registration Act* can be regarded as the final attempt to erase the Khoekhoe and the San bureaucratically in South Africa. The Act defines a "Coloured person" as "a person who is not a white person or a native" (Section 1 (iii)). The Act thus removed the indigenous status of

---

[18]   In Chapter 5, I will elaborate on what the institutionalisation of apartheid meant.

the Khoekhoe and San, who were included in the "Coloured" classification. "Native" in the Act is defined as "a person who in fact is or is generally accepted as a member of any aboriginal race or tribe of Africa" (Section 1, (x)). From this, it is clear that the Khoekhoe and San were now considered either mix-descendant or "civilised" to the extent they could not be considered "Hottentot" or "Boesman" or they did not exist anymore. Hence, the "native" or "aboriginal race" was reserved for "black African" people.

The Act also defined a "white person" as "a person who in appearance obviously is, or who is generally accepted as a white person, but does not include a person who, although in appearance obviously a white person, is generally accepted as a coloured person" (Section, [xv]). For being "white" the criteria was twofold. The first was that it must be "generally accepted". This means other "white people" must accept one or regard one as "white" to be considered "white". The second criterion was based on appearance. The Act highlighted that "Coloured people" who look white could not be considered White. The Act also gave the Director of Census the responsibility for classifying people into different racial groups (Section 5[1]). It was thus the Director's responsibility to determine who was "White", "Coloured", or "Native" in the Union. The Act instructs the Director to issue people with identity cards that include their racial classification.

Conclusion

This chapter shows that race in South Africa was constructed through pseudoscientific methods. These methods allowed Europeans to place them at the top of their "civilisation" ladder and every other nation below them. They had the godlike ability to move "races" up or down the ladder to suit them politically. The "civilising" mission of the Khoekhoe and San started in 1652. It began with Krotoa, who became Eva, the "civilised Hottentot". Over 300 years, the Khoekhoe and San were systematically dispossessed of their lands and livestock and subjected to the most horrendous acts of violence.

To survive their oppression, the Khoekhoe and San had to collaborate in their oppression to survive. Hence, new survival strategies were borrowed from the coloniser. To survive, the Khoekhoe and San opted for missionary education that stripped them of their Being. Some scholars might even argue that this is assimilation. However, if one has a closer look at "assimilation", one would recognise that it was greatly restricted to the spheres of Western influence: in the colonial and apartheid public domains. However, the culture, religion, and language were passed on to the next generation within the family unit.

For example, Adam Kok III's wife spoke Dutch but preferred the Griqua dialect and ensured that it was spoken within her circle of influence (Besten, 2006, p. 169). This was a form of resistance. And it is because of resistance that many people in South Africa still speak Khoekhoe and San languages. Therefore, collaboration is not in the absence of resistance. Resistance is always present.

Furthermore, no laws until 1828 policed "difference" in a racial sense. It was only after 1828 that racial consciousness based on "difference" was institu-tionalised through law. Before 1828, it was class that policed the boundaries of difference. Identities in the frontier societies were more fluid and integrated than in the colony. In the colony, the difference between "Christian" (White/ European), "Hottentot" (Khoekhoe), "Baster" (mixed-Khoekhoe), "Kaffir" (black indigene) and the slave was clearly demarcated and kept this way through class. However, the colony had some integration because many were married and chose life partners across racial and class barriers. Therefore, race was operational during this period, but it yet had to merge into its modern form of, race. However, part of the apartheid race project was born in South Africa, another in Europe and another in the Southern states of the United States of America (Lalu, 2022). This informed and influenced the racial consciousness of South Africa. However, the institutional nature of apartheid can be traced to the American South. Apartheid institutionalised the race consciousness that was already operational in South Africa for centuries.

Moreover, it was in the missionary societies that the first version of the "coloured" identity was formed and was later institutionalised by the colonial state and the apartheid state. This is the version that Adhikari (2002, 2004) encounters and writes about. However, *Ordinance 50 of 1828*, marks the birth of the "coloured" identity in law and the Khoekhoe and San's bureaucratic erasure. Yet, this does not mean the Khoekhoe and San ceased to exist. On the contrary, they thrived on the margins and the cracks of the colonial and apartheid states.

Furthermore, the "Hottentot", "Hotnot", or "Boesman" slurs did not end with the bureaucratic erasure. During the apartheid, the Khoekhoe and San people were continuously reminded that they were the "backwards" and "savage Boesman" or "Hottentot". For example, school textbooks and history books reiterated their subordination and subjected them to the "coloured" identity. In 1979 Abraham A.J. van Niekerk published *Tasāl van die grasvlakte*. In today's terms, it is considered to be young adult literature. This was one of the books found in primary school libraries during apartheid. This book presents the "Bushmanland" as an "empty" frontier ready to be captured and tamed by the Afrikaner "trek Boer". The book follows the story of Tasāl, a "wild bushman" who was spared during a Commando attack. After the attack, he was "apprenticed" on a "trek Boer's" farm. As expected, Van Niekerk's book softens the genocide of the San. The book also shares many parallels with the Louis Anything account.

If one compares van Niekerk's account with the Louis Anything report, there are many similarities and two possible explanations for this. Firstly, he could have studied the Anything report to write the story of Tasāl. Secondly, it can be that Van Niekerk knew about the extermination, which is plausible because he grew up in the Bushmanland. Books like *Tasāl van die grasvlakte* re-establish the colonial frame of the "wild bushman" and plundering "savage" and was an attempt to reiterate the subordination of the Khoekhoe and San. Through books like *Tasāl van die grasvlakte,* the apartheid government ensured that the Afrikaners were portrayed as the "civilising" figures who tamed South Africa and its indigenous people. The book also reminded "Coloured" people during apartheid of their "barbarous" ancestry, something they forever had to be ashamed of.

The Khoekhoe and San were, and still are, daily reminded that they are "Hotnot" or "Boesman". This daily reminder and the structural violence that came with it led to a temporary public rejection of the Khoekhoe identity. Nevertheless, as one will see in the next chapter, the culture of the Khoekhoe and the San people never ceased to exist. It just moved to spaces out of reach of the colonial and apartheid governments. The next chapter will focus on one such case: the ǀkhâba ra. The ǀkhâba ra kept the history and identity of the Khoekhoe alive.

4

Asbrood en Hardevet: Resisting Coloured-ism

The previous chapter dealt with the framing and bureaucratic erasure of the Khoekhoe and San in South Africa. With framing also comes violence; in most cases, the audience is complicit in the violence, even though some might argue that they were manipulated into participating. This chapter draws on the second limitation to show that audiences are complicit in some violent acts. In this regard, documentary filmmaking reflects a reciprocal process between the audience and the filmmaking. Many times, filmmakers are feeding audiences their biases. Thus, the second limitation addresses the subjectivity of the audience. However, the film is one of many mediums that can tell one about the audiences' subjectivity. For centuries, mediums such as song, dance, and theatre produced specific works for certain audiences.[1]

In this chapter, I am guided by the following question: What can audiences tell about a particular society? I believe that the audience is symptomatic of society. Audiences tell one more about society than one would like to believe. My discussion in this chapter starts with discussing the origins of the so-called *rieldans*. This dance is often described as energetic and one of the oldest traditional dances in Southern Africa. However, this historically significant dance has become a spectacle of its former self. It is currently under the paternalistic guidance of the Afrikaanse Taal- en Kultuur Vereniging (ATKV).[2] Not only is the ATKV claiming responsibility for the revival of the dance, but it dictates how the dance must be performed. This is to satisfy a predominantly white Afrikaner audience.

---

[1] This chapter is dedicated to Oom George Slaverse. Oom George lived in Carnavon and was one of the few historians of the *ǀkhȃba ra*. Oom George passed away in 2021. Also, "Asbrood en Hardevet" can be translated to "Ash Bread and Harden Fat."

[2] This chapter is an ethnographic account of my experiences growing up in Namaqualand, as a member of the Bitterfontein Traditional Dancers and as an ATKV 'rieldans' judge from 2018 to 2019.

The Problematic Historical Narrative

I wanted to make a documentary film *Wie se dans is dit?* However, after visiting Barrydale, my original film idea developed into "Steek My Weg" (Hidden Away). "*Wie se dans is dit?*" would have been about the "*rieldans*" or *|khâba ra* as it is known in Namaqualand. The "*rieldans*" over recent years have become associated with the ATKV. Many recent newspaper articles and even researchers are referring to the role the ATKV played in the "revival of the rieldans". Problematically so, the dance became the cultural symbol through which the so-called Afrikaans-speaking rural "coloured" community identified themselves.

The annual ATKV Riel Dance Competition thrusts the dance into the national spotlight. The ATKV drew up the competition rules, which had to be performed a certain way. There had to be four men and four women dancing. Groups had to, through the dance, illustrate how the Khoekhoe and San used to live. Groups received specific points when illustrating a certain number of animals and Khoekhoe and San practices. They were penalised if they did not adhere to this essentialist cherry-picking of a people's culture. The name changed. "*Riel*" instead of *|khâba ra* was used. As the "*riel*" became the artefact through which the so-called Afrikaans rural "coloureds" identified themselves, it lost its historical significance. As the competition increased in popularity and the rules became more cast in stone, more and more groups started to disagree with the competition rules. They felt the competition was a misrepresentation of their culture. They criticised the music and the essentialist cherry-picking of the Khoekhoe and San cultures. However, the ATKV's attitude towards the unhappiness of the "*rieldans*" community was dismissive, revealing their paternalistic attitude. After all, they believed they were responsible for the "revival" of the dance.

The competition indeed increased the popularity of the dance, but they were not responsible for the revival of the dance. The revival of this dance did not start with the ATKV. It started with Florence Filton in Vredendal around 2004. At the time, she worked for the Western Cape's Department of Cultural Affairs and Sport. Filton was born and raised in the Kamiesberg in Namaqualand. Growing up, she was an avid dancer of the *|khâba ra*. The dance had a cultural significance for her and the community she grew up in. Many years later, when working for the Department of Cultural Affairs and Sport, she realised that the dance was not performed as much as it used to be; it was disappearing. Through her work in the Department of Cultural Affairs and Sport, she started a project teaching the *|khâba ra* to learners of various schools in Namaqualand, the Olifants River, and the Cederberg. She also taught the cultural and historical significance of this dance. She visited various regions in Namaqualand, Cederberg, and Bushmanlad to document different variations of this dance. I was part of this documentation process in 2006 and 2007.

However, the ATKV created a metanarrative in which they claimed responsibility for the revival of the dance, and that narrative made its way into the media and some Afrikaans books. Since the ATKV's metanarrative is available on their website, some Afrikaans authors used the ATKV's metanarrative to describe the dance. For example, Chris N van der Merwe, in his book *Die Houtbeen van St Sergius: Opstelle oor Afrikaanse romans*, quote the metanarrative of the ATKV at length.

Translated version

The riel dance can rightly be regarded as the oldest type of dance in Southern Africa because the contemporary form is traced directly to the Khoi-San, the first inhabitants of the region. Some time ago, the Khoi-San danced around the fire after a good harvest or hunting trip and at their various festivals. Much of the choreography is performed in a circle today. In Nama, the dance is known as the *Ikhapara*. It is especially known for its clever footwork and energetic pace (Van der Merwe, 2014, p. 251).

Ilse Salzwedel's book *Onvertelde Stories van Afrikaans* uses an amended version of the ATKV metanarrative:

Translated version

The riel dances can be traced back to the Khoisan, who danced in a circle around a fire to celebrate a harvest or a good hunt. Later, the Namas began to imitate them. In Nama, it is called khapara. The riel requires ingenious footwork and loads of energy. The reel dance of Scottish immigrants also influenced the dance, and that is where the *reel dance* comes from (Salzwedel, 2013, n.p).

In the ATKV's metanarrative, the dance was practised around a fire, in a circle, after a hunt, and it was "Khoisan" because of the footwork. The first issue with the metanarrative is its problematic reference to it as a "Khoisan" dance. The term "Khoisan" merges two distinct yet very similar societies – the Khoekhoe and San. However, they did not practice the same dance. For example, early colonial documents only document the Khoekhoe performing a dance when they received visitors. Much later, William Burchell, Wilhelm Bleek, and Lucy Lloyd also wrote about the San performing dances. Whether the Khoekhoe shared a dance with the San is not clear.

The second issue in the ATKV's metanarrative that needs addressing is the claim among *"rieldans"* scholars and commentators that it is the oldest dance form in Southern Africa. This claim is from Vasco da Gama's documentation of a "reed dance" that the Hessequa performed in 1497 at Mosselbay. Centuries later, Pieter van Meerhof also documented a "reed dance" performed in 1661 in Namaqualand (Du Preez, 16 December 2014). Van Meerhof describes the dance as follows:

> Between 100 and 200 fine persons arranged themselves in a circle, each holding a hollowed reed in the hand, some long, some short, some thick, some thin. In the middle stood one with a long staff, and he sang while the others blew into their reeds and danced in a circle, making many beautiful movements with their feet (Van Meerhof cited in Du Preez, 2014, December 16).

Others like Britz (2019) and Parkington et al. (2015) use the dancing figure in rock art as evidence of its pre-colonial San and Khoekhoe roots.

The third issue is the interchangeable usage of "*rieldans*" and |*khapara* (|*khâba ra*).[3] Growing up in Namaqualand, I knew this dance as the |*khâba ra*. Britz (2019) argues that the reference to "*rieldans*" is derivative of the phrase "hotnotsriel" or Hottentot's reel, which traces it to a colonialist description of the dance. The |*khâba ra* traces its roots to the Khoekhoe or the Nama. The |*khâba ra* also shares similarities with the *Namastap*, a Nama-specific dance. In addition, Britz argues that "the riel was primarily performed at social dance parties held on farms" (2019, p. 24). This is understandable if one considers that Dutch colonists impoverished and dispossessed the Khoekhoe of their land and were forced into serfdom by the *Hottentot Proclamation of 1809*. Thus, it makes sense why this dance is connected to "Coloured" farmworkers. Here, some farmers must have seen a resemblance to the Scottish reel. It might also be on these farms that the racist term "*hotnotsriel*" was used to describe the dance.

The fourth issue is the difference between the dance and the music. Here again, there are various styles to play "*riel*" music, and the most popular of these styles is the "*optel en knyp*" (pick up and pinch). Pieter van der Westhuizen made this particular style popular in the late 1980s and the early 1990s. However, that is not the only "*riel*" music style. Among many riel musicians, there is a belief in a "pure *riel*" sound, which is also problematic. Suppose the claim is that this dance is the oldest in Southern Africa. In that case, one has to consider European musical influences on the performance of the dance. Thus, this claim has to be region-specific when they speak of a "pure riel" sound. The tempo of the dance and the music are different in Namaqualand, Cederberg and Bushmanland. The music informed the style and speed of the dance. For example, the "*kortriel*" is faster than the "*platriel*".

---

[3] |*Khâba ra* is the correct spelling of the dance. |*Khâba ra* in Khoekhoegowab means to give salutations.

The closest resemblance the |khâba ra has to the Scottish reel is the "*bokriel*." The "*bokriel*" is faster than the "*platriel*". However, the "*bokriel*" is named after the nimble movements of goats. The "*platriel*" is much slower and kept its older form – a form I am speculating was performed on the musical bow. Peter Takelo explained, "*Ons dans op die snar*" (We dance on the sound of the string). For me, this is a significant emphasis. Some colonial accounts speak of the musical bow, which sometimes accompanied the reed dance. The string thus has a historical significance for these artists. Peter Takelo is particularly critical of some of the "riel" leaders' understanding of the "riel" culture, which led to what he calls the bastardisation of the culture. This bastardisation is the influence of the drums and electronic piano on the performance of the dance.

Revisiting the Historical Narrative

With these four issues in mind, I revisit the historical narrative of the dance. For the ATKV's metanarrative, it seems that the |khâba ra or "*rieldans*" originates in what colonial writers called the "Reed-dance." As mentioned earlier, the description of the "Reed-dance" goes as far back as 1497, which Vasco da Gama documented. It appeared that the Hessequa performed it at Mosselbay. The second time it was mentioned was by Pieter van Meerhof on an expedition to the Namaqualand (du Preez, 16 December 2014).

It seems that Pieter van Meerhof encountered the Namaqua in 1661. That was the second time the "reed dance" was entered into colonial texts. Van Meerhof undertook several expeditions to establish a trading network with the Namaqua. The Namaqua was rich in livestock and minerals, especially copper. Of the early colonial explorers, van Meerhof was the most successful in finding the Namaqua (Ballantyne & Burton, 2005, p. 97). I believe his success was with the help of Krotoa.

Pieter Cruyhoff led several expeditions after Van Meerhof could not make contact with the Namaqua. It was only in 1682 that the Colony again made contact with the Namaqua (Carstens, 2011, p. 26). In the Tachard account of 1682, the "reed-dance" was performed when the Colony made contact with the Namaqua again.[4]

---

[4] It is important to note that Tachard narrated this from secondary sources. Tachard never physically met the Namaqua.

Next day one of their Captains came to us: He was a Man who for the tallness of his Stature and a certain fierceness in his looks, was respected by his Country - People, he brought along with him fifty young men, and as many women and Girls. The Men carried each of them a flute in their hand made of a certain Reed very well wrought, which rendered a pretty pleasant sound. The Captain having given them the sign, they fell a playing all together upon these instruments, with which the women and girls mingled their voices, and a noise which they made by clapping of their hands. These two Companies were drawn into two rings one within another. The first, which was the outmost, and made up of the Men, encompassed the second of the ring of the women, that was within them, both men and women danced this in a round, the Men turning to the right hand and the Women to the left, whilst and Old Man stand in the middle with a stick in his hand beat the time and regulated their dance. The Music at a distance seemed too pleasant nay and harmonious too, but there was no kind of regularity in their dance, or rather it was a mere confusion (Tachard, 1688, pp. 73-74).

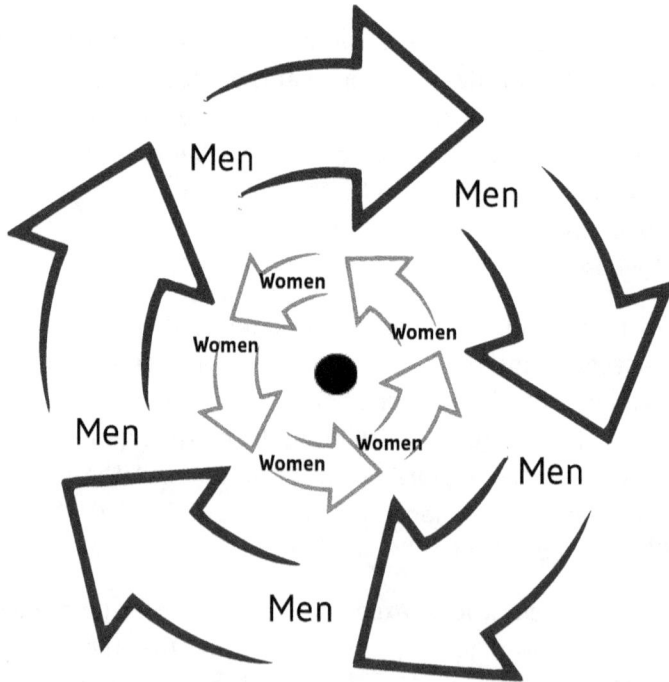

Figure 5   My visual reconstruction of the 'reed dance' dance

George Schmidt also encountered the "reed-dance" in the Caledon district, and the Hessequa performed it. I estimate that it was when Schmidt tried setting up a Mission Station at Baviaans Kloof. That must have been between 1737 and 1743. Hahn (1881) also mentions that a Free Burgher named Hop and Ryk van Tulbagh encountered the dance in Namaqualand. Then, after them,

Jonker Afrikaner welcomed James Alexander with this dance (Hahn, 1881).[5] So it appears that there was a significance to the "Reed-dance", and it was performed when a stranger was welcomed.

> I cannot conclude this chapter without adding some remarks on Khoikhoi poetry, and on the so-called 'Reed-dance,' ǂãb, to which in the following chapters repeatedly reference will be made.
>
> The Khoikhoi have two kinds of poetry, sacred and profane. The sacred hymns, as well as the profane songs, are sung accompanied by the so-called Reed-music or Reed-dancers. The sacred hymns are generally prayers, invocations, and songs of praise in honor of *Tsuǁgoab*, Heitsieibib and the moon; and such sacred songs and the performance with dancing is called *ǀgeib* while general profane songs are called *ǁnai-tsanati*, and to perform them with a dance on reed-pipes, or better, bark pipes, is *ǂaba xaĩre*. The profane reed-dances or reed-songs are of a very different nature. Either the fate of a hero who fell in a battle or lost his life on a hunting expedition, is deplored; and on such an occasion a performance is connected with it ..." (Hahn, 1881, pp. 27-28).

Thus the "Reed-dance" was part of what Hahn called the profane songs. It was only called profane because it could not be classified with the poetry associated with prayers or *ǀgeib*. The "reed-dance" among the Khoekhoe was called *ǂaba xaĩre*. Hahn's text clearly shows that the "reed-dance" was part of a cluster of dances that the Khoekhoe used for archivisation. These dances were called *ǁnai-tsanati*.

Thus, the "reed-dance" in colonial accounts is a description of the "reed-pipes" the Khoekhoe used as musical instruments to perform the dance. In colonial accounts, the nature of the documented performance could have been very different. At times, it could have been *ǂaba xaĩre*, at other times, it could have been other dances in the *ǁnai-tsanati* cluster. However, one can now ascertain that whenever a reference was made to the "reed-dance", it was a reference to the *ǂaba xaĩre*.

However, there is a caution. The dances the Khoekhoe performed during the full moon and the new moon were prayers.

> He [Kolb] had observed how they performed dances in honour of the new moon, and how they address the moon in singing: 'Be welcome, give us plenty of honey, give grass to our cattle, that we may get plenty of milk.' In offering this prayer they look toward the moon (Hahn, 1881, p. 41).

---

[5]   Hahn's account is based on the notes of James Alexander. Both James Alexander and Theophilus Hahn are contemporaries of the Afrikaners. Alexander of Jonker Afrikaner and Hahn of Jan Jonker Afrikaner. Jan Jonker Afrikaner is the son of Jonker Afrikaner.

From Hahn's study of the Khoekhoe's religion, one comes to know that the moon (⫽Khab) was also considered to be !Khab a deity; a deity who promises immortality (Hahn, 1881, p. 42). Thus, when encountering the sacred moon dance in colonial texts, one has to treat it as a prayer. For example: "Many of the early writers further state that at new moon and at full moon the people spent the night in dancing, singing and merry making" (Schapera, 1933, p. XIII; Leftwich,1976, p. 225). Leftwich (1976) references Hahn, but Leftwich did not investigate whether there was a difference between the "Reed-dance" and the sacred moon dance. The sacred moon dance is a ⎹geib, and was part of the Khoekhoe's general religious practices. Thus, "merry making" is not the best way to describe the dance during the new and full moon.

For a moment, let me return to the incident where Dorothea was expelled from the Genadendal missionary because she was dancing and singing in the mountains. The missionaries must have suspected that when the Khoekhoe danced and sang, these practices included praying to !Khab. In *The Genadendal Diaries*, it is clear that the missionaries were against singing and dancing. Thus, they banned these practices and called them the "Devil's work".

Khoekhoe poetry	
⎹Geib Sacred and religious poetry Sacred moon dance	⫽Nai-tsanati Archival and Historical Poetry ǂaba xaĩre (reed-dance) ⎹khâba ra

Figure 6   My visual representation of the Khoekhoe poetry

The ⫽nai-tsanati had a different purpose, and this was storytelling and archiving:

> For the last fifteen years these epical myths have been sung and performed exactly in the same way as the "Songs of Sanaχab and Gei⎹aub," men who distinguished themselves in the late Namaqua and Damara war. I was present at one of these ceremonies, and as an old Namaqua told me that, in his young days, Heitsi–eibib and Tsūi⫽goab were honoured in the same way.

> One sees the whole fight, in which dancers and pipe-blowers are actors. We see the cows and sheep driven off by the horsemen, and we see them retaken; at last the daring and plucky Gei⎹aub receives a mortal wound by a bullet of the enemy. They strip him naked, and leave him a prey to the vultures, which soon approach and commence to devour the body. At last, the friends having slain the enemy, return and collect his bones in a grave, and sing a very doleful burial song (Hahn, 1881, pp. 103–104).

Storytelling and archiving were, therefore, central to the *Inai-tsanati*. Hence, when early colonialists encountered the dance, they did not understand its significance and labelled it the "reed-dance" dance. Thus, to understand the story and the archive, one needed to understand the symbolism and to understand the symbolism, one needed a translator. Even though Hahn could understand the language, he still needed a translator for the symbolism.

Since the dance is about the history of the Khoekhoe, it was performed whenever a stranger of important stature visited the Khoekhoe. For example:

> Thus the first Moravian missionary, George Schmidt, who came to the *//Heisiqua* Hottentots in the Caledon district, was received with a reed-dance. The Dutch Governor van der Stell, on his journey to the Copper Mountains, the present Copper Mines, was honoured in the same way. Hop, a burgher of Stellenbosch, who in Governor Ryk van Tulbagh's time went on an expedition to Great Namaqualand, received the congratulations of the *//Habobes* at the foot of the *//Kharas* mountain in a grand reed-dance performance. Alexander received the same honours from this Namaqua host, the famous Jonker Afrikaner *IHaramŭb* (Hahn, 1881, p. 28).

This was clearly a custom, but the early colonialists were ignorant and did not ask the Khoekhoe about this custom. Moreover, a dance was performed by the Goringhaiqua after the first Khoekhoe-Dutch War with Gogosoa in attendance. It is unclear whether this was the "reed-dance", but it certainly was a *Inai-tsanati*. Reading the description of how the dance was performed, I believe this dance was a post-war custom and could have been part of the Khoekhoe's archiving process.

> … they began to dance and jump about continuously with strange gestures and in a peculiar manner, almost like the bakers over here work dough in the trays with their feet, by stamping, now with the one foot and then with the other, their buttocks sticking out, and the head always inclined on the side of the ground. The women were no less jolly during the dancing of the men, clapping their hands and all along singing the self-same song of ha, ho, ho, ho for well-nigh two hours on end. The sound of this singing and handclapping of women could easily be heard a gunshot away from the fort. They shout loudly and make an uproar in the same way at night, whenever they observe the approach of some wild beast like the lion or leopard, so that the beast, horrified by the unfamiliar din, skinks away (Dapper, 2011, p. 21).

It is clear that this was not the *ǂaba xaĩre* or "reed-dance" because no musical instruments were mentioned in this dance performance. In all the cases where the "reed-dance" was mentioned, men played an instrument during the performance of the dance. For example, Hahn explains that with Ryk van Tulbagh's journey to Namaqualand, the dance was performed by women. "The men stand in a circle together and blow on a hollow pipe or similar instrument, and the women, clasping hands, dance round the men" (Hahn, 1881, p. 44). Thus, it seems that when performing the ǂaba xaĩre, the reed musical instruments were always part of the performance.

From Dapper's account, it also seems that specific dances were used to protect them and their livestock against wild animals. According to de Grevenbroek (2011, p. 251):

> Where meadows and pastures invite the flocks and herds, there they scatter themselves with their little buts, living the life of wandering friars. Till even shadows fall they pasture their flocks; at night they enclose them, as I said above; then to the clapping of hands and stamping of feet, with wanton gestures they ply the dance beneath the presiding moon far into the stilly hours of the night.

In Dapper's account, it was also mentioned that the dance was performed in a similar fashion. "They shout loudly and make an uproar in the same way at night, whenever they observe the approach of some wild beast like the lion or leopard, so that the beast, horrified by the unfamiliar din, skinks away" (Dapper, 2011, p. 21).

So far, I have found no concrete evidence that the San performed the "reed-dance". The description of the San's rain dance is very similar to the Khoekhoe sacred moon dance (Lewis-Williams, 1990). However, even though these two dances share a resemblance in terms of footwork and movements, it cannot with certainty be said whether the Khoekhoe and San shared dances of symbolic meaning. For example, William Burchell (1822b, pp. 63-66) describes a different dance performed by the San in Volume 2 of his *Travels in the interior of Southern Africa*. On two occasions, this dance was performed in a hut. Why the dance was performed in a hut is a mystery and open to speculation.

Moreover, it is unclear whether the ǂaba xaĩre or "reed-dance" is the |khâba ra or "rieldans" that various colonial texts refer to (Dapper, 2011; Grevenbroek, 2011; Hahn, 1881; Tachard, 1688; Ten Thyne, 2011). The |khâba ra or 'rieldans' definitely share similarities with the ǂaba xaĩre. For example, they share the "voetwerk" and the mimicking of certain animals and events. As I have pointed out earlier, mimicking and symbolism are central parts of the ǂaba xaĩre. However, even with these similarities, I cannot conclude that this is indeed the same dance. Given this, I believe that the |khâba ra was one of the dances in the |nai-tsanati cluster and that the |khâba ra was used as a dance that gave salutations; |khâba ra, after all, means giving salutations.[6] "|Khâba" means to salute, and "ra" indicates the present continuous tense. Hahn (1881, p. 20) also mentions

---

[6] Please see W.H.G. Haacke. (2010). *Khoekhoegowab is veral die taal van die Damara, Haiǁom en Nama*. Macmillan Education Namibia Publishers (Pty) Ltd.

that – ra indicates custom. To salute or give salutations would make sense to describe this dance because *"hand speel"*, a form of greeting, is still a central feature of the dance.

Thus, I believe that the *|khâba ra*, unlike the *ǂaba xaĩre*, was an intra-Khoekhoe dance. The *|khâba ra* was not used to greet visitors, travellers, or guests. In Namaqualand and Bushmanland, the *|khâba ra* was usually performed annually among families who had not seen each other for some time. At the end of each year, families who lived on farms scattered across the Bushmanland and Namaqualand usually visited each other. During these visits they would share their stories, which were incorporated into the *|khâba ra*. It is probably here that farmers encountered the dance and described it as the *"hotnotsriel"*, and what was birthed is today popularly known as the *"rieldans"*.

The Second Limitation and the Violence of the Audience

So, how does the second limitation relate to the *|khâba ra* and the "coloured" identity? As I mentioned earlier, the second limitation concerns the audience's subjectivity. I believe that the audience is symptomatic society. Therefore, audiences can tell much about a particular society's perversion. Given this, let me discuss the second limitation.

Let me start with the Kuleshov effect. The Kuleshov effect is the juxtaposition of two unrelated or two different shots that create meaning for the audience (Barratt et al., 2016). For example, when a shot of someone looking in the distance is juxtaposed with a shot of a grazing cow, it might create the impression that the person is looking at the cow in the distance. The audience will create meaning whether or not the filmmaker intended to do so. Some documentary filmmakers realise the danger of this effect, especially when making films about marginalised groups. Filmmakers generally try to resolve this through narrative documentary films. Here, a story is constructed, aiming to get the audience invested in the story.

Narrative documentary films use the classic three-act story structure, with a beginning, middle and end (Bradbury & Guadagno, 2020). The idea is to create conflict because it is believed that conflict creates "good" documentary films. Conflict in a story is about a "want" and an "obstacle". The main character wants something and something or someone is standing in the way of getting it. Hence, the story centres on resolving this. In narrative documentary films, one also needs a main character, and the aim is to get the audience invested in this character.

However, narrative documentary films raise questions about the authenticity of some scenes. Sometimes, documentary filmmakers stage scenes to construct a story and conflict. For example, there was a debate in our documentary class about whether some scenes in the award-winning documentary film *Family* were staged. The scene in question was that of the phone calls.[7] The film's protagonist searching for his father. Hence, he made a series of phone calls to various family members to find out if they knew his father or whether they could give him a message. As the audience watched the film, we sensed that some of the phone calls might have been staged. They seemed to be shot at once, not over time as the film depicts them. It is here that this award-winning documentary film lost its authenticity for us.

This leads me to the next issue: point of view (POV). POV asks through whose point of view the audience encounters the characters or experiences the story (Barratt et al., 2016). Since documentary filmmakers use the word "character" to describe the human subject being filmed, it masks the power relations with the filmmakers. However, the audience is not entirely powerless and wields significant power. Documentary filmmakers are aware of this power, hence their desire to construct a story that also creates an audience.

Sometimes, the characters can reverse the power relation the filmmakers and the audience wield. For example, the documentary film *Bobbi Jene* reverses the subjective power relation of the audience.[8] *Bobbi Jene* brings sexuality, dance, and the performative together in a powerful way.[9] It makes the audience an unintentional voyeur. For me, one of the most interesting yet uncomfortable scenes is where Jene masturbates completely naked in front of an audience in an art gallery. It renders the question as to who the voyeur was. Was it the filmmaker, or was it the audience? If it was the audience, which audience was it? The ones watching the live show or the ones watching it on screen? In this case, it leaves the question of who wields power open-ended and, in a sense, returns power to the character.

Many documentary filmmakers will consider these three factors when writing their treatments, funding proposals and festival applications. Documentary filmmakers and the industry are aware of the likes and dislikes of specific audiences and encourage filmmakers to tailor their films according to the subjectivity of their specific audiences. However, not all audiences will applaud a particular documentary film. For example, a predominantly white audience will receive a documentary film about black people differently than

---

[7]   Phie Ambo and Sami Saif, *Family* (Denmark, 2001).

[8]   Bobbi Jene, *Bobbi Jene* (Sweden, 2017).

[9]   Bobbi Jene is also the name of the main character in the film.

a predominantly black audience. For a predominantly white audience, such a documentary might be something novel. However, for a black audience, it might mean pain and shame. Given this, representation matters, misrepresenting particular groups may bring forth violence.

However, who is responsible for this violence? In *Black Skin, White Masks*, Fanon argues that the family represents the world and that "the family is a miniature of the nation" (Fanon, 2008, p. 109). According to Fanon, "As the child emerges from the shadow of his parents, he finds himself once more among the same laws, the same principles, the same values" (Fanon, ibid.). Fanon sees the family as the basis of the nation, and it is "projected onto the social environment" (Fanon, 2008, p. 110). In this sense, "behaviour toward authority is something learned. And it is learned in the heart of the family" (Fanon, 2008, pp. 110-111). Thus, the shaping of individual consciousness starts in the family.

Fanon, reading Freud, argues that trauma is expelled from the consciousness and stored in the subconsciousness and that these "Erlebnisse are repressed in the unconsciousness" (Fanon, 2008, p. 112). Erlebnisse is a traumatic event. For Fanon, after slavery, the question was: "Has there been a real traumatism?" (Fanon, ibid.).[10] The trauma did not stop after slavery. New forms of control and repression were institutionalised and structurally continued. In addition, he argues that "we observe the opposite in the man of color. A normal Negro child, having grown up within a normal family, will become abnormal on the slightest contact with the white world" (Fanon, 2008, p. 111). James Baldwin also observed this abnormality.

> Leaving aside all the physical features one could quote, leaving aside rape or murder, leaving aside the bloody catalogue of oppression, which we are one way too familiar with already. What this does to the subjugated is to destroy his sense of reality. This means in the case of an American Negro, born in that glittering republic, and the moment you are born, since you do not know any better, every stick and stone and every face is white, and yet have not seen the mirror you suppose that you are too.[11]

---

[10] I have to note that Fanon wrote this before he lived in colonial Africa; hence, his analysis here is restricted to the "black man." Here, one must see the 'black man' or the "Negro" as oppressed. Biko had also observed that the oppressed share a universalised oppressed spirit. Hence, Biko famously wrote: "Being black is not a matter of pigmentation – being black is a reflection of a mental attitude." Reading Fanon's *Black Skin, White Masks*, one may contribute this universalism to the Hegelian dialectic. Also, see Bulhan's *Frantz Fanon and the Psychology of the Oppressed*.

[11] Peck, R., Grellety, R., Peck, H., Baldwin, J., Adebonojo, H., Ross, B., Ross, T., ... Magnolia Home Entertainment (Firm). (2017). *I am not your Negro*.

Baldwin made this observation after seeing how African Americans were represented in the media. Why is this then the case? Fanon contributes this to the collective unconscious. Fanon believes it is a "collective unconscious" that holds the trauma. Therefore, to understand the "black" man's trauma-tisation, one must understand the "collective unconscious" and the "collective catharsis".

Fanon, reading Jung, argues that in the collective unconscious, the black man stands for "Evil and Ugliness", only because of his skin colour. Since Jung argues that the collective unconscious is based on instinct and thus biological, Fanon believes Jung made an error and that the collective unconscious results from habit, not instinct. If the collective unconscious results from habit, it is also cultural. Hence, Fanon calls the collective unconscious "the unreflected imposition of culture" (Fanon, 2008, p. 147). Even though Fanon contributes this unreflected imposition of culture to white people, he also argues that black people can have a "white" collective unconscious. For example, "An Antillean is made white by the collective unconscious, by a large part of his individual unconscious, and by the virtual totality of his mechanism of individuation" (Fanon, 2008, p. 149). Hence, one sees the rejection of blackness later in the black man's life.

A striking example in South Africa would be the response of Katlego Mapoyane in an interview in 1992. It was just after the "end of apartheid", and Katlego was one of the few black kids who attended an exclusive private school with white children. Al Jazeera started a documentary series that tracked the lives of a group of children after apartheid. The first documentary in the series aired in 1992, and after that, every seven years, they released an episode catching up with these children to show the progression of their lives. In 7Up (the first instalment), Katlego was asked whether he was an African.[12] He was seven years old, and his answer was no. The interviewer asked why not, and he asked the interviewer whether he sounded African. For me, this is an apt example of what Fanon meant when he wrote: "Little by little, one can observe in the young Antillean the formation and crystallisation of an attitude and a way of thinking and seeing that are essentially white" (Fanon, 2008, p. 114). For Katlego, he could not be African because he did not sound African.

In the previous chapter, one sees that people of Khoekhoe and San origin were forced to reject their identities because of the racist connotations of these identities. They also rejected parts of their culture because it was remnants of the "Hotnot" and the "Boesman." This rejection led them to assimilate into

---

[12]   Angus Gibson and Jemma Jupp, 7Up (United Kingdom, 1992).

whiteness reluctantly. Assimilation to whiteness, therefore, happens in the collective unconscious. In the collective unconscious, the "Negro is forever in combat with his own image" (Fanon, 2008, p. 149).

Furthermore, Fanon argues that there must be a collective catharsis if there is a collective consciousness. Collective catharsis is a channel through which society releases strong and repressed emotions.[13] According to Fanon:

> In every society, in every collectivity, exists – must exist – a channel, an outlet through which the forces accumulated in the form of aggression can be released … The Tarzan stories, the sagas of twelve-year-old explorers, the adventures of Mickey Mouse, and all those "comic books" serve actually as a release for collective aggression. The magazines are put together by white men for little white men. This is the heart of the problem (Fanon, 2008, pp. 112-113).

Collective catharsis is, therefore, the release of collective aggression towards a particular subject. This subject is the black man or those who are oppressed. According to Baldwin, "It comes as a great shock around the age of five or six or seven that Gary Cooper was killing off the Indians when you were rooting for Gary Cooper, that the Indians were you" (Baldwin, 2017).

One notices this collective aggression towards the Khoekhoe and the San from the photos that were taken of the Nama and Herero prisoners on Shark Island in Namibia during the genocide and of the photos taken of *Dia!kwain*, *||Kabbo*, *|A!khunta* and others during the San genocide in South Africa. The purpose of these photographs was to document genocide. However, more problematic for me is that a scientific and a general European audience existed for this sadistic perversion. These audiences released a collective aggression toward a particular subject they encountered in "comic books". From an early age, black people have no choice but to combat their image to prevent extermination.

Given this, documentary filmmakers must ask whether some of their documentary films project a type of salvation toward black people. Do their films buy into the colonial sentiment that black people need saving from their "savage" or "backward" selves? Or are their films about voyeurism – a sadistic aggression towards a black figure to temporally satisfy the perversions of a particular audience?

Is there a possibility that documentary filmmakers may project or reproduce the stereotypes of their collective unconscious? I would answer yes simply because the collective unconscious is false consciousness. According to Baldwin, "The

---

[13] I believe that the chapter "On Violence" in *Wretched of the Earth* is about the collective catharsis which he theorises in *Black Skin, White Masks*. Thus, the violence of the 'native' in "On Violence" can be read as cathartic.

industry is compelled, given the way it is built, to present the American people, a self-perpetuating fantasy of American life. The concept of entertainment is difficult to distinguish from the use of narcotics" (Baldwin, 2017). From Baldwin's explanation, this "self-perpetuating fantasy" appears to be a false consciousness reproduced in the collective unconscious, and more importantly, it is the movement-image that perpetuates this false consciousness.

Bernard Stiegler (2011), in *Technics and Time 3*, argues that one's conscious stream coincides with the cinematic stream. Thus, it is difficult for a person to distinguish between the two streams. Evidently, one becomes caught up in the cinematic moment, and the moment something horrific happens on-screen, one's emotional response is genuine; one experiences "real" fear, disgust or betrayal. It is only afterwards that one realises that it happened on screen. For example, in the *Act of Killing*, I felt the fear of the "characters" in the film.[14] For a moment, I was there with the "characters" and was just as tormented by Anwar Congo and the rest of the gangsters.

One finds the explanation for this phenomenon in Henri Bergson's *Matter and Memory*. Bergson argues that one's consciousness interprets and relates to reality in terms of images. In cinema, the movement is generally reproduced in 25 frames per second. This means that a device took 25 photos in very short succession, and when one plays it back at the right speed, it produces a "movement" on screen (Deleuze, 1986). Interestingly, when one consciously recalls "movement", it is only one image. In a Bergsonian sense, one's consciousness cannot recall movement. Movement, therefore, can only be experienced in the present and in dreams (the subconscious). Cinema replaces and adds new images to one's "real" images of one's lived experiences. Thus, it is possible to recall distorted images mixed with reality and cinema. This creates a false consciousness, which explains Baldwin as a "self-perpetuating fantasy". This false consciousness also constitutes the audience.

It is for this false consciousness that documentary filmmakers are tailoring their films. Hence, some documentary films produce a universal "black figure". This is the figure the audience expects. A friend and fellow researcher once explained the subtext of many award-winning documentary films: "The white person is always behind the camera that the 'black figure' transfers his or her hope to." The white filmmaker is the Good Samaritan who cares about the "black figure". The white filmmaker and the black human subject believe this because the collective unconscious has programmed society to believe that black people are incapable of doing anything for themselves. In the collective

---

[14]   Joshua Oppenheimer, *Act of Killing* (Denmark, 2012).

unconscious, the "black figure" is the subject of pity, pain and suffering. Hence, a white colleague of mine could say that *Strike A Rock* "beautifully and brilliantly depicted the life of women Nkaneng." This was because the film ticked all the basic conditions of a good film about black people. It lived up to the expectations of the audience. Hence, it was worrisome to see that I was the only one who felt uncomfortable about the portrayal of the "black figure". I looked around for support but was greeted with silence, shame, and resentment. The collective unconscious did its job.

However, not all is lost. Butler (1997) explains that by reiterating one's subjection comes resistance. There will be a moment of crisis for the black person or the oppressed, where they will question their subjection. For Fanon, it was when he went to Europe. It was here he was labelled "Negro". He soon discovered that he was not white and that all the comics lied to him. He is the "Negro".

> Look, a Negro! (Fanon, 2008, p. 84).

For Fanon, this was when he realised that he was black and could not escape the depiction of him as a "Negro", an awareness that left him rejecting his 'blackness' and combatting his image.

> I sit down at the fire and become aware of my uniform. I had not seen it. It is indeed ugly. I stop there, for who can tell me what beauty is? (Fanon, 2008, p. 86).

In *28Up*, Katlego was asked the same question as when he was seven. This time, he affirmed that he is African.[15] Some "Coloured" people also became aware after 1950 that they were still regarded as "*Hotnot*" and "*Boesman*". They realised that missionary education and conversion to Christianity did not translate into "whiteness". After all that pain, shame, and humiliation, they were still seen as the uncivilised "*Hotnots*" and "*Boesmans*". Some of those who regarded themselves as "mixed", "*Bruin*", "*Baster*", and "*halfnaaitjie*" thought if they embraced their so-called "European" ancestry, it would give them the right to discriminate against those who still regarded themselves as Nama, Griqua, "*Hottentot*" and "*Boesman*". Hence, a class attitude among the so-called coloured people emerged. This is the racial sentiment Adhikari (2002, 2004) and Besten (2006) is writing about. This class attitude was grounded in "whiteness".

After becoming aware of his "Negro" identity, Fanon's "real apprenticeship" began (Fanon, 2008, p. 115). Fanon observed how different a black person's reception of Tarzan in the Antilles is from that in Europe. In the Antilles, black people associated with Tarzan and his fight against the bad "Negros",

---

15   Angus Gibson and Jemma Jupp, *28Up* (United Kingdom: Al Jazeera, 2013).

but in Europe, every black person becomes the bad "Negro". The "real apprenticeship" deals with the reality that "the black man must be black in relation to the white man" (Fanon, 2008, p. 110).

Kyk 'n Boesman! (Look, a Bushman!)

Hence, when the apprenticeship begins, "the racial drama" for the white man is unconscious. For the black man, it is conscious. During the *Strike a Rock* screening, I was conscious, and it seemed everyone else was unconscious. I was conscious of the pain and the hurt that film would cause Black mothers, fathers, sisters, and brothers. I was conscious of the Black child's innocence and pain. After the screening, I also became conscious that I was regarded as the aggressor.

Kyk 'n Hotnot! (Look, a Hotnot!)

I was confused, but later, like Fanon, I became conscious that I am a phobogenic object, "a stimulus to anxiety" (Fanon, 2008, p. 117). The white person encounters this phobogenic object before the actual encounter because many books, films, television shows, and cartoons have been made about this object. I was the 'uncivilised' savage that the media portrayed. As a result, the white person always fears this object and is always ready to defend themselves against this object.

> I thought he was going for a gun. And I shot him in the side, in the chest (crying). I thought he was going to kill me (crying). I have never been so scared (Crying and sobbing uncontrollably) (KJRH -TV [Channel 2], 2017).

Betty Shelby's victim was an unarmed black man. Shelby shot and killed Terence Crutcher, surrounded by four other police officers. She continued shooting Terence as he fell to the ground. However, before Shelby shot Terence Crutcher, he was tased by her colleague. So she killed Crutcher in anticipation. Crutcher was Shelby's phobogenic object. She was unconsciously trained to expect violence from black men. She was so blinded by her fear of the phobogenic object that she did not realise she was the real aggressor. She claimed she suspected Crutcher was under the influence of drugs, and she feared he might have a gun. The police officers, after the incident, searched Crutcher's vehicle for weapons and drugs and found none.

One of the most common imaginary constructs or stereotypes of black men is that they are all biological. According to Fanon, "In relation to the Negro, everything takes place on a genital level" (Fanon, 2008, p. 121).

I am afraid of black people – more specifically, dark-complexioned black men. ... My fear of black men is visceral, rooted in the physical and completely at odds with my utopian desires. (Bentley, 2017).

The stereotype, Fanon explains, has been perpetuated by white people in stories, books, and cinema. The lynching of the Negro, for Fanon, is a sign of sexual revenge. "We know how much of sexuality there is in all cruelties, tortures, beatings." (Fanon, 2008, p. 123). The sadist or voyeur is not aware of this. They are trapped in a collective unconscious that informs their desires. "The Negro is castrated. The penis, the symbol of manhood, is annihilated, which is to say that it is denied" (Fanon, 2008, p. 125). Hence, "To suffer from a phobia of Negroes is to be afraid of the biological. For the Negro is only biological. The Negroes are animals" (Fanon, 2008, p. 125).[16] In a scene from Annalet Steenkamp's documentary film, I Afrikaner, her brother told one of the Black men working on his farm not to perform sexual acts on the farm animals while he was away.[17] Annalet's brother did this, knowing his sister was filming him. Needless to say, the worker was confused and did not know what he was talking about. Annalet's brother, a white male, needed to emasculate the Black male to re-assert his dominance in front of his sister – a dominance the world had to see. And Steenkamp included this part in the filming, knowing it would emasculate and humiliate a Black man.

With this in mind, I am returning to the |khâba ra and the so-called coloured identity. As Oom George Slaverse explained, there was a time when this dance was performed strictly on farms, and sometimes the dancers were paid with alcohol to perform it for white Afrikaner farmers on their farms. These farmers were not interested in the culture of the Khoekhoe or what the dance represented – they wanted a spectacle. They wanted "Coloured" people to live up to being the "drunkards" the white society labelled them, the same society that refused to pay them full wages and paid them half their salary in alcohol. This, in turn, decimated their social structure and made them a different kind of controllable slave: an alcoholic. They named this spectacle "Hotnotsriel".

As seen earlier, the audience reflects a particular consciousness. Hence, the ATKV and its mainly white audience are not interested in the culture of the Khoekhoe. They are interested in the spectacle and annually stage it. Since they are interested in the spectacle, they dismiss the feedback from the "riel

---

[16] As one saw from the previous chapter, that biological and sub-human frame of the colonised or the oppressed is a result of coloniality. Consequently, the framing and rendering of the colonised as a sub-human result from coloniality, and this frame can be unmasked using the first limitation as an analytic framework.

[17] Annalet Steenkamp, I Afrikaner (Netherlands, n.d.).

community". On several occasions, the "riel community" made it clear that the ATKV Riel Dance Competition does not represent their culture. However, since the ATKV and its audience were affected by the collective consciousness of apartheid, the Khoekhoe and San were reduced to "*Hotnots*" and "*Boesmans*". This audience needed a collective catharsis. Hence, they reproduce the sadistic violence they were exposed to as children. They need to see the spectacle to feel better about themselves. They must remind themselves they are the "saviours" of those performing the "*Hotnotsriel*".

Conclusion

As I have argued in the previous chapter, the final attempt to erase the Khoekhoe and the San and their history happened in 1950. In 1950, the Afrikaner-led National Party passed the *Population Registration Act*. This Act created three racial groups: "Black", "Coloured", and "White". The so-called Coloured racial group consisted of the Khoekhoe, the San, and those of "mixed-racial" origins. Thus, after 1950, the Khoekhoe and the San genocide in South Africa was complete. They no longer existed – they were erased. Or so it seemed.

History books were rewritten, and textbooks taught a history that emphasised the superiority of whites in South Africa and their racial domination over the Khoekhoe and San. Racial slurs like "*Hotnot*" and "*Boesman*" led to a further rejection of the Khoekhoe and San identities. It also created a class difference among the so-called Coloured people. Those of "mixed origin" deemed themselves better than those of Khoekhoe and San. Those who considered them closer to white called other "Coloured" people "*Hotnot*" and "*Boesman*". Because of this intra-coloured racism, many "Coloured" people of Khoekhoe and San origin rejected their "Native" identity.

So, how does one make sense of the so-called Coloured people's return to their Khoekhoe and San identities? My observations in this regard are twofold. Firstly, if one follows Butler's theorisation of subjection, one notices that subjection can only be successful if continuous reiteration occurs. Without continuous reiteration, the oppressed subject cannot be formed. After the *Population Registration Act of 1950*, "Coloured" people had to reiterate this oppressive subject identity. This reiteration was enforced by various other acts such as the *Prohibition of Mixed Marriages Act, Act No 55 of 1949; Immorality Amendment Act, Act No 21 of 1950*; amended in 1957 (Act 23); *The Group Areas Act, No 41 of 1950; Reservation of Separate Amenities Act, Act No 49 of 1953;* and the *Extension of University Education Act of 1959.*

Chapters 5 and 6, show that one of these acts created a "Coloured" university: The University of the Western Cape (UWC). At UWC, apartheid aimed to create a servant to serve the apartheid project better. In this instance, apartheid education took a leaf from the missionary "civilising" education. Apartheid education wanted to create and birth a uniform "Coloured" subject, as missionary education tried to "civilise" the Khoekhoe and San. In addition, these Acts ensured that they were reminded in the public sphere that they were "Coloured". However, in the social sphere, where identities were differently regulated, they were reminded that they were "*Hotnot*" and "*Boesman*". Moreover, in the education sphere, both primary and secondary, they were reminded that they once were "backward savages"; they were "*Hottentots*" and "*Boesman*" who had to be tamed and "civilised.". Psychologically, they were programmed to combat their own image, which led to the rejection of their Khoekhoe and San ethnic identities.

However, as Butler explains, resistance also comes with the reiteration of one's subject position. Fanon says that this is when the "real apprenticeship" begins. The resistance against the "coloured" identity is not a post-apartheid phenomenon. It started very early on, and it took place at various sites. One of these sites was culture, where the so-called Coloured people preserved their Khoekhoe and San identities.

For example, it was kept alive by people like Oom Pieter van der Westhuizen. Oom Pieter van der Westhuizen, in the 1980s and 1990s, took the ǀkhâba ra culture to some of the most remote corners of the Cape Province. In 1990, Oom Pieter performed his "Bokkie sê my reg" album in Rietpoort at the small Roman Catholic Mission, where the white students took photos of me. I could not afford a ticket, but I did not want to miss out because by then, I knew the chorus of "Sout Manne, Sout" by heart. So I sneaked in. That evening, his show changed my life because I could feel what it meant for the community. Decades later, I am still listening to the same album, and it surprises me every time how carefully the album was curated. It captured the spirit of a people. I found a subtle resistance message in his album that the apartheid state could not recognise. If they did, the album would have been banned. For example, in "Asbrood En Hardevet" (Ash Bread and Hardened Fat), he leaves the following:

> Ek durf nie nou omdraai (I dare not turn around)
> Die pad lê voor (With the road ahead)
> Moet nou net nie my keer (Don't stop me now)
> Ek sien 'n horison al nader kom (I see the horizon near)
> Ons kan nie meer verloor (We have nothing to lose)

Hier gaat ek nou (So, here I go)

My knieë vou (And, yet, my legs are weak)

Hou maar aan net wat ek het (I will keep what I have)

Al moet ek sterf (Even if it means my death)

Ek gaan tog erf (My inheritance awaits)

Al is dit net asbrood en hardevet (Even if that is just ash bread and hardened fat)

There is a cultural difference between *sagtevet* and *hardevet*. *Sagtevet* refers to the sheep's fat that surrounds the animal's muscles. It is located between the skin and the muscles. When it rains, and sheep have enough to eat, they have a lot of excess fat for the dry season. This type of fat was cut into small pieces and cooked. The dried small pieces are *kaiings*. *Kaiings, sagtevet,* and bread combined is a delicious cultural meal. *Sagtevet* is also used as a spread on bread because it is soft. *Hardevet*, on the other hand, is always present in the animal's body and surrounds the organs. It is not that tasty and becomes hard. It cannot be used as a spread, and the *kaiings* are not that tasty. The fat and *kaiings* were stored for hard times because they did not go off and could be used over a long time. The best way to eat *hardevet* and the hard *kaiings* was with *asbrood* or *roosterbrood*. When the bread is warm, the fat melts. The smokey and wooden flavours of these asbrood or roosterbrood complimented hardevet to make it an enjoyable meal. Therefore, the song "Asbrood En Hardevet" is about hard times and the looming struggle ahead.

Thus, when we think of the *|khâba ra*, we have to think of it with the music and the poetry accompanying the dance. Dancers, until today, still incorporate the "askoek" (ash bread) move in their dancing repertoire. The *|khâba ra* is an archive. Therefore, the purpose of the *|khâba ra* is to archive the history and stories of the Khoekhoe people. So how does one read and access the knowledge in this archive? I would suggest that one take a Derridean approach. Jacques Derrida argued that "there is no political power without control of the archive, if not memory" (Derrida and Prenowitz, 2013, p. 11). Thus, an analysis of the *"leef wêreld"* or the plane on which the memory of this archive is accessed brings forth the political.

In the *"leef wêreld"* of their daily lives, the Khoekhoe and San formed and performed their subjectivity. At first, their pre-colonial lives informed the plane on which memory was stored. On this plane, they archived their history, stories, and culture. During colonialism, as farmworkers, they added more memories to this archive. Sometimes, they were forced to perform their colonial life to their oppressors. In post-apartheid South Africa, another layer was added to this *"leef wêreld"*, and the *|khâba ra* now raises new issues such as HIV Aids, gender-based violence, the Barrydale Redfin Minnow and religion. This shows an ever-evolving story grounded in the dance's basic footwork and steps, performed over the ages. This plane can only be accessed through the |khâba ra.

However, colonialism and apartheid tried to eradicate the African archive because it "affirms the past, present, and future; it preserves the records of the past, and it embodies the promise of the present to the future" (Manoff, 2004, p. 11). However, destroying this archive (|khâba ra) was difficult since the information was stored in the body as dance choreography and passed down through generations. When physically destroying a people's history, present, and future did not work, the credibility of the Khoekhoe and San archives was questioned. Their history was always treated with scepticism and suspicion. The reason was that it did not resemble the European archive. European archivisation disputed the historical records of Africa. The historical record was questionable if not in a library or museum.

Still, these efforts to destroy the Khoekhoe people and their archives were unsuccessful. The |khâba ra preserved the history of a people on the margins of the colonial and later the apartheid state. Dance and sound preserved the memories and histories of the Khoekhoe and San. Since these dances and sounds were deemed backward, they were marginalised within the apartheid state and educated elites. The |khâba ra survived because the Khoekhoe resisted the apartheid states' "Coloured" classification, which prevented the Khoekhoe's complete and total destruction. The |khâba ra now offers those robbed of their Khoekhoe identity an opportunity to reclaim their ethnicity and, thus, their indigeneity.

Act 3
The Resolution

5

Ending and Beginning

Since this book is about how the Khoekhoe and San were framed in colonial and apartheid texts and how that contributed to their bureaucratic erasure over time, I want to turn my attention to the University of the Western Cape. The University of the Western Cape was created for "Coloured" people by the *Extension of University Education Act of 1959*. It officially opened its doors in 1960. Apartheid's aim for UWC was to produce the middle-class apartheid "Coloured" subject. At UWC, they were supposed to learn how to "administrate" "Coloured" people. They would become teachers, lawyers, dentists, nurses, clergy, and social workers. However, studying business, finance, economics, and medicine was not meant for them; those fields were reserved for white people. Thus, the destiny of an apartheid-educated student at UWC was to administrate "Coloured Affairs" and be subservient to white people.[1]

However, this was a destiny the students at UWC refused. At UWC, students resisted the "coloured" identity. This is evident from their participation in SASO, the 1970 Desmond Damas tie affair, the 1973 student walk-off, the 1976 Soweto uprising and its impact on UWC, the 1980 student revolt, "Hek toe" during the 1980s, and Professor Jakes Gerwel declaring UWC the "intellectual home for the left" in 1987, and "Khoisan revivalism" in the 1990s. Hence, in 1990, when Former President Nelson Mandela was released from prison, the ANC was unbanned, and the abolishment of apartheid, it seemed as if UWC successfully resisted and escaped its destiny. The first democratic elections further confirmed this, and this was crowned when President Mandela received an honorary doctorate at UWC.

---

[1]   This chapter is an autoethnographic account of my experiences as a university staff member.

Thus, UWC staff and academics who completed their degrees in the 1980s and the 1990s and who matured as academics during the Brian O'Connell era were shocked when UWC students during #FeesMustFall (FMF) called for the "decolonisation of the university" and declared that UWC was no more the "intellectual home for the left." At first, they resisted because they firmly believed they had dealt with it in the 1970s, 1980s, and 1990s. Many identified as black, participated in the struggle and were staunch Marxist supporters. However, as students persisted, they were forced to have another look at the institution.

This chapter has another look at the institution and focuses on the third limitation: the invisibility of the filmmaker/researcher (architects). The invisibility of the "architects" highlights the subliminal and structural nature of power. For me, institutionalisation is the best explanation of this structural nature of power. And one way to unmask it is to actively engage the invisibility of the "architects" of the structure.

The Third Limitation

In documentary films, audiences tend to scrutinise the characters, not the filmmakers. This begs the question: why is this the case? I have asked this question to many well-respected directors and editors of documentary films. The answer they tend to give me relates to ethics, point of view (POV), and audience. For example, the film *The Act of Killing* investigates the limits of morality and raises a question regarding dignity. In *The Act of Killing*, there is a scene where the main character and others re-enact a village raid. They did it with civilians, and the people were not actors. Given the history of mass killings in Indonesia, the re-enactment was so violent and intense that children cried. The civilians were traumatised, and it opened up old wounds.

This particular scene in *The Act of Killing* raises two pertinent questions regarding the power of the filmmakers. Firstly, why did the filmmakers continue filming when they saw that the re-enactment traumatised people? Secondly, why were the images of the crying children included in the cut of the film? Was the purpose of those scenes merely empathy? In class, we were asked how we felt about the scene, and I responded that I appreciated the inclusion of the crying children. If it were not included, it would have been a greater ethical dilemma if I had found out later that the filmmaker had cut this scene.

In the opening chapter of this book, I mentioned that the portrayal of children in *Strike a Rock* was problematic because it stripped children of their agency and, thus, their dignity. Therefore, if I had to compare the inclusion of children in *The Act of Killing* to that of *To Strike a Rock*, I would be guided by the following question: Does their inclusion take dignity away, or does it return dignity? *The Act of Killing* returned dignity to the children. The inclusion of children crying unveiled the filmmaker. If it were not included, the filmmaker would have gotten away with the violence that, that particular scene caused. Including crying children makes the filmmakers responsible for their role in this violent act.

Furthermore, one of the most problematic discourses in documentary films is using "character" to describe human beings. In documentary filmmaking, "character" allows the filmmakers to distance themselves from the human subject they are filming. If documentary filmmakers use "person" or "people", that would position them closer to the human subject. It is almost similar to psychotherapy; the therapist is encouraged to use the term 'client.' By using the term 'client', psychologists can separate them from the person in front of them. Thus, the aim is to be "objective". But can the filmmakers of documentary films be objective? I think documentary films cannot be entirely objective. There would always be a level of subjectivity. As I have mentioned earlier, documentary filmmakers yield significant power in producing a film. Sometimes, films may create unintentional voyeuristic subjects. Therefore, it is important for documentary filmmakers to reveal themselves. Technically, they are part of the actuality being filmed. They are altering reality.

I think the Foucauldian notion of discourses and power also explains this. By reducing human subjects to "characters" in the filmmaking process, the filmmaker is in a powerful position to decide what happens to the "character/s" (the human/s) in the story. And this brings me to the edit of the film. The filmmakers decide which cuts to use and in which sequence the cuts are used. The filmmaker decides how, when and where the "character" would appear. The filmmakers ultimately play god with the images of human beings after they signed the release forms.

However, some filmmakers are visible and put their voices and perspectives in their films. Usually, these are called advocacy documentary films. I found these films guide and enforce the view of the filmmaker. An excellent example of such a film is *Miners Shot Down*. The director's history and politics strongly influenced the direction and storyline of the film. *Miners Shot Down* relied primarily on interviews and archival footage of the Marikana massacre. Advocacy films generally rely on a solid narrative. Thus, one may argue that *Miners Shot Down* poses a question regarding the intention of the director and the filmmaker.

With this in mind, I decided to make a documentary film that would engage the filmmaker' subliminal and complicated relationship has with the audience and the humans being filmed. The name of the film is ENDING AND BEGINNING, and David Hlongwane's sculpture at UWC inspires it. ENDING AND BEGINNING engage the subliminal power relations between architects, people, and society. For example, before FMF at UWC, the struggle of cleaners, security guards, and poor students was known to the university management. However, this reality was stored in the subconscious of the middle-class university staff. As a result, they have become "unaware" of the sculpture and the plight of poor students. Thus, the university's middle-class staff was in a trance and completely unaware of these struggles. It took several protest marches and the destruction of university property to take them out of this flux.

Once they were out of this flux, some resurrected their "struggle credentials" and joined the students. Some rejected the movement and objected to the destruction of university property. Students were reminded that these facilities were built for them and helped them attain a middle-class future, which is at least better than that of the cleaners and security guards. Some did not take any sides and were just grateful that the university closed its operations so that they could temporarily escape their mundane and boring careers. Some pointed out that this is a middle-class struggle and that the real problem is basic education.[2] For that brief moment, we at UWC became conscious and aware of the suffering of the poor at the university, but after a while, we slipped back into a trance and forgot about the poor.[3]

---

[2] I took this stance, and I still believe that our problem in South Africa lies with basic education.

[3] In 2019, when we thought we dealt with all the issues students' raised during FMF, a series of protest marches started again. This time around, it was about accommodation. In 2019, the Cape Peninsula University of Technology (CPUT) signed an agreement with South Point, a private student residence, to exclusively provide accommodation for CPUT students in 2020. However, in 2019, UWC students could also stay at South Point. When UWC students were informed that they could not stay at South Point in 2020, they first approached the university management to intervene. However, when they did not receive any feedback after two months, they started a series of protest marches. Could these protest marches have been anticipated? I believe it could have been. The Senate was informed about the accommodation crisis in the first sitting of 2018. Instead, it sparked a debate centred around "What is the university for?" After that debate, the university management acquired more bed spaces for students. They also built a new residence to accommodate more students. In addition, in 2019, the university management was timeously informed about the CPUT agreement and what would happen to UWC students. However, it did not act on it, which led to the continuation of protest marches on campus in 2020. The states' Covid-19 lockdown brought an end to these protests on campus.

ENDING AND BEGINNING have the same effect on the audience because it breaks the fourth wall several times and directly addresses the filmmaker. This is an intentional attempt to make the audience aware that someone is filming a particular "reality" and that they (the audience) are not part of the on-screen "reality"; that they are an audience. Hence, when the main character calls out the filmmaker's name several times, the audience realises they are not "Jacob" and temporarily feels betrayed. However, a couple of frames later, they are back in a cinematic flux. Cinematic flux is from Deleuze's *Technics and Time 3*. When the audience's conscious stream becomes entangled with the images on the screen, it is considered a cinematic flux. This phenomenon, for me, is the best explanation of the subliminal nature of power, a power that institutionalises people.

The "Ghetto" as a Site for Institutionalisation

David Hlongwane's statue highlights a post-apartheid reality: the current post-apartheid project cannot escape its apartheid frame. And its inability to escape the frame reproduces apartheid in more nuanced ways. This frame gave rise to a psychic condition called institutionalisation. This is a psychic condition that started in slavery. The best description of this condition is found in Kendrick Lamar's critically acclaimed album *To Pimp A Butterfly*. On Track 4, he raps the following:

> I'm trapped inside the ghetto and I ain't proud to admit it
>
> Institutionalized, I keep runnin' back for a visit
>
> Hol'up, get it back
>
> I said I'm trapped inside the ghetto and I ain't proud to admit it
>
> Institutionalized, I could still kill me a nigga, so what?

(Kendrick Lamar Duckworth, 2015)

"Institutionalised" is a term rappers use to describe a psychic condition that they witness amongst African American males after they are released from prison. These ex-prisoners continue to live as if they are still in prison. Kendrick is aware of this because his uncle was "institutionalised".[4] Here the "institution" in "institutionalised" refers to the prison system in America. In this song, Kendrick Lamar extends the borders of the prison to that of the "ghetto". In America, a "ghetto" describes a neighbourhood where African Americans were forced to live. In another song, Kendrick describes the "ghetto" as an orphanage and says living in the "ghetto" "is quite a routine".

---

[4]   He raps about his uncle's institutionalisation on "Poe Man's Dream" on his album *Section 80*.

This routine describes the prison-like system in which African Americans are forced to live.[5] He dedicates another album, *Good Kid, Mad City*, to describe this world young African Americans are trapped in and how they negotiate it daily. They are restricted to certain gang-controlled areas and cannot move from one block to another without risking their lives. They also cannot leave the ghetto because racial profiling makes them the target of police. Therefore, they are trapped inside the ghetto and cannot get out. This forces many of them to get involved in gang activities.

Two levels of violence control African American neighbourhoods. The first is at a nation-state level. After slavery, many neighbourhoods were created for African Americans. City planning and the police ensure that African Americans stay in the neighbourhoods created for them. The second is at a neighbourhood level. Here, various gangs control African Americans, young African American males turn into Crips and Bloods (Adamson, 2000). This creates an endless cycle of violence. This violence sends young African American males to prison, which creates the psychic condition Kendrick recognises that he is trapped in.

> I'm trapped inside the ghetto and I ain't proud to admit it
>
> Institutionalized, I keep running back for a visit.

It is extremely dangerous for a world-famous hip hop artist to return to the "ghetto". Many successful rappers have been killed in neighbourhoods like Kendrick's. For example, in 2019, Ermias Joseph Asghedom, also known as Nipsey Hussle, was shot and killed in the neighbourhood he was trying to uplift. Therefore, even though it is extremely dangerous for Kendrick to return to the "ghetto", he cannot stop himself from returning for a visit. Although he was never imprisoned, he, too, is institutionalised.

Slavery as the Origin of Institutionalisation

Reading Frederick Douglass' *Narrative of the Life of Frederick Douglass, An American Slave*, one realises that institutionalisation originates in racism and slavery. Slavery restricted the movements and desires of slaves. A master controlled slaves. The master dictated where, when, and what the slave could do. The master was the sovereign power that controlled the slave. The slave was property, and the law dictated that the master could do whatever they pleased with their property. Slaves, born into slavery, lived in a slave society where they were subjugated and socialised into slavery. Since human beings are not born with any sense of bondage, at one point, slave children had

---

[5] The song is titled "Sing About Me, Dying of Thirst" on the *Good Kid, Mad City* album.

a sense of freedom. However, as they grew up, they became aware of the limitations to their sense of freedom. For example, Frederick Douglass, born into slavery, tells us in his memoir about his first encounter with the cruelty of slavery, and that experience changed him.

> I was so terrified and horror-stricken at the sight, that I hid myself in a closet, and dared not venture out till long after the bloody transaction was over. I expected it would be my turn next. It was all new to me. I had never seen anything like it before (Douglass, 1845, p. 6).

The "bloody transaction" he is reflecting on is the whipping of his aunt Hester. The event left him with lifelong scars and illustrated the unregulated violence that was at the disposal of the master. This violence restricted the boundaries of the slave. The slave had to regulate and negotiate their movements at the will of the master. However, this changed after the abolishment of slavery. The master did not have the sovereign power to control the movements or determine the limits of the freedom of the freed slave. This right shifted to the state because the state now had to extend rights and obligations to freed slaves.

However, slaves did not enjoy the same levels of freedom as those regarded as their masters not long ago. One must remember that slavery created a black and a white other and justified the treatment of both racial groups in the white supremacy doctrine. After the abolishment of slavery, white people in the Southern states wanted to continue being the recipients of racial privilege. This racial privilege had to come at the cost of the human dignity of the black other. For such a continued privilege, an institution had to be created to ensure white people's sense of illusionary racial superiority in the South continued. Various measures were institutionalised to achieve this. The first was the 13th Amendment to the Constitution. The 13th Amendment conditionally abolished slavery.

> Neither slavery nor involuntary servitude, except as a punishment for crime whereof the party shall have been duly convicted, shall exist within the United States, nor any place subject to their jurisdiction.

Slavery was, therefore, never wholly abolished in the United States of America. The 13th Amendment left a back door open. Slavery and involuntary servitude could be used as a "punishment for crime". Hence, freed slaves were arrested for petty crimes, convicted and imprisoned. These inmates became the workforce for many state and private sector projects in the South. This labour was free and plentiful (DuVernay, 2016).

Moreover, abolishing slavery did not change the attitudes of most white people in the South. In fact, Jim Crow Laws were introduced in 26 Southern states to defend and support the idea of white supremacy. The place of the "Negro" after the Civil War was conceptualised by Henry Gardy in his book *The New South*. Gardy was an unmistakable white supremacist, and his writings were very influential in passing the Jim Crow Laws. Gardy, for example, writes:

> First – that the whites shall have clear and unmistakable control of public affairs. They own the property. They have the intelligence. Theirs is the responsibility. For these reasons they are entitled to control. Beyond these reasons is a racial one. They are the superior race, and will not and cannot submit to the domination of an inferior race (Gardy, 1890, p. 239).

Gardy recognised the importance of state control for the continuation of white supremacy. The state became the sovereign power over "excess bodies".[6] Hence, the state legislated and implemented laws for these "excess bodies". With its monopoly on violence, the state made it possible to shape the consciousness of society. Gardy proposed the "separate but equal" doctrine that would later influence institutionalising apartheid in South Africa.

Christianity also played a crucial role in institutionalising slavery. Frederick Douglass paints a picture of how religion was instrumental in slavery.

> I have said my master found religious sanction for his cruelty. As an example, I will state one of many facts going to prove the charge. I have seen him tie up a lame young woman, and whip her with a heavy cowskin upon her naked shoulders, causing the warm red blood to drip; and, in justification of the bloody deed, he would quote this passage of Scripture – "He that knoweth his master's will, and doeth it not, shall be beaten with many stripes" (Douglass, 1845, p. 48).

In the Bible, the slave is an infrahuman and devoid of humanity. The white supremacy doctrine borrowed this from the Bible to justify slavery.[7] Hence, for the successful transition of the white supremacy doctrine (that institutionalised slavery), Gardy drew on religion to make racial discrimination seem like something God ordained.

> But the white and black carpenters, working together on the same building, go to separate homes at night, to separate churches on Sunday. White and black mechanics in the same shop send their children to separate schools. White and black farmers in the same field ride to market in separate cars. This distinction may seem trifling, but it is natural. It responds to an instinct planted by the Almighty in the two races. It is the wisest and best course (Gardy, 1890, pp. 249-250).

[6]   Parikh (2022) explains that "excess bodies" was born from the narrative of 'overpopulation'. Those who live in 'overpopulated' areas are the problem. They are the "excess" that consumes too many resources.

[7]   An infrahuman is an incomplete human. See the Tanner lectures of Paul Gilroy for a description and history of the infrahuman.

The Lockean notion of Natural Law supported Gardy's doctrine; hence, 26 Southern states could pass Jim Crow laws because black people "did not have 'human rights' because they were not part of humanity" (Tischauser, 2012, p. xi).[8] Jim Crow laws were operational from 1881 to 1964, and they separated Americans based on race.[9] These laws segregated almost all possible human contact. It segregated neighbourhoods, schools, churches, sexual relations, and businesses. It created the psychological condition Kendrick describes in his album. More importantly, these laws and the work of Gardy aided racists in South Africa in developing a "separate but equal" policy (apartheid) that subjugated Black people to an inferior racial status.

Institutionalising Apartheid in South Africa

As we saw in Chapter 3, in South Africa, we also had laws that restricted the movements of slaves, the Khoekhoe and San. The colonial state appointed "Masters" over their bodies. Movements and violence was used to ensure the slaves, the Khoekhoe and San, restricted their movement in the boundaries of their oppression. Chapter 3 highlighted how the colonial and apartheid states instituted the "coloured" identity through a series of laws that spanned close to 150 years. However, it was apartheid laws and violence that finally bureaucratically erased the Khoekhoe and San and trapped them in the "coloured" identity. In this section, I will briefly examine how the "architects of apartheid" institutionalised apartheid in South Africa.

J.W. Sauer, Minister of Native Affairs in the Union of South Africa government, was a staunch supporter of racial segregation and drew on the work of Gardy to introduce the *Natives Land Act of 1913* (Giliomee, 2003, p. 303). This Act restricted native South Africans to only 7% of South Africa's land. It also restricted black people from owning land in the 93% set aside for white people in South Africa. Other staunch "separate but equal" supporters included Hertzog, Malan, and Verwoerd.

Hertzog's thinking was also informed by William H. Thomas (Giliomee, 2003, pp. 301-302). Thomas was of mixed racial origin and denounced black people in the hardest and crudest ways. He regarded black people as culturally, morally, physiologically and intellectually inferior to white people. He did not see himself as black but as mulatto and thus better as the "Negro"

---

[8] Only after the Second World War and with the Jewish Holocaust in mind, the United Nations passed a Universal Declaration for Human Rights.

[9] I want to draw the reader's attention to the following: Jim Crow laws were longer institutionalised in the USA than colonialism in central Africa.

(Smith, 2019). In addition to the work of Thomas, Hertzog justified racial discrimination through religion, which in turn influenced Malan, who was a great follower of Hertzog and "became converted to the gospel of General Hertzog's 'Afrikanerism.' A new call – to serve his people as well as his God – rang in his ears" (Robins, 1953, p. 16).

While Sauer, Hertzog and Malan were born in South Africa, Verwoerd was born in Amsterdam. Verwoerd was only two years old when his parents moved to South Africa after the South African War. During the war, Verwoerd senior sympathised with the "Boers" and "he served on a committee which helped Boers visiting the Netherlands for aid in their cause against the British" (Hepple, 1967, p. 13). The Verwoerd family settled in Wynberg, Cape Town, where they lived for ten years before moving to Bulawayo in Southern Rhodesia (now Zimbabwe) to take up a missionary position. The Verwoerd family stayed there for two years before moving back to South Africa to settle in Brandfort. This was at the height of the *Bittereinder* rebellion in South Africa (Hepple, 1967, p. 15).[10]

Once Verwoerd completed high school, he joined the University of Stellenbosch to study theology but changed to psychology and sociology and completed his doctorate in psychology. His dissertation was on the blunting of emotions and was the first written in Afrikaans (Giliomee, 2003; Hepple, 1967; Lalu, 2022). After his doctoral studies, he studied at three universities in Germany, where he continued to study psychology and philosophy. After Verwoerd got married, he and his wife toured the United States, and they then returned to South Africa to take up a teaching position at the University of Stellenbosch (Giliomee, 2003; Hepple, 1967).

Apartheid was not the grand design of Verwoerd. Instead, Verwoerd's contribution was shaping the psychological design of apartheid. Verwoerd's contribution to the apartheid project was overhauling "the hotchpotch of laws, regulations, and conventions of racial discrimination and adapted what needed to his overall purpose" (Hepple, 1967, pp. 110-111). Verwoerd's studies gave him insights into designing an apartheid project that reflects the psychology of a white society that believes in racial superiority and inferiority.[11]

---

[10] The *Bittereinder* Rebellion resulted from the Union of South Africa's decision to support Brittan in the First World War against Germany. *Bittereinder* is an Afrikaans word that means to the bitter end. The *Bittereinders* were a faction in the Afrikaner community who did not accept the defeat against the Brittan in the South African War.

[11] Ironically, Verwoerd was killed by Dimitri Tsafendas, who was declared insane by the state.

He also authored three critical pieces of legislation that laid the foundation for the National Party's notion of "separate development" (apartheid) (Giliomee, 2003, pp. 508-511; Hepple, 1967, p. 116). These laws were the *Bantu Authorities Act of 1951*, the *Natives Laws Amendment Act of 1952*, and the *Bantu Education Act of 1953*.[12] As President, he also passed the *Promotion of Bantu Self-Government Act of 1959,* which was an extension of the *Bantu Authorities Act*. This Act divided Black people into eight distinct ethnic groups and facilitated the resettlement of Black people in eight different reservations or "homelands". I have to point out that the *Bantu Authorities Act* is similar to the Hottentot Proclamation of 150 years before.

Verwoerd's nuanced understanding of psychology and sociology helped design a system of racial classification that led to social stratification. The laws introduced during apartheid clearly aimed at restructuring the social makeup of South Africa, which reflected the Afrikaner conceptualisation of race (Lalu, 2022). They knew that black and white would be institutionalised if such a system were enforced long enough. Black and white people will believe that these differences are "natural". Verwoerd, thus, carefully conceptualised petty apartheid to succeed grand apartheid as everyday life (Lalu, 2022). Petty apartheid was, therefore, institutionalised to alter the collective consciousness of South Africa. Thus, to accept racial difference as natural.

Therefore, in retrospect, we can see that race was created in South Africa to elevate white people's sense of racial superiority. White people forced black people to call them "Baas" (Master), "Nooi" (Madam), "Klein Baas" (Little Master) and "Klein Nooi" (Little Madam). This was to alter and subjugate the psyche of black people. Black people who refused and resisted the white supremacy doctrine were subjected to unimaginable violence. I know this because I saw my grandparents live through this. Sadly, this is still happening in South Africa. If you travel to rural South Africa as a black person, you will experience this violence. You will always be treated worse than the white "Oom" and "Tannie". They will remind you are "black".[13]

In addition, these laws played an important role in communicating and institutionalising apartheid in South Africa. Norbert Wiener defines the law "as the ethical control applied to communication, and to language as a form of communication, especially when this normative aspect is under the control of some authority sufficiently strong to give its decisions and effective

---

[12]   There were many more laws that institutionalised apartheid. Please see Appendix 1.

[13]   In 2023, I released Bergsig in collaboration with the Institute for Justice and
       Reconciliation. The film addresses this continuous violence and its generational effect on
       "Coloured" people.

social sanction" (Wiener, 1988 p. 105). It is the authority that sets the ethical parameters. The authority decides what is ethical and what is not. The supporters of apartheid wanted to control the state by implementing a set of laws to give them "ethical control" over black and white people. In law, they found the answer to communicate their doctrine of apartheid. Wiener argues that "the problems of law may be considered communicative and cybernetic" and that "they are problems of orderly and repeatable control of certain critical situations" (Wiener, 1988, p. 110). If this is the case, then the aim of the law was institutionalisation. Institutionalisation prevented the repetition of certain critical situations. It aimed to eliminate errors and, if an error did occur, to automatically rectify it without any ambiguity.

Moreover, any law's effectiveness is whether Judge A's interpretation can be reproduced by Judge B (Wiener, 1988, p. 107). Reproducibility ensures the continuation of institutionalisation. The Jim Crow system clearly inspired the architects of apartheid. Thus, even though racial segregation started in colonial times in South Africa, apartheid borrowed many institutional characteristics of the Jim Crow system when creating apartheid laws. This is why reading accounts of racism from the American South feels so familiar. We are institutionalised the same way Kendrick Lamar, his uncles, and friends are.

Therefore, even though one may remove the discriminatory aspects and racism from the law, this would not eradicate nor stop the discrimination against black people in society. Institutionalisation altered the collective unconscious of South African society; the South African society is institutionalised; since social stratification is complete, we are the institution. We will continue upholding and recreating the structure of the institution. This is a result of the psychic life of power.[14] Therefore, racism and discrimination will continue, especially since racism and discrimination were spatially and materially defined. Black and white people's spatial and material reality of has not changed much since 1990. For discrimination and racism to stop, we must change of black people's spatial, material, and psychological conditions.

Higher Education as an Institutionalisation Site

Education is the institution most present in one's life, shaping a large part of one's psyche and life. It plays a vital role in shaping one into a citizen and transfers the ethical norms of this type of citizenship. Therefore, one has to think of Bantu Education and especially the university system under apartheid, as a

---

[14] See Butler's book *The Psychic Life of Power* for a detailed discussion.

site of segregation. The *Extension of University Education Act of 1959* established colleges and university colleges for "non-white" persons. It also prohibited the admission of "non-white" students to certain universities classified as white. This Act created university colleges for Black, "Coloured", and Indian people. This Act segregated and racialised Higher Education in South Africa. Hence, various universities were created to accommodate specific racial and ethnic groups. For example, the University of Durban-Westville was created for Indian people. The University of Zululand for Zulu and Swazi people and the University of the Western Cape for "Coloured" people (Iaga Ramoupi, 2022, p. 128).

In this segregated university system, the South African Students' Organisation (SASO) and Steve Biko's Black Consciousness project came to life. Biko recognised the psychology behind the apartheid project when he wrote: "At the heart of this kind of thinking is the realization by the blacks that the most potent weapon in the hands of the oppressor is the mind of the oppressed" (Biko, 2017, p. 74). Also, considering how Biko paints the picture of the apartheid institution, one can argue that it can be considered a counter psychological project to apartheid.

> I think the black man is subjected to two forces in this country. He is first of all oppressed by an external world through institutionalised machinery, through laws that restrict him from doing certain things, through heavy work conditions, through poor pay, through very difficult living conditions, through poor education, these are all external to him, and secondly, and this we regard as the most important, the black man in himself has developed a certain state of alienation, he rejects himself, precisely because he attaches the meaning white to all that is good, in other words, he associates good and he equates good with white (Biko, 2017, p. 111).

From Biko's explanation, one notices that institutionally apartheid South Africa looked very similar to the American South under Jim Crow laws. It also created a similar psyche. For example, "The homes are different, the streets are different, the lighting is different, so you tend to begin to feel that there is something incomplete in your humanity, and that completeness goes with whiteness" (Biko, 2017, p. 111). For Biko, the apartheid project located humanity in whiteness.

Apartheid was the project that saw the "need" to "develop" Black people separately in homelands. For that, the *Promotion of Bantu Self-Government Act of 1959* was created. In this "model of development," White people considered themselves the "civilised" race and Black people the "uncivilised" race. Only when Black people assimilated and mirrored white people's sense of "civilisation" was humanity conditionally bestowed on these assimilated Black people.

Black Consciousness challenged this notion of development with "Black is beautiful." It encouraged black people to rise and attain their "envisaged self" (Biko, 2017, p. 74). It excluded white people from this project but extended blackness to the so-called Coloured and Indian people in South Africa. It also challenged the fear that apartheid instilled in black people through violence. According to Biko (2017, p. 108), "We must remove from our vocabulary completely the concept of fear. Truth must ultimately triumph over evil, and the white man has always nourished his greed on this basic fear that shows itself in the black community." Biko, like Fanon, recognised that this fear resulted from the Hegelian dialectic, which led to the subjugation of black people. Fear keeps the subjugated in an institutionalised state of mind. Fear reminds the subjugated where to go and where not to go. Fear keeps the oppressed in their familiar boundaries of oppression.

Resisting the "Coloured" Identity at UWC

From 1971 to 1973, UWC was rocked by student protests. These protests started over a disagreement over the SRC constitution. According to Lalu (2012, p. 42), in October 1967, the UWC council authorised the SRC constitution. However, it did not get the required votes in 1969 because students also wanted to be affiliated with national and international organisations such as SASO. However, the university refused. So, the students drew up their own Constitution in May 1971 that reflected their wishes. The students' constitution also authorised mass meetings, referenda, and surveys. This matter eventually led to a case at the Supreme Court in November 1972. Unfortunately, the court ruled in favour of the administration, but students rejected the ruling. This led to the 1973 student walk-off.

An important precursor to the 1973 student walk-off is the Desmond Damas tie affair in 1970. During the 1960s and the early 1970s, UWC student was prescribed by the apartheid state to dress in a particular way. Part of the criteria was that men should wear a tie. After refusing to wear a tie, Desmond Damas was suspended for three weeks during March/April 1970. According to Damas (2010, p. 22), "On my return to campus, I still refused to conform and was summonsed to appear before the University Council. At this meeting, I challenged the rector on the same issues I challenged my lecturer." Damas believed the dress code prescribed for UWC students was that they were treated as children. He pointed out that students at white universities were allowed to dress in casual clothes. Since Damas was not apologetic and refused to conform to the dress code, his studies were terminated (Damas, 2010, p. 23).

This led to a dress code and tie boycott at UWC, fuelling the anti-oppression sentiments that already existed among UWC students. According to Damas (2010, p. 23), "For the first time in the history of Bush, marches were held on the campus. Placards were displayed, petitions were delivered to the rector, and students openly demonstrated by burning their ties." Since the protests were ongoing and received much publicity, UWC lifted the suspension with a fine and never enforced the dress code again.

If the Desmond Damas tie affair was the catalyst, then the prevailing conditions at UWC led to the 1973 student walk-off. According to Lalu (2012, p. 46):

> The limitations of student life that were at issue, especially the restrictions in the hostels, the strict dress code for students, the conditions in the library, regulations relating to sporting activities, the authoritarianism that prevailed amongst administrators, the state of the bookshop, and the conditions of the toilets on campus, all these were highlighted in the students' grievances.

In addition, students demanded a "*nie-blanke*" (non-white) rector and a more representative staff. They also wanted the non-white staff at UWC to be paid at the same scale as their white counterparts. Students of the 1971 to 1972 protests believed that UWC's academic programme failed to address the South African reality. During the 1970s, protesting students opted for informal structures of education, education that they normally would not receive from their white lecturers. Students read Fanon, Marx, and Biko. Thus, it was SASO in the 1970s that diagnosed the structural violence at UWC – a violence that was structurally institutionalised during its birth.

The 1973 student movement demanded that Prof CJ Kriel step down as rector. He eventually did, but none of the reforms students hoped for was implemented. According to Grootboom (2010, pp. 106-107):

> Then it happened, after debate after debate, the students walked off campus. Some never returned. After that June 1973, things were never the same. We got a new rector, Professor Wynand Mouton – from the Orange Free State. He signed the SRC constitution without batting an eyelid. The students were totally disempowered. We did not expect it.

It is clear that UWC rejected the "coloured" identity early on through Black Consciousness and Marxism. One of the leading Black Consciousness and Marxist figures at UWC is Prof. Jakes Gerwel. In 1972, after completing his degree in Afrikaans-Nederlands at UWC, he was appointed a lecturer in Afrikaans and Nederlands. In 1979, he received his doctorate, and in 1982, he was promoted to professor (Daily Dispatch, 1999). When Gerwel joined UWC in the 1960s, he got into Black Consciousness. However, he also believed that Black Consciousness was not everything (Willemse, 2013, p. 126). Gerwel realised there was more to the struggle for liberation than race. There were structural inequalities that Black Consciousness was unable to solve. Marxism resolved these structural issues.

Thus, when he was appointed in 1987, he declared UWC "the intellectual home for the left" (Gerwel, 1987). Gerwel aspired to build a university that would not reproduce a social order that is "undemocratic, discriminatory, exploitative and repressive" (Gerwel, 1987). Hence, he opened the doors of UWC to all races and people from various socio-economic backgrounds. As a result, UWC identified itself with the struggle of the working class and was "committed to the values and the vigour of critical scholarship" (Gerwel, 1987). From then on, it was not a "Coloured" university anymore, and it was known as the university of the left.

Another way some academics at UWC resisted the "coloured" identity was through the "Khoisan revivalism" movement. One of the central figures in the "Khoisan revivalism" movement is Henry Bredenkamp, considered by many to be the "father of Khoisan revivalism". Bredenkamp started working at UWC in 1975 as a lecturer-researcher at the Institute for Historical Research (Verbuyst, 2022, p. 88). Bredenkamp was one of the black academics to focus on the history of the Khoekhoe and San. In particular, white males dominated the Khoekhoe and San studies field during those years. And in many instances, they wrote about the Khoekhoe and San as extinct. After reading the works of Richard Elphick on the Khoekhoe and San, Bredenkamp decided to focus his research on the Khoekhoe and San. He ensured they were written back into history (Bredenkamp, 2022). Bredenkamp was also the leading figure who organised the "ground-breaking Khoisan Identities and Cultural Heritage Conference in 1997" (Verbuyst, 2022, p. 61). This conference births what scholars call the "Khoisan Revivalism" movement.

This movement was born at the university and started with academics; at a university that was supposed to reiterate its oppression, it resisted it with Khoisan revivalism. In this sense, "Khoisan revivalism" could be seen as resistance. However, after the conference, "Khoisan revivalism" lost steam in the university. Bredenkamp also did not successfully change the IHR into a centre for Khoisan studies (Verbuyst, 2022, p. 122). One of the people against the idea of the Khoisan centre was Jakes Gerwel. At the time, Gerwel believed the "Khoisan revivalism" promoted "recidivist neo-ethnicity". It did not promote "trans-ethnic nation-building." (Verbuyst, 2022, pp. 122-123). I think

Gerwel was right. In Chapter 1, I pointed out a danger regarding the "Khoisan" terminology. If we are not careful, it could reproduce the racist "coloured" identity as a "Khoisan" identity.

If UWC early on resisted itself as a "Coloured" university, why did the FMF movement at UWC call for the "decolonisation of the university" and declare that UWC was no longer the "intellectual home for the left"? What happened? Where did UWC go wrong? In the following sections, I will critically examine the FMF movement at UWC. It will also look at why students called for the decolonisation of UWC. However, before I get there, I have to give a contextual background of the #RhodesMustFall and #FeesMustFall movements.

A Contextual Background to RMF and FMF

The demographic profile of higher education in South Africa before RMF and FMF started, had not changed much since 1993. For example, *the Education White Paper 3: A Programme for the Transformation of Higher Education of 1997* (WP3) mentioned that "In 1993, the overall participation rate in all post-Standard ten programmes in public and private institutions was about 20%.[15] However, the participation rate for white students was just under 70%, while that for African students was about 12% (NCHE Report, 1996:64)" (section 2.22). This picture did not change much by 2012.

By 2012, the participation of Black students at institutions of higher learning was 16%. From 1993 to 2012, there has been only a 4% increase in the participation rate of Black students at university. This begs the question, why such a marginal increase? To answer this question, one has to consider the effects of the *Bantu Education Act of 1953*, the *Coloured Person's Education Act of 1963*, the *Indians Education Act of 1965* and the *Extension of University Act of 1959*. These four pieces of legislation shaped apartheid education and the futures of Black, Indian and "Coloured" people in South Africa. In addition, one also has to consider the amount of money spent on each student during apartheid. For example, R644 was spent on White, R189 on Indian, R42 on Black, and R139 on "Coloured" students (Villette, 2016).

I must highlight that the 1993 participation rate of Black students in university does not surprise me. The apartheid system was designed to discriminate against and oppress Black people. As a result, Black people were not given equal opportunities to enter university. However, the 16% participation rate of Black students in 2012 does raise questions. For answers, one has to turn to the

---

[15] Standard 10 is now referred to as Grade 12 in South Africa.

WP3. If one looks at what the WP3 envisioned, it becomes clear that the central focus of the WP3 was rapid economic growth and not redress. For example, according to section 2.25, preference was given to science, engineering, and technology. The narrative was that science and technology were to bring about rapid economic growth to recover from economic decline during apartheid. In addition, the WP3 also allowed higher education institutions to decide their transformation targets (section 2.28). These were transformation targets in terms of staff and students.

Furthermore, 20 years later, the *Post School Education and Training* (PSET) white paper was born. The PSET highlights the following:

> Black students at formerly whites-only institutions have often been victims of racism, and female students have been victims of patriarchal practices and sexual harassment. Poorer students have to fit in with systems that were designed for students from relatively privileged backgrounds. Opportunities in rural areas are far more limited than those in urban areas and informal settlements are also victims of under-provision. The majority of disabled students continue to experience discrimination in terms of access to post-school education and training opportunities, and the system as a whole has inadequate facilities and staff to cater for the needs of the disabled. Education for adults has been marginalised and neglected, and has seldom provided a vocational component for those seeking to enhance their occupational skills (PSET, 2013, p. 1).

With this in mind, PSET set a particular target for enrolment. According to PSET (2013, p. xiv), "Participation rates in universities are expected to increase from the current 17.3% to 25% – that is, from just over 937 000 students in 2011 to about 1.6 million enrolments in 2030. As participation increases, universities must simultaneously focus their attention on improving student performance." The Department of Higher Education and Training (DHET) expects as more students enrol to universities, their performance must also improve. The PSET frames performance as "access," "success", and "throughput."

Sadly, the PSET does not speak about the under-representation of Black students at university. The department envisioned a 25% increase in student participation rates would more or less mean a proportional increase across all racial groups in South African universities. More simply, the 25% increase would not mean that by 2030, 25% of all students at South African universities will be Black. It could stay proportionally the same at 17.3%. The aim is only to develop the capacity of universities to take on an increase of 25% of students. Like the WP3, the PSET focuses on economic growth.

Moreover, before 2018, the big question was whether free tertiary education would be possible. For example, before FMF, the plan was "to progressively [introduce] free education for the poor in South African universities as resources become available" (PSET, 2013, p. xiv). Thus, the aim was always to provide free education to the poor and not everyone, but there was no clear funding plan to realise this aim. If one looks at the aims of the PSET in this regard, one has to ask whether universities have the capacity and the resources to achieve this. PSET identified National Student Financial Aid Scheme (NSFAS), fees, third-stream income and subsidies to fund tertiary education.

The PSET also had foresight into the "missing middle" phenomenon, which became a popular phrase to describe the children of the middle-class in the aftermath of the first phase of FMF. For example, the PSET indicated that "Of particular concern is finding ways to assist those students whose parental incomes are too high to qualify for funding from NSFAS but are too low to qualify for loans from private financial institutions" (PSET, 2013, p. 8). However, the "missing middle" phenomenon did not disappear after President Zuma's announcement in 2018 that there will be free education for tertiary students whose household income is less than R 350 000 annually.

For example, at UWC, in 2019, the second phase of the FMF started and was driven by "missing middle" students who were financially excluded from the university and needed accommodation. The PSET also had foresight into this. For example, the PSET proposed "capping university fees to keep them more affordable, both for individual students and for NSFAS and other funders" (PSET, 2013, p. 8). Unfortunately, these measures were not implemented by the time the FMF started. Interestingly, raising university fees at historically white universities (HWU) led to the FMF movement. Black students could not afford to continue studying at these universities, and FMF was born. It started at the University of the Witwatersrand (Wits) and spread throughout universities in South Africa (Booysen, 2016).

In hindsight, one could argue that if the aims of the PSET had been implemented, the RMF and FMF movements could have been deferred. However, RMF resulted from institutionalised racism, and FMF later raised the remaining structural issues Black students faced (Godsell & Chikane, 2016). At UWC, three issues need attention in the coming years. These issues are (1) the transformation of institutional power, (2) the dignity of black students, and (3) the question regarding the "decolonisation of the university".

Institutional Power

FMF was a very violent phenomenon on both sides of the spectrum. Students' violence was mainly directed toward the university property. In addition, most students' grievances were directed toward the university, not the state. This begs an obvious question: Why was the violence directed toward the institution? For example, if one looks at the memorandum of understanding by UWC students, one notices that 23 of the 32 grievances focused on institutional transformation. For example:

> The University is not a differently abled friendly environment and has ignored the many cries made by the Differently Abled Students Association (DASA) for many years (FMF Memorandum of Understanding, 2015, Grievance 9).

> The outsourcing of essential services such as transport, catering, cleaning and security services (FMF Memorandum of Understanding, 2015, Grievance 14).

> The wasteful expenditure by senior executive managers, where we have seen hosting of extravagant events while students are literally starving on residences (FMF Memorandum of Understanding, 2015, Grievance 15).

More importantly, one cannot ignore the issue of race at UWC. For example:

> The racial academic profiling that happens when our assessments are being marked where it is evident that those who have African surnames get lower marks than other students yet their content is the same (Grievance 6).

> The University must start a programme to create black academics in order to assist to transform the academic staff of UWC so that it reflects South African demographics (Demand 22).

The reality is that UWC's institutional power is largely still in the hands of "Coloured", White and Indian staff. For example, 31% of the university's top and senior management is "Coloured", 26% White, 23% Foreign, 13% Indian, and 7% Black. As one goes down the grading system, the number of Black people in lower positions increases. For example, 14% of the professionally qualified and experienced specialists are Black, 48% are "Coloured", 16% White, 15% Foreign, and 7% Indian. Amongst the technical skilled and academically qualified are 20% Black, 74% "Coloured", 3% White, 2% Indian and 1% Foreign. Finally, among the semi-skilled staff, 31.2% is Black, 65.4% is "Coloured", 0.4% is Indian, 1.1% is White, and 1.9% is Foreign (University of the Western Cape, Five Year Employment Equity Plan, 2021, p. 27).[16]

---

[16] Please see Appendix 2 for a detailed breakdown of UWC Staff's Racial Profile.

Therefore, power is invested in the hands of "Coloured", White, Indian, and Foreign administrators. Hence, it is no surprise that at UWC, one sees the Black cleaner, the Black security guard and the Black student at the bottom of the system. To make sense of the violence in his neighbourhood, Kendrick Lamar explains: "America is a reflection of me; that is what a mirror does." Before Lamar, Fanon, and Biko indicated that the violence of the oppressed mirrors the violence they experience at the hands of the oppressor. Thus, to answer the question. At UWC, FMF mirrored the structural violence Black students faced daily.

At UWC, the security and cleaning services are outsourced, and companies employ security guards and cleaners. Therefore, the university is not directly responsible for the demographic profile of security and cleaning services. However, the demographic profile of security guards and cleaners indicates the failure of the "post-apartheid" South African society's ability to transform. Something Gerwel warned the university about in his 1987 Inaugural Address. He recognised the role the university had to play in transforming society. For him, the university is responsible for addressing the structural issues created by colonialism and apartheid. The university could not sit along the sidelines and had to get involved. Therefore, through its outsourcing policy, the university has become a site for reproducing systemic racism and inequality against Black people in South Africa. For Black students, is UWC home, but is it "a place of quality, a place to grow"? Is it still the *"home* of the intellectual left"?

Interestingly, the 32-point memorandum of FMF was similar to the demands of the students of 1973. Both movements were against the structural violence at UWC. Students of the 1971 to 1972 protests believed that UWC's academic programme failed to address the South African reality. This is another similarity with FMF's decolonisation call in 2015. During the 1970s, protesting students opted for informal structures of education, education that they normally would not receive from their white lecturers. A similar programme started during FMF at UWC. Strikingly, the FMF students and the students during the 1970s read the same material. They read Fanon, Marx, and Biko. Thus, both SASO in the 1970s and FMF diagnosed the structural violence at UWC – a violence that was structurally institutionalised during its birth. Finally, students in 1973 demanded a "nie-blanke" (non-white) rector and a more representative staff. They also wanted the non-white staff at UWC to be paid at the same scale as their white counterparts. The FMF student movement made the same demands. Why the similarity between 1973 (apartheid) and 2015 (post-apartheid)?

For me, it is clear that institutional power at UWC has not transformed. This is mainly because of how the transformation of Higher Education in South Africa was conceptualised in key policy documents after 1994. If one critically looks at the WP3, several issues become apparent. Firstly, the 'historical' scope of the white paper is limited to apartheid and does not include colonialism. Higher Education in South Africa started as exclusively reserved for white people during colonialism. For example, the University of Cape Town was established in 1829 and is the first university in South Africa (Ndelu, 2017; Penrith, 1972). However, only in the 1920s were a small group of Black students admitted to the university – almost 100 years later.

Secondly, from the WP3, it is clear that the focus after apartheid was to develop the economy. There was a considerable emphasis in WP3 on "development" and the drive to be part of the global economy. The "development" task was assigned to the university. The university had to prepare the labour force needed for rapid economic growth. The university also had to focus on science and technology. The belief was that "development" was driven by "science and technology." Therefore, economic growth was, and still is, primarily seen as the best way to meet the demands of the "transforming" South Africa.

Thirdly, the WP3 also uses words such as "historically advantage" and "historical disadvantage" to describe the people who were oppressed during colonialism and apartheid. For example, "*historically advantaged* institutions will require additional resources to deal with the learning needs of *disadvantaged students* as a result of the changing composition of the student body, with large and increasing numbers of black students enrolled in these institutions" (WP3, 1997, Section 2.20).[17] I want to highlight that the "development discourse" masks the Hegelian master-slave dialectic in the same manner words like "historically advantage" and "historically disadvantage" masks the oppression of black people in South Africa. This carefully worded policy document created the *Higher Education Act of 1997*. This new law was supposed to change the higher education landscape in South Africa after 1997. However, genealogically the *Higher Education Act of 1997* shares many similarities with the *Extension of University Education Act of 1959*. For example, power in both Acts is vested with the minister of Higher Education. In addition, both Acts place institutional power in the University Council and Senate. Finally, both Acts ensure that the state controls the governance structures of the public university.

---

[17] The italics are my emphasis.

Fourthly, in the WP3, the Council for Higher Education (CHE) was conceptualised as a powerful institution, but not in the *Higher Education Act of 1997*. In the *Act*, power shifted towards the minister. The *Act* gives the Minister the right to appoint the chairperson of the CHE and the ordinary members. In addition, the WP3 envisages the CHE as the driver of transformation in Higher Education, but not in the *Act*. The WP3 envisages the transformation of the university governance system as a necessity and not an option (WP3, 1997, Section 3.1). However, this responsibility was given to the Minister and not the CHE. The minister was to drive transformation (WP3, 1997, Section 3.8). Therefore, even though the WP3 created the CHE to help facilitate the transformation of governance in higher education, it did not have any significant power to bring about any real change.

Moreover, the emphasis was on transforming the university's governance structures at a national and council level. This is why the WP3 envisages the university council as the highest decision-making body. This is something the *Act* ensures. According to section 27 (6), "At least 60% of the members of a council must be persons who are not employed by, or students of, the public higher education institution concerned." However, it does not mean that when 60% of the council consists of non-university staff and students, the governance structure of the university has been "transformed". Also, the supposed transformation of the university council did not automatically translate into institutional transformation. Institutional power is primarily vested in the University Senate, the Executive Management Committee (EMC), and Institutional Forum. Therefore, even though the emphasis was on transformation, it mainly focused on transforming the governance structures, not the university as an institution.

Fifth, the WP3 indicated in 1997 that public expenditure growth rates could not be maintained with the economic growth rate. The WP3 also indicated that "Fee-free higher education for students is not an affordable or sustainable option for S.A" (WP3, 1997, Section 4.7). The argument back then was that fee-free higher education was only possible with a higher economic growth rate. Because of this reality affected the disparity between the admission of wealthy and poor students, where the wealthy student is mainly white, and the poor student is mainly black. This is another reason why the participation rate of Black students is still below 20%. To get around this dilemma, the WP3 made some important suggestions. For example: "the cost of HE should be shared equitably between public and private beneficiaries" (WP3, 1997, Section 4.7) and "It is important, however, that the direct cost to students should be propionate to their ability to pay" (WP3, 1997, Section 4.8). The *Higher Education Act* ignored these recommendations. Hence, the PSET's attempt in 2013 to rectify some of these issues.

One notices that the discourse in the PSET shifted. For example, the PSET shifted to the "progressive narrowing of the gap between the rich and the poor" and "eradicating the legacy of apartheid" (PSET, 2013, p. viii). It was also framed in line with the *National Development Plan 2030* (NDP) and the *New Growth Path*. Besides the new terminology, epistemologically, the PSET, like the WP3, is a neoliberal document. For example, concepts such as "expansion" and "modern economy" in these documents reproduce the university system as the training ground for people who want to enter the capitalist economy. In her groundbreaking work on the Jewish Holocaust, Hannah Arendt argues that "expansion" informed Cecil John Rhodes' desire to colonise parts of Southern Africa.[18]

In addition, one of the main shortcomings of the PSET is its inability to question the postcolonial and post-apartheid power structure in South Africa. The PSET states that "It is close to twenty years since South Africa discarded the apartheid regime and replaced it with a democratically elected government" (PSET, 2013, p, 4). For me, this points to the heart of the problem. Changing a regime is more than just replacing people and changing Acts. As Spivak (2012) explained, it is the constant chipping away of the edifices and structures that colonialism and apartheid created.

However, the democratically elected government and its plan to transform Higher Education are envisaged from the same discourse that produced colonialism and apartheid. In reality, the democratically elected government struggles to transform the post-apartheid society into an equitable, fair and non-racial society. Apartheid was a project that racially discriminated against non-whites and created an ideal society in which white people were elevated, in every aspect, above all other racial groups in South Africa.

Unfortunately, the WP3 and PSET fell short of their transformation plan, resulting in the university being one of the least transformed institutions in post-apartheid South Africa. For example, the rationale behind creating a Department of Higher Education and Training (which birthed the PSET) was to combine post-school training and education in the Department of Labour and higher education into a single institution. Hence, the "post-school system as conceptualised in [the PSET] consists of all the institutions, public and private,

[18] See Arendt, H. (2007). *The origins of totalitarianism*. Duke University Press.

for which the DHET is responsible" (PSET, 2013, p. 5). The power to develop Higher Education in SA seems to be vested in the DHET. However, it is not the case. Since institutions of Higher Education are autonomous, they can bypass the transformative agenda of the DHET. In addition, the PSET did not recommend any structural changes to the institutional powers of universities. The result was that universities such as UWC could not respond expeditiously to black students' needs, partly leading to the FMF movement.

If one compares the outcomes of 1973 and 2018 at the UWC, I get a sense that history is repeating itself and will repeat itself in the future again. This is because we have not dealt with the frame that was institutionalised in 1960. It is that frame that produces structural violence at UWC.

The Dignity of Black Students

Starvation is a powerful weapon in the hands of the oppressor. Hence, to understand the importance of dignity in a 'postcolonial' society, one must look at the Herero and Nama genocide in German South West Africa. The technology and methodology the German intellectuals developed during the Herero and the Nama genocide were later used by the Nazis in the Jewish Holocaust. One of the most detailed accounts of the Herero and Nama genocide is *The Kaiser's Holocaust,* which reads like Ellie Wiesel's *Night*.[19] If you compare the two accounts, there are striking similarities between the two accounts.

Herero and Nama Genocide

I have seen women and children with my own eyes at Angra Penqueña [Lüderitz], dying of starvation and overwork, nothing but skin and bone, getting flogged every time they fell under their heavy loads. I have seen them picking up bits of bread and refuse food thrown away outside our tents … most of the prisoners, who compose the working gangs at Angra Penqueña, are sent up from Swakopmund (Olusoga and Erichsen, 2010, p. 211 [transport rider]).

Cornell reported that food was so scarce on Shark Island that when rations were distributed, the prisoners 'fought like wild animals and killed each other to secure a share (Olusoga & Erichsen, 2010, p. 215).

---

[19] Ellie Wiesel was in the Nazi death camps, and this is another indication of how the technology and the methodology for the Jewish Holocaust were experimented with and developed during the Herero and Nama genocide in Namibia.

Jewish Holocaust

There followed days and nights of travelling. Occasionally, we would pass through German towns. Usually, very early in the morning. German laborers were going to work. They would stop and look at us without surprise. One day when we had come to a stop, a worker took a piece of bread out of his bag and threw it into a wagon. There was a stampede. Dozens of starving men fought desperately over a few crumbs. The worker watched the spectacle with great interest.

...

In the wagon, where the bread had landed, a battle had ensued. Men were hurling themselves against each other, trampling, tearing at and mauling each other Beasts of prey unleashed, animal hate in their eyes. An extraordinary vitality possessed them, sharpening their teeth and nails. A crowd of workmen and curious passersby had formed all along the train. They had undoubtedly never seen a train with this kind of cargo. Soon, pieces of bread were falling into the wagons from all sides. And the spectators observed these emaciated creatures ready to kill for a crust of bread. (Wiesel, 2013, pp. 100-101).[20]

Starvation, thus, was one of the key "weapons" in the genocides of Namibia and Germany. In Africa, it demonstrated the power the authorities had over the oppressed colonial subject. There was also a pornographic element to the genocide. People did not only throw bread at the "prisoners". They also stood watching them fighting over the crumbs.

As a poor student at UWC, I was faced with starvation, and there were days that I, and many other students at UWC residences, did not have any food to eat. Yet, we survived in our ways. One of the keyways to get food was to attend seminars and events where they provided the attendees with food. Every time at these events, the buffet was stormed by students. Students tried to get as much food as they could onto their plates. Later, when I was appointed as a staff member and coordinated a mentoring programme at UWC, I saw this also happening at mentor training. Mentors would "fight" over "seconds". Many of my fellow staff members could not understand why this happened. However, I could because I was one of those students who pushed and fought my way to "seconds". For me, it raises the question: Does the university system starve black students in an attempt to control their psyche? One thing that has not made sense to me over these years at UWC was that hundreds of thousands of Rand were available for staff functions. Nevertheless, there was

---

[20] Strikingly from Ellie Wiesel's account is the audience formed to consume the violence they created. This is another indication that the audience's subjectivity reproduces the state's violence.

never enough money to subsidize meals on campus. What does that say about the institution? Why are there no dining halls where students can get at least one meal a day for free?

With this in mind, I proposed in 2018 to the Senate that we should use the departmental staff function budgets to subsidize food on campus. Even though the Senate decided to look into my proposal, nothing came of it. Grievance 15 of the FMF Memorandum of Understanding echoes my sentiment: "The wasteful expenditures by senior executive managers, where we have seen hosting of extravagant events while students are literally starving on residences." It is clear students also noticed it and wanted the university to reflect on it. Some units have had attempts over the years to deal with this issue. However, there have recently been attempts at an institutional level to address this issue.

Furthermore, students in the "missing middle" are not recipients of NSFAS, and the allowances of these students are not enough either. I know of these students whose allowances were less than R1,000 a month in 2015. The only option they had was to find a supplementary income. Hence, the Work Study programme at UWC is popular among needy students. Apart from the tuition, books, and food, there are additional costs that one has to consider, like toiletries, medical aid, sanitary pads, and more. Therefore, NSFAS and the monthly allowances of "missing middle" students are insufficient to cover their university expenses.

How do students survive? Some students said that they would rather sleep because it helps them forget and suppress hunger. They also reported that they lack energy and cannot go to class. Most of these students do not raise the issue of hunger because poverty and hunger left students with many deep scars and a sense of powerlessness. The only strand of dignity left is not to say anything and make a plan; sometimes, making a plan involves prostitution.[21] Universities have a moral obligation to protect students' dignity because humiliation was one of the key "weapons" of colonialism and apartheid. Colonialism and colonisation intended a complete psychological annihilation of the oppressed. Therefore, university staff must ask themselves whether they are unintentionally feeding off the stories that poor students are telling them and whether they are reproducing the perverted system of colonialism. I will return to this argument later in this chapter.

Let me turn to a larger epistemological issue that is related to starvation. During the FMF campaign at UWC, on one of the walls on campus was written "land ngoku," which means "land now". For me, this is an interesting vantage

---

[21]   I was a student affairs practitioner for nearly a decade, and several students have indicated that they opted for sex work to buy food.

point to look at the root causes of FMF. As mentioned earlier, FMF started at HWUs among black students who could not afford tertiary education at these institutions, and it later spilt over to other institutions across South Africa. So what does "land ngoku" say at a Historical Black University? It points to a systemic issue around decolonisation.

In South Africa, black people were dispossessed of their livestock and lands and systematically impoverished by the colonial and apartheid states. Black students know this. The university, after all, teaches them this. They know the disparity between black and white land ownership results from colonialism and apartheid. They are aware that they are poor as a result of this. They also know that during the negotiations, the African National Congress (ANC) and other liberation parties failed to return the land to the oppressed (Alexander, 2004; Dlamini, 2015). Instead, a settlement was reached between the negotiating parties. It was first captured in the *Interim Consitution of 1993* and later in Section 25 of the *South African Constitution of 1996*. Section 25 states that no one may be deprived of private property and that any land expropriation needs compensation.

For Fanon, decolonisation was about land. "For a colonized people the most essential value, because the most concrete, is first and foremost the land: the land which will bring them bread and, above all, dignity" (Fanon, 2001, p. 34). Human dignity is closely linked to the object of land. Without this particular object, humans cannot be human. Humans would have no place to stay or be unable to produce anything to eat. The enslaved person and the colonised did not have the right to this object since the oppressor knew it was this object that would set the colonised free. As we saw, they were forced into "Hottentot" reserves and "Bantustans", where they could be controlled and could not escape. They had to be trapped because their labour was too important for the survival of white supremacy.

Thus, one must never forget that colonialism was about land. Even the Germans had to admit during the Nama, Herero, and San genocide that the genocide was about dispossessing the Khoekhoe, San, and Herero of their lands (Olusoga & Erichsen, 2010). If colonisation was about land, then decolonisation must be about the land. Thus, it is crucial to understand that although certain institutions have made concrete efforts to decolonise the curriculum, a larger systemic issue also needs attention. Moreover, as Gerwel warned in 1987, the university cannot sit on the sideline regarding this issue.

Decolonising the University

This brings me to the decolonisation debate. The current efforts in South African universities to "decolonise the university" is not a new phenomenon on the African continent. Mkandawire (1995, p. 75) argues, "Since independence there have been at least three generations of indigenous researchers." [22] The first generation was the scholars who had trained abroad in mostly American universities. This happened directly after independence. The aim was "to provide the first set of indigenous scholars in the 'indigenisation' of African universities" (Mkandawire, 1995, p. 75). Indigenisation here can also be read as "Africanisation". The first generation returned and laid the foundations of what is considered to be the postcolonial "African university". This generation also supported "the state's 'developmentalist' ideology and some even rationalised the authoritarian cast with which the 'developmentalist' ideology was to be moulded by pointing to supposedly universal exigencies of development" (Mkandawire, 1995, p. 76). This generation also had their articles accepted in major journals and books published by international publishers. This generation also established the Council for the Development of Social Science Research in Africa (CODESRIA).

The second generation was also trained abroad but mainly after completing their "undergraduate studies at their national universities" (Mkandawire, 1995, p. 76). However, this generation did not necessarily return to the postcolonial African university for several reasons. Firstly, "the indigenisation programmes had been virtually completed" (Mkandawire, 1995, p. 77). This meant this generation could not find employment in the university. Secondly, from the mid-1970s to the 1990s, "academia and the state were virtually at each other's throats" (Mkandawire, 1995, p. 77). This was because academia had become critical of the state, and many scholars had to leave the continent for their safety.

The third generation was produced in Africa, both undergraduate and postgraduate. According to Mkandawire (1995, p. 79), the third generation qualified under challenging circumstances. The third generation was also the so-called "born free" generation since they were born after independence and reached adulthood in "independent Africa". This generation lacked "international exposure, having not acquired a sure footing in the international research world and are much less 'marketable' internationally than their predecessors" (Mkandawire, 1995, p. 79). However, the third generation

---

[22] By indigenous, Mkandawire refers to scholars of African descent born on the African continent. Mkandawire, in this article, does not join the indigeneity-autochthony debate that Mamdani engages in *When Victims Become Killers*.

addressed the postcolonial "African university" challenge. This generation did not and could not leave the continent like the first and second generations. According to Mkandawire (1995, p. 80), through public action (strikes and demonstrations), this generation returned the university to the national agenda and demanded better working conditions, libraries, and teaching load. In addition, the third generation initiated "an autonomous discourse and reflection on Africa" (Mkandawire, 1995, p. 81). This period produced some of the most prolific African scholars.

When Mkandawire wrote this article, it was a year after South Africa's first democratic elections. There was optimism regarding the fall of settler colonialism in Africa and yet pessimism because of the Rwandan genocide. This led to introspection regarding the efforts that were made since independence. For example, in 1996, Mamdani's groundbreaking book *Citizen and Subject* was published. The book moved away from the developmentalist perspective of decolonisation that marked an earlier period. Instead, Mamdani, in *Citizen and Subject,* showed the importance of revisiting the history of colonialism and highlighted that politicisation of "ethnic" identities during colonialism and the failure to depoliticise these identities led to the Rwandan genocide.

It is here that I enter the debate. First, applying a Foucauldian and Butlerian reading of power, leads one to the discursive production of the postcolonial subject. This discursive production occurs in an epistemology that maintains Africa's colonial power relation. Mkandawire, in his 1995 text, shows the global power structure of knowledge production. For example, to get published in established and accredited journals in the Global North is to write into particular discourses. Writing outside and challenging these discourses meant the rejection of one's paper.

Secondly, the Mkandawire text also points to the importance of capital and epistemology. Whoever funds the university controls the university. This raises the question of how independent the university is from the state and capitalism. Considering this, the postcolonial subject comes into existence in this global and dominant epistemology, which explains its desire for "development" and "modernity". Modernity is a result of the developmentalist discourse in postcolonial Africa, and the developmentalist discourse is a reincarnation of Africa's "civilisation" colonial discourse. Mamdani (2019, p. 17) argues that the African university started as a colonial project. At the heart of its desire was to conquer society, and it operationalised the colonial "civilising mission". In Chapters 2 and 3 of this book, I showed how they would participate in producing knowledge that rendered indigenous groups in South Africa as "backward" and "savage". The Khoekhoe and San are still trapped in the "hunter-gatherer" and "pastoralist" frames. Earlier in this Chapter, I also discussed how the Afrikaner intellectuals conceptualised apartheid in the university and how that was used to restructure South Africa. According to Mamdani (2019, p. 17), "Its ambition was to create universal scholars, men and women who stood for excellence, regardless of context, who would serve as the vanguard of the 'civilising mission' without reservation of remorse." The University of the Western Cape was created as a "Coloured" university to realise this ambition. Since the Khoekhoe and San were bureaucratically erased, the UWC aimed to bring forth the excellent middle-class "Coloured" subject. Jansen argues that "knowledge is never neutral ... [and] draws its authority from power" (2019, p. 2). If this is the case, the university, the primary site of knowledge production, is not neutral. The university can no longer sit on the sidelines. They have a moral obligation to attain the ideals of a post-apartheid South Africa.

Thus, decolonisation raises the question: Can "Africans" be agents of their destinies to reconstitute "African" subjectivities on their own historical and cultural terms? For me, central to answering this question rests on the implosion of the past, present, and future. In *I Am Not Your Negro*, Raoul Peck uses the archive to conflate the past and the present into one. *I Am Not Your Negro* is a documentary film that focuses on the unpublished manuscript of James Baldwin titled *Remember This House*. The manuscript is about the death of his friends Malcolm X, Martin Luther King and Medgar Evers. Using what I believe to be a Fanonian framework, Baldwin argues that the "White people did not act, for the way they act because they are white; but for some other reason" (Baldwin, 2017).[23] Since Baldwin says this early in the film, Peck takes us on a journey as to why Baldwin would argue this.

Baldwin uses the American history of colonialism, conquest, and cinema to explain his conclusion. According to Baldwin:

> Heroes, as far as I could see, were white, and not merely because of the movies, but because of those land of in which I lived, of which movies was simply a reflection ... These images are designed not to trouble but to reassure. They also weaken our ability to deal with the world as it is – ourselves as we are (Baldwin, 2017).

Peck powerfully uses the voice of Samuel L. Jackson and the horse chase scene in the film *Stagecoach* (1939) to make this point, and this effectively questions whether white people were the heroes they portrayed themselves to be in a film such as *Stagecoach* and in a land that is not theirs. This raises the question as to why white people would do this. Baldwin suspected "that all these stories are designed to reassure us that no crime was committed. We made a

---

[23] I believe this is a result of the collective unconscious.

legend of a massacre" (Baldwin, 2017). The massacre Baldwin refers to was the extermination of Native Americans on the American continent by white conquerors. Once again, it raises the civilising mentality of colonialists. These massacres were possible because of their mindset. This mindset dates back to the Valladolid debate of 1550-1551 between Las Casas and Sepulveda over the legality of waging war as a just means to Christianise the Native Americans. The real reason was neglected in the debate. Conquest was about land. Native Americans were exterminated for their lands, and colonialists depicted this as a "civilisation" mission. Hence, white Americans are not the saviours and the heroes they pretend to be on screen. They are the ones everyone is scared of – the real danger. Moreover:

> To watch the TV screen for any length of time is to learn some really frightening things about the American sense of reality. We are coolly trapped in what we would like to be and what we actually are, and we cannot possibly become what we would like to be until we are willing to ask ourselves just why the lives we lead on this continent is mainly too empty, so tame and so ugly (Baldwin, 2017).

This again directs one to the psyche of the oppressed and the oppressor.

Lwazi Lushaba, in a Public Lecture, "Unpacking Decolonised Quality Education: Student Perspective and Institutional Responses" at the University of the Western Cape, argued that there were two types of colonies in Africa: colonies of domination and colonies of settlement.[24] According to Lushaba, colonies of domination attained their independence much earlier than colonies of settlement. In colonies of settlement, colonists exterminated the indigenous population and took over their lands to settle, as in the Americas. In Africa, colonies of the settlement thus required an armed liberation struggle. Hence, the armed liberation struggles in South Africa, Namibia, Rhodesia, and Mozambique.

In contrast, colonies of domination needed a colonial administration and very few white colonial administrators. The intention was to have a few settlers. In *Citizen and Subject*, Mamdani argues that a form of "direct and indirect rule" was used to administer the colonial state in Africa.[25] However, unlike Lushaba, Mamdani argues that "indirect and direct rule" was universally implemented across Africa. For Lushaba, the difference is the settlement of Europeans in some colonies. These white settlers were prepared in Europe to settle in Africa, so they studied Africa and her people. For Lushaba, the work

---

[24] I have to note that Mamdani also made this observation and indicated that colonies of domination were restricted to central Africa, and colonies of settlement were restricted to Southern Africa.

[25] In *Citizen and Subject*, Mamdani draws from Lord Lugard Dual Mandate, a chief colonial administrator in India and later in Nigeria, to explain how this administration worked.

of Lord William Malcolm Hailey was instrumental in preparing the settlement. Lord William Malcolm Hailey's book *An African Survey* laid the foundations for preparatory education for colonial administrators. It also laid the foundations for Anthropology that had to determine the effects of African societies on Europe, how African people resisted and how to respond to resistance. The aim was to respond progressively, and it needed more than just proverbial "the barrel of the gun".

Ben Turok, in his lecture titled: "Deconstructing decolonization: African perspectives, historical insights & lessons for the future" at the University of the Western Cape, indicated that in South Africa, the colonial power was internal and that the legacy of internal colonialism is still strong in "post-apartheid" South Africa. According to Turok, there is still a system that reproduces colonialism and colonisation daily in South Africa. This raises a question about the sites for reproducing colonialism and colonisation. Considering this, one must first investigate internal colonialism and how this reproduction occurs. Here, Lushaba's theory on cognitive domination helps explain "internal colonialism".

I would argue that internal colonialism is a psychic operation kept in place by spatial segregation. It is in this spatial reality that colonial subjectivities are reinforced. According to Fuss (1994, p. 21), "Space operates as one of the chief signifiers of racial difference here: under colonial rule, freedom of movement (physical and social) becomes a white prerogative." The spatial reality of South Africa's segregation past is still in post-apartheid South Africa, which has now become entangled with capitalism. There are spaces of integration, such as shopping malls, schools, and churches, and spaces of no integration.

However, if one looks closely, one notices that public places such as shopping malls are also segregated spaces. In restaurants, the waiters are primarily black, and the people they serve are mostly white. Thus, in shopping malls, capital maintains the racial *status quo* set up during apartheid and colonialism. Neighbourhoods in which white people live have big roads and streets. They have a lot of space. In the neighbourhoods where black people live, the streets are narrow, and they have a lot less living space, which constantly reminds them of "white supremacy" and "black inferiority".[26]

Internal colonisation also results in a segregated psyche. This is also something Kendrick Lamar observed. Peck ends *I Am Not Your Negro* with Lamar's song "Blacker the Berry" from the *To Pimp A Butterfly* album. One of the striking verses on the album is the second verse. Lamar observes the following:

---

[26] Not much has changed since Fanon made this observation in the 1960s.

I mean it's evident I'm irrelevant to society

That's what you're telling me, penitentiary would only hire me

Curse me till I'm dead

Church me with your fake prophesizing that I'mma be another slave in my head

Institutionalize manipulation and lies

Reciprocation of freedom only live in your eyes

You hate me, don't you? (Kendrick Lamar Duckworth, 2015)

I return to institutionalisation. Internal colonialism can, therefore, be seen as institutionalisation. Colonialism and apartheid colonised the psyche of Khoekhoe and San people with the "coloured" identity. An education system was designed first to turn them into "civilised" Hottentots and later into "Coloured" people. Universities like UWC during apartheid fell under the Department of Coloured Affairs (Iaga Ramoupi, 2022, p. 127). The aim was to create the middle-class "Coloured" subject to serve white people's interests. Or, if I may borrow Lamar's explanation, the aim was to turn them into slaves in their heads. And yet many resisted this frame. They refused to be institutionalised. Hence, UWC resisted its "coloured" identity from very early on. However, as FMF indicated, much work still needs to be done. The apartheid institution is not entirely dismantled yet.

Conclusion

The architects of apartheid used state power (with its monopoly over violence) to create laws that institutionalised racism and white privilege in almost every aspect of life for the benefit of white people. Every institution that created identity was racialised with the white supremacy doctrine of "separate but equal". From Frederick Douglass' to Fanon's to Biko's accounts of oppression, I see a dialectical relationship between the black other and the white other. Central to the separate but equal doctrine is white privilege, where white privilege means that white people have to control every aspect of life to maintain the material advantage they received on the back of slavery, colonialism, and apartheid.[27]

---

[27] What became known as South Africa started in 1652. It was birthed in colonial conquest and slavery. Apartheid further developed this notion of South Africa; a state where the indigenous are landless and white people are the landowners; where indigenous work as cheap labour and white people are the employers of that labour. A recommended reading is Morley Nkosi's book, *BLACK WORKERS WHITE SUPERVISORS: The Emergence of the Labor Structure in South Africa.*

In white privilege, the black other is always the infrahuman, and the white other is always the saviour of the black other. The institutionalisation of white privilege created a psychic condition where the white other always felt superior over the black other. The black other is trapped inside the ghetto, institutionalised, believing they are inferior. The black other only exists in relation to whiteness, and this relationship is constantly re-established and reiterated. If the white other failed to do so independently, they could always draw on the institution's powers to re-establish their privileged position. Hence, a white woman can call the police on a black child to reassert her power and sense of superiority. In the process, the black child is introduced and reminded of their people's place in the institution.

Our laws are not predicting the future; but curating the "separate but equal" doctrine and, in this sense, the past. According to Wiener (1988, p. 110), "Whenever such a theoretical agreement fails to exist, we shall have some sort of no-man's land that faces us when we have two currency systems without an accepted basis of exchange" (Wiener, 1988, p. 110). The land question in South Africa is an example of this. Everyone knows that colonialism and the 1913 *Native Land Act* disowned black people of their last remaining lands and designed a system that impoverished black people to such an extent that they had to become the cheap labourers of white people. The negotiated settlement of 1993, and later the 1996 *Constitution*, did not resolve this issue. The *Constitution* states, "No one may be deprived of property except in terms of law of general application, and no law may permit arbitrary deprivation of property" (S 25 [1]) and "property is not limited to land" (S 25[4] [a]). For black people, the historical question is not property but land, the object. Therefore, the *Constitution* collapses the historical question of land into property. This has taken the South African "post-apartheid" society to that "no-man's" land that faces us when we have two currency systems without an accepted basis of exchange." With this, I return to *ENDING AND BEGINNING* and the statue of David Hlongwane. David Hlongwane's statue at UWC perfectly captures institutionalisation in South Africa. It periodically and temporarily takes institutionalised subjects out of their trance. However, that fleeting moment of awareness is too short to altering the collective institutionalised unconsciousness of the majority. Thus, we continue living in an institutionalised South Africa, waiting for the post-apartheid.

6

I am an African

The future of a new and more inclusive South Africa kicked off with *The Convention for a Democratic South Africa* (CODESA) negotiations in 1991. It was clear early on that the Khoekhoe and San were excluded from the negotiations (Verbuyst, 2022). The CODESA I and II and the subsequent *Multi-Party Negotiation Process* (MPNP) negotiations focus on creating a post-apartheid democracy based on non-racialism. However, there was the ethnic representation of the other indigenous groups in South Africa. To put this representation in context, one must briefly discuss the "Bantustan" or "Homeland" system during apartheid South Africa.

Apartheid created several homelands for indigenous groups, and this was an attempt to drive apartheid's "separate development" ideology home. The *Bantu Authorities Act of 1951* laid the foundations that institutionalised ten different "Homelands" or "Bantustans" for Black people in South Africa. On the other hand, the *Promotion of Bantu Self-Government Act of 1959,* gave these "Homelands" pseudo-independence. These Acts aimed to strip Black people in South Africa of their inherent and natural South African citizenship and force onto them a "homeland" citizenship. It was to make them foreigners in South Africa. As we saw in Chapter 3, this was a page from the playbook of British colonialism.

Furthermore, the *Bantu Authorities Act* resembles the *Hottentot Proclamation of 1809.* The *Hottentot Proclamation* established "Hottentot reverses." As I mentioned earlier in this book, this *Proclamation* established a pass system for the Khoekhoe people in South Africa. In 1909, the *Mission Stations and Communal Reserves Act* was enacted to better manage and control certain

Mission stations and communal reserves. This act came about after a Parliamentary Select Committee in 1896 was established to consider the future of the Namaqualand Mission Reserves (Sharp, 1984, p. 6). Later, this act was renamed the *Coloured Persons Communal Reserves Act of 1961*. As I showed earlier, the Griqua states, in particular, laid the foundations for the "Bantustans" that came into existence during apartheid. The apartheid combined the pass laws for slaves and Khoekhoe and San with the practice of pseudo-independence of the Griqua state.

Moreover, as indicated earlier in this book, these Acts erased the "Hottentot" (Khoekhoe) and "Bushman" (San) and replaced them with "Coloured". There-fore, unlike Black people in South Africa, "Coloured" people of Khoekhoe and San ancestry were bureaucratically erased, and so was their ethnicity. In the apartheid administration, the Khoekhoe and San did not exist as a political entity; in the same manner, other ethnicities, such as the Xhosa, Tswana, Zulu, and Sotho, existed. The Khoekhoe and San did not have Traditional Authorities in the same manner as under the *Bantu Authorities Act*. Hence, they did not have the same level of representation during the negotiations.

Moreover, the "Bantustans" were rejected from very early on. One of the key objectors was Steve Biko. According to Biko (2017, p. 95), "At this stage of our history, we cannot have our struggle being tribalised through the creation of Zulu, Xhosa and Tswana politicians by the system." Biko recognised the politics of ethnicity and spoke out against it very early. He urged Black people to "constantly pressurise the Bantustan leaders to pull out of the political cul-de-sac that has been created for us by the system" (Biko, 2017, p. 95). Hence, Biko's alternative was a politics of black consciousness – a politics that countered the fragmentation of Black people along ethnic lines. Biko saw the possibility for the Black majority to take control of the state if they let go of their ethnic and racial differences. For him, it was only under a united front that they could defeat the apartheid regime. It eventually happened, but that ideal cost him his life. However, the ethnic identities that were enforced and maintained by the "Bantustans" remained.

In addition, leading up to the negotiations, ethnicity was weaponised. At the time, there were real concerns about an ethnic war in South Africa. Thus, rightfully so, to prevent a full-scale ethnic war, the focus for a post-apartheid South Africa needed to be non-racialism. However, since the ANC needed the support of "Bantustan" leaders, they had to accommodate traditional leaders. Therefore, the ANC's notion of non-racialism is inclusive of ethnic authorities in the post-apartheid government. Hence, the negotiations ensured the continuous benefit of Traditional Authorities in post-apartheid South Africa. The 1993 Interim Constitution, which laid the foundation for the 1994 elections, made provisions for traditional leaders and authorities in South Africa. However, nowhere was provision made for the Khoekhoe and San to form part of the traditional leaders and authorities. Thus, from the start of post-apartheid South Africa, the post-apartheid reality of the Khoekhoe and San was pretty much the same as it was under apartheid and colonialism.

Furthermore, in his "I am an African" speech, Thabo Mbeki recognised the Khoekhoe and San struggle against colonialism. He rightfully points out that this struggle led to genocide.

> I owe my being to the Khoi and the San whose desolate souls haunt the great expanses of the beautiful Cape – they who fell victim to the most merciless genocide our native land has ever seen, they who were the first to lose their lives in the struggle to defend our freedom and independence and they who, as a people, perished in the result.

> Today, as a country, we keep an audible silence about these ancestors of the generations that live, fearful to admit the horror of a former deed, seeking to obliterate from our memories a cruel occurrence which, in its remembering, should teach us not and never to be inhuman again (Mbeki, 08 May 1996).

If one has a closer look at this extract of Mbeki's speech, it is clear that the silence of this genocide was haunting Mbeki. He had to admit that this silence was to erase the cruelty of the genocide from the country's memory. Thus, acting as if the Khoekhoe and the San did not exist was post-apartheid South Africa's attempt to eject the memory of this horrible deed from the collective consciousness.

Ironically, Mbeki's "I am an African" speech was a pivotal moment in the post-apartheid history of South Africa. It was delivered in Parliament when the new *South African Constitution* of 1996 was adopted. The new Constitution ushered in an era of non-racialism and constitutionalism. It was labelled one of the most progressive constitutions the world has ever seen. Nonetheless, the document did not recognise any of the Khoekhoe and San languages as official languages, thus excluding them from the prospect of an all-inclusive post-apartheid South Africa – sending the Khoekhoe and the San back to the fringes of society, as they were under colonialism and apartheid.

In South Africa, the obvious marker of indigeneity is language. Thus, one cannot claim indigeneity if one does not speak an indigenous language in South Africa. Most Khoekhoe and San people in South Africa do not speak Afrikaans by accident. After their lands were taken and many exterminated, they were forced to work on the colonists' farms, where they were forced to speak Dutch. Since the Dutch they spoke were not fluent, it was labelled as "kombuis-Afrikaans" (kitchen-Dutch), which is still widely used in "coloured" communities. "Kitchen-Dutch" was a violent exchange between the colonists and the indentured. As Oom Hans Springbok explained, "Hulle het onse taal uit ons geslaan" (They beaten our language out of us).[1] When the Afrikaners experienced an identity crisis with the arrival of the British settlers, they appropriated "kitchen-Dutch" and developed what we now know as Afrikaans. Whenever they spoke their native language, they were subjected to horrendous acts of violence to stop them from speaking their language. These frontier farmers also stripped them of their indigenous names. Instead, they were given European names that were easy to pronounce. Names such as Eva (Krotoa), Harry (*Autshumao*), David Hoesar (*Dia!kwain*), Klaas Stoffel (*/A!kunta*), Rachel (*!Kweiten-ta-//ken*), Klein Jantjie (*/Han‡kass'o*), and Ou Jantje Tooren (*//Kabbo*) (Bank, 2006; Schoeman, 2006; Krog, 2004). Forcing the Khoekhoe and San people to speak Dutch and reclassifying them as "Coloured" people stripped them of their indigeneity.

However, the silence did not stop with the *Constitution* and continued with the Truth and Reconciliation Commission (TRC). The scope of the Commission was only limited to apartheid crimes. It did not focus before apartheid. The report explicitly states that the mandated timeframe was 1960 to 1994. In addition, the Commission also believed that this short period represented "the bloodiest in the long and violent history of human rights abuse in this Subcontinent" (Truth and Reconciliation Commission of South Africa report, 1998, p. 25). This belief that 1960-1994 was the bloodiest period in South Africa's history is grossly overstated. The narrow scope of the Commission erased 300 years of oppression in South Africa. The genocide of the Khoekhoe and the San fell outside the scope of the Commission. Hence, they had to continue living with the pain, shame, and memories of their attempted erasure.

However, as they resisted their apartheid erasure, they continued to resist their post-apartheid erasure. Many of the Khoekhoe and San leaders and activists, over a span of 25 years, tirelessly petitioned the South African government to recognise them in the same manner as the state recognises other traditional leaders and ethnicities in South Africa. Their petition finally led to the *Traditional and Khoi-San Leadership Act of 2019*. The Act aims to recognise traditional and 'Khoi-San' communities and establish political structures to recognise

---

[1]   See Mokwena, L. (Producer) & Cloete, J. (Director). (2022). *The Broken String*. [Cape Town TV (Broadcast)]

communities and leaders. Once this process is completed, the Khoekhoe and San will form part of Cooperative Governance & Traditional Affairs in South Africa and have government representation.

In addition, the Department of Cooperative Governance & Traditional Affairs established a Commission on Khoisan Matters in 2021. However, this Commission's scope only focuses on the traditional structures of Khoekhoe and San (Section 57). These traditional structures will translate into political structures and will be incorporated into Cooperative Governance & Traditional Affairs. Even though all of these are positive measures, the danger of the *Traditional and Khoi-San Leadership Act of 2019* is that it will politicise the Khoekhoe and San identities, and that has the possibility of erasing some of them. Since the Khoekhoe and San erasure happened on such a large scale, many "Coloured" people of Khoekhoe and San descent do not know of their ancestry. This was because it was hidden from them by their grandparents and great-grandparents. Therefore, the *Traditional and Khoi-San Leadership Act of 2019* could exclude many Khoekhoe and San people from gaining recognition and regaining their identities.

Moreover, the problem in South Africa is that the Khoekhoe and San identities are considered racial. They are ethnic identities like Xhosa, Zulu, and Tswana are ethnic and not racial. The racial argument was made by Leonhard Schultze, and apartheid contributed by removing the remaining Khoekhoe and San ethnicities from the Population Registration Act of 1950. It was here where the Khoekhoe and San identities became "extinct" and vanished from the public domain. The ethnic identity is in the domain of the ethnic. Meaning one can marry into an ethnic identity or be initiated into an ethnic identity. This practice was the norm in pre-colonial Khoekhoe and San societies. Hence, enslaved people, white people, San, Xhosa and Tswana were all accepted into the Khoekhoe and San identities. It was also the other way around. The Khoekhoe and San were incorporated into all other indigenous groups in South Africa. Hence, the wide range of Khoekhoe and San DNA.

These practices stopped when pseudoscience regarded them as a "yellow race" with distinct racial features that differed from the other indigenous groups. The Khoekhoe and San people are the only ones in South Africa who have to prove they are genetically connected to the Khoekhoe and San. It would be a ridiculous assertion to ask a Tswana or Zulu person in South Africa to prove that they are Tswana or Zulu genetically. However, asking people of Khoekhoe and San origin to prove they are genetically Khoekhoe or San is not considered to be ridiculous. The genetic test confirms the image universities and museums created of the Khoekhoe and San. Thus, the Khoekhoe and San identities have not been dislodged from their racialised categorisation. This image reinforces the racial stereotypes of Khoekhoe and San people in South Africa.

Being regarded as the "bastards" of white people is tied into a racial argument that erasures the Khoekhoe and San and their ethnic identity. This is what the *Khoisan Traditional Leaders Act* is trying to achieve. They want to move the "Khoisan" identity from the racial domain to the customary domain. Even though this is a brilliant initiative and the most appropriate response, we will still go a long way before we have changed most South Africans' perceptions about the Khoekhoe and San identities. Many believe they are extinct, and they do not exist anymore. The only ones whose "Khoisanness" are not disputed are those who speak a native language and who look and dress the part. The rest who were forcefully included into the "coloured" identity "Khoisanness" are rejected because they do not act and conform to the racist and stereotypical notion of being Khoisan.

Furthermore, what does decolonising the university have to do with the Khoekhoe, San and "Coloured" people? Some students during #FMF have pointed out that the South African higher education system needs to be Africanised. Where does this leave the Khoekhoe, San and their descendants that were classified "Coloured"? In addition, what would happen to the knowledge of the Khoekhoe and San that is presented in the university as "indigenous knowledge". The university system in South Africa did not become the custodians of this knowledge ethically.

Moreover, what would happen to the Khoekhoe artefacts that are locked in university archives? The university also did not become these artefacts ethically. It contains the spirit of a people and needs to be set free. Needless to say, the relationship between the Khoekhoe, San, and the university is not great. For example, many Khoekhoe and San communities do not trust researchers or universities after the Hoodia debacle. A debacle that caused Oom Dawid Kruiper much pain in his community.

Furthermore, Mamdani (2019) suggests that the decolonisation efforts must focus on African languages. Of all the African languages in South Africa, Khoekhoe and San are the most marginalised. The Constitution does not even recognise them as official languages.

Therefore, decolonisation has everything to do with the Khoekhoe, San, and "Coloured" identities. One identity that needs urgent decolonisation is the "coloured" identity. However, at UWC, little attention has been given to the Khoekhoe and San. The last genuine effort to establish a Centre dedicated to the Khoekhoe and San was when Bredenkamp was still at UWC. When he left, so did the Khoekhoe and San agenda. In addition, Khoekhoe and San languages are not part of UWC's focus. UWC's efforts are in stark contrast to the efforts that are taking place at UCT. UCT has a dedicated centre that focuses on the Khoekhoe and San issues and is spending a lot of resources on developing the Khoekhoe and San languages. I am a beneficiary of UCT's efforts. In 2020, I was able to complete a Foundational Course in Khoekhoegowab. That course helped me significantly in writing this book. It allowed me to read and write the language that was beaten out of my ancestors.

In conclusion, is there a future beyond the "coloured" identity? I think so. During my 2018 presentation at Wits University, I played a clip of one of the ǀkhâba ra instructors teaching kids in Bitterfontein the dance. After my presentation, someone told me she had learned a similar dance in the Xhosa community where she grew up. She explained that the dance was still practised in parts of the Eastern Cape. The dance she was referring to is the umxhentso. I also later found out that there are two dances with a similar "voetwerk" in the Tswana culture. They are the phatisi and setapa. In addition, the San has a similar dance: the n/um tchai. For me, this indicates a fluid and integrated pre-colonial society. In this society, different ethnic groups lived next to and with each other.

I, therefore, believe the problem with identity in postcolonial and post-apartheid South Africa is philosophical. Before colonialism, identity and belonging were fluid. The becoming process was different and was not marked by the capitalist (liberal and neoliberal formations of identity and belonging). In an attempt to get past politicised identities, we have to revisit Hobbes, Locke, Rosseau, Hegel, et al. with postcolonial and decolonial thinkers. This is an attempt to arrive at a new concept of the human in South Africa. In South Africa, the human is still racialised in Hegel's master-slave dialectic. In this dialectic, the civilising figure is always regarded as the complete human. The indigene is always viewed as the "savage" that needs civilisation.

This leads me to the question: would Biko's notion of black consciousness have taken us past the master-slave dialect? Would it take us to a new version of the human not related to whiteness? I argue that it would not. In the previous chapter, I explained that white people in the American South wanted to maintain the *status quo* between master and slave. Hence, they designed the Jim Crow system that ensured this relationship. This system and the experience of racism in the American South were combined with the racist system already in place in South Africa to produce apartheid. Apartheid means a permanent separation between races. Therefore, after slavery, the master-slave dialectic evolved into a master (white)- slave (black) dialectic in South Africa. However, unlike the master-slave dialectic, where the slave can become the master, in the white-black dialectic, white can never be black and black can never be white. They will always be separated by race. Race thus fossilised the master-slave dialectic.

The human, in its liberal and neoliberal formations, is rendering everyone else as "excess bodies." White men and women retain their humanness through capital, status, and race. Other groups of people can attain capital and status, but they will never attain complete humanness because they are not white. Thus, black people will never fully attain complete humanness in the current neoliberal formation. Finally, will the Khoekhoe and San identities or any other ethnic identity liberate black South Africans from the master-slave dialectic? I believe the possibility for such a liberation exist, because these identities never originated in Western thought.

Appendix 1

UWC Fees Will Fall Memorandum of Understanding

Memorandum of Understanding

We the students of the University of the Western Cape are part of the National Campaign under the banner of Fees Must Fall. We believe that the right to education as enshrined within the Constitution of the Republic of South Africa should not come at the expense of the poor through Institutional Autonomy. We furthermore believe that the same notion of Institutional Autonomy limits the very same rights to access to education by the poor and working class students.

While we are constantly reminded of the glaring inequalities within our communities and the role of Universities in alleviating our people from poverty, we can only question the hypocrisy of our University Management and the Government. If we are to lead our country to greener pastures with the doors of learning being inaccessible due to exorbitant fees, what leaves the students of 2015 and beyond to do? It leaves us with little choice but to engage in a manner which is known to us and that is characterised by our recent history, the class of 1976.

Therefore, as the students of the University of the Western Cape under the banner of UWC Fees WILL Fall movement, we feel strongly aggrieved by the following:

1) Free Education – Central Thesis
2) The upfront payments of 30% of outstanding debt plus full registration fees upon registration, this in itself seek to exclude students from middle income families that do not have bursaries nor do they qualify for government bursaries.

3) The fact that students based on outstanding debt, can only register for 1st semester modules and have to endure the same trauma of Student Credit Management ques to get financial clearance for 2nd semester.

4) The exorbitant fees of KOVACS Residence and the ridiculous fines that students need to pay, once a rule has been contravened and having to pay for all additional services such as the laundry facility.

5) The fact that at UWC we have a physical division between the "Rich and the Poor" in the form of the fence that divides KOVACS Residence from the rest of the UWC community, which has created great animosity amongst UWC students.

6) The racial academic profiling that happens when our assessments are being marked where it evident that those who have African surnames get lower marks than other students yet their content is the same.

7) The fact that some faculties expect students to write more than three tests of the same year level in the space of a week.

8) The writing of tests after five pm when the majority of our students rely on public transport to travel to and from school.

9) The University is not a differently abled friendly environment and has ignored the many cries made by the Differently Abled Students Association (DASA) for many years.

10) International students are subjected to paying exorbitant amounts at the beginning of the year.

11) The high fees paid by the University through NSFAS and Bursaries to Private Accommodation Landlords that provides substandard accommodation to our students and the University have no policy that regulates Private Accommodation.

12) The increments of our University's Executive Management salaries each year that are paid by student fees but yet students don't have the financial means to take care of themselves.

13) The Rector and the Deputies earn in total a sum of approximately 12 million per annum, whilst students are struggling to register and sustain themselves on campus.

14) The outsourcing of essential services such as transport, catering, cleaning and security services.

15) The wasteful expenditures by senior executive managers, where we have seen hosting of extravagant events while students are literally starving on residences.

16) Application fees that seek to exclude learners from learners wishing to enter our Institution.

17) Unsafe route between the university and Belhar where a large number of student live and they are exposed to robbery on a daily basis.

18) There is no platform made available by the university to enable students to tap into entrepreneurship.

19) Clinic prices are too expensive and it is difficult to access the clinic due to the fact that bookings have to be made way in advance.

20) Bookshop prices are exorbitant and therefore students don't afford compulsory study

21) Library closes when students still want to study.

22) Students have very limited access to stadium.

23) Nursing students are liable to pay for vacation accommodation while they are completing their academic programme.

We, the students of the University of the Western Cape therefore demand the following:

1. We demand scrapping of all students debts.
2. No student will be prevented for graduating because of outstanding fees.
3. Students should not pay any registration fees.
4. No students will be denied room in res because of outstanding fees.
5. We demand the immediate scrapping of the use of our surnames and names on all University assessment and demand that only student numbers are used.
6. Students must be able to register for the whole year in January.
7. We demand scrapping off of R150 of student card and each student must receive one free student card every year.
8. The price of KOVACS Residence should be reduced and standardized to the prices of our University Residences and things such as laundry facilities should be free.
9. The University must ensure the safety and security of our students that reside in Private Accommodation by ensuring that the University has a Private Accommodation Policy in place that would protect the interest of students
10. The university must start a process of buying houses in the surrounding community and make them UWC communes. This will ensure that more bed spaces are created at a lower cost than building a new residence and the university would be able to provide shuttle services as it does in off campus residence.
11. While we are waiting for institution to buy Kovacs we demand the immediate removal of the fence and gate that separates Kovacs from the rest of UWC community.
12. Shuttle services should be provided for students residing in Belhar private accommodation.
13. The Vice Chancellor and his entire executive should not be getting any further salary increments, it's not justifiable.

14. The University must review the outsourcing of essential services such as cleaning, catering, etc. and employ workers and pay them a decent salary.

15. An investigation must be launched into the wasteful expenditure by University Executives and any person implicated must be investigated and go through the disciplinary processes.

16. Application fees must be scrapped and we demand the immediate return of physical application forms instead of only having online application.

17. We demand immediate renaming of New Life Science building to Steve Biko Life Science Building.

18. We demand the immediate scrapping of the picketing policy as it is an apartheid style policy that seeks to suppress the voice of students and can never be acceptable in this current democratic dispensation.

19. We demand immediate halting of the Institutional Operating Plan (IOP) process until students are given an opportunity to extensively engage on the IOP.

20. Each faculty must have an academic intervention programme for struggling students before it is allowed to academically exclude students.

21. UWC must provide space on the campus where students can be allowed to operate their own small businesses.

22. The University must start a programme to create black academics in order to assist to transform the academic staff of UWC so that it reflects South African demographics.

23. We demand immediate scrapping off of expensive clinic prices and students must have efficient access to the clinic at all relevant circumstances.

24. We demand immediate scrapping off of expensive bookshop and students must be charged lowest reasonable amount for study material.

25. We demand that the library operate 24/7.

26. We demand that students have access to use gym facilities in stadium.

27. We demand scrapping off of vacation accommodation fee to nursing students.

28. We demand immediate dissolution of the SRC as the no longer represent students views of students.

29. Any student that is participating in the movement must be immune from prosecution by the office of the proctor based on acts committed during this period.

We call upon the University Executive to respond to our Memorandum of Understandings by no later than the **30-10-2015 (Friday) at 13h00 at the Student Centre.** Failure on the side of the University to respond, we will continue protesting until our grievances have been given attention.

Revolutionary Regards

UWC Fees Must Fall Student Movement

Appendix 2

UWC Staff Racial Profile

This information was obtained from Five Year Employment Equity Plan. 1 October 2020 to 30 September 2025. Please see page 27. I had to re-enter the information on page 27 into MS Excel. From this, I was able to re-analyse the data that is presented here below. Please note the report made several calculation mistakes. I have rectified these mistakes with my calculations.

⁂ A – African

⁂ C – Coloured

⁂ I – Indian

⁂ W – White

⁂ FN – Foreign National

Table 1   Original Table in the report on page 27

	A	C	I	W	FN	Total
Top and Senior Management	10	42	17	35	31	135
	7%	31%	13%	26%	23%	
Professionally qualified and experienced specialists and mid management	117	393	56	132	127	825
	14%	48%	7%	16%	15%	
Skilled technical and academically qualified workers, junior management, supervisors, foremen, and superintendents	138	508	16	21	7	690
	20%	74%	2%	3%	1%	
Semi-skilled and discretionary decision making	83	174	1	3	5	266
	31,2%	65,4%	0,4%	1,1%	1,9%	

THE ATTEMPTED ERASURE OF THE KHOEKHOE AND SAN

	A	C	I	W	FN	Total
Total Permanent Staff	348	1117	90	191	170	1916
	18%	58%	5%	10%	9%	
Temporary Staff	46	133	18	41	27	265
	17%	50%	7%	15%	10%	

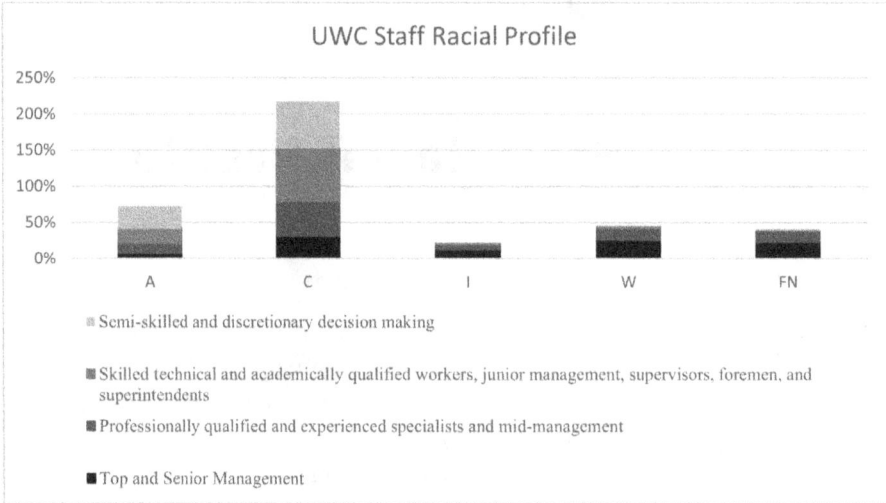

UWC Staff Racial Profile

- Semi-skilled and discretionary decision making
- Skilled technical and academically qualified workers, junior management, supervisors, foremen, and superintendents
- Professionally qualified and experienced specialists and mid-management
- Top and Senior Management

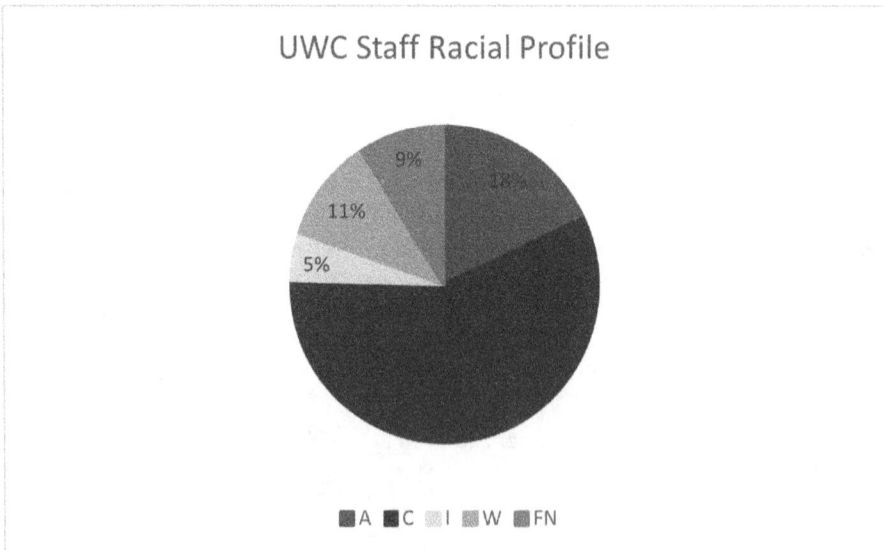

UWC Staff Racial Profile

A C I W FN

References

Secondary Sources

Abrahams, Y. (1994). *Resistance, pacification and consciousness: a discussion of the historiography of Khoisan resistance from 1972 to 1993 and Khoisan resistance from 1652 to 1853.* (Thesis). The University of Cape Town, Faculty of Humanities, Department of Historical Studies.

Abrahams, A. (2000). *Colonialism, dysfunction and dysjuncture: The historiography of Sarah Bartmann.* (PhD Thesis). The University of Cape Town.

Adams, T.E. & Holman Jones, S. (2011). Telling stories: Reflexivity, queer theory, and autoethnography. Cultural Studies? *Critical Methodologies,* 11(2):108-116. https://doi.org/10.1177/1532708611401329

Adams, T.E., Ellis, C. & Jones, S.H. (2015). *Autoethnography. Understanding Qualitative Research.* Oxford.

Adamson, C. (2000). Defensive localism in white and black: A comparative history of European-American and African-American youth gangs. *Ethnic and Racial Studies,* 23(2):272-298. https://doi.org/10.1080/014198700329051

Adhikari, M. (2002). *Hope, fear, shame, frustration: continuity and change in the expression of coloured identity in white supremacist South Africa, 1910-1994.* (Thesis). The University of Cape Town, Faculty of Humanities, Department of Historical Studies.

Adhikari, M. (2004). 'Not Black Enough': Changing Expressions of Coloured Identity in Post-Apartheid South Africa. *South African Historical Journal,* 51:1, 167-178. https://doi.org/10.1080/02582470409464835

Adhikari, M. (2014). *The anatomy of a South African Genocide: The extermination of the Cape San People.* UCT Press. https://doi.org/10.58331/UCTPRESS.30

Adorno, T. & Horkheimer, M. (1993). *The Culture Industry: Enlightenment as Mass Deception.* Continuum.

Aizenman, N. & Gharib, M. (2019). American With No Medical Training Ran Center for Malnourished Ugandan Kids. 105 Died. *NPR.* https://bit.ly/3ZEbTiB

Alexander, N. (2004). The Politics of language planning in post-apartheid South Africa. *Language Problems & Language Planning*, 28(2):113-130. https://doi.org/10.1075/lplp.28.2.02ale

Allen, R.J. (2013). Beginning, Middle, End of an Era: Has Technology Trumped Aristotle? *Journal of Film and Video*, 65(1-2):9-22. https://doi.org/10.5406/jfilmvideo.65.1-2.0009

Arendt, H. (2007). *The origins of totalitarianism*. Duke University Press. https://doi.org/10.1215/9780822390169-017

Arnolds, H. & De Jager, A. (2013). Lifeworld of The Karoo People Expressed in the Riel Dance – A Geographical Perspective. *Confluences 7: Dance, Religion and Spirituality*. UCT School of Dance Woolsack Drive. https://bit.ly/3PzHlK4

Arribas-Ayllon, M. & Walkerdine, V. (2008). Foucauldian Discourse Analysis. C. Willig and W. Stainton-Rogers (Eds.), *The SAGE Handbook of Qualitative Research in Psychology*. SAGE Publications Ltd. https://doi.org/10.4135/9781848607927.n6

Autesserre, S. (2009). Hobbes and the Congo: Frames, Local Violence, and International Intervention. *International Organization*, 63:249-280. https://doi.org/10.1017/S0020818309090080

Bam, J. (2021). *Ausi Told Me: Why Cape Herstoriographies Matter*. Fanele.

Balie, I.H.T. (1988). *Die geskiedenis van Genadendal: 1738-1988*. Perskor.

Ballantyne, T. & Burton, A. (2005). *Bodies in Contact: Rethinking Colonial Encounters in World History*. Duke University Press. https://doi.org/10.1215/9780822386452

Bank, A. (2006). *Bushmen in a Victorian World. The remarkable story of the Bleek-Lloyd Collection of Bushman folklore*. Double Storey Books.

Barnabas, S. & Miya, S. (2019). KhoeSan Identity and Language in South Africa: Articulations of Reclamation, *Critical Arts*, 33:4-5, 89-103. https://doi.org/10.1080/02560046.2019.1702071

Barratt, D., Rédei, A.C., Innes-Ker, Å. & Van de Weijer, J. (2016). Does the Kuleshov effect really exist? Revisiting a classic film experiment on facial expressions and emotional contexts. *Perception*, 45(8):847-874. https://doi.org/10.1177/0301006616638595

Benjamin, W. (1996). Critique of Violence. In: M. Bullock & M.W. Jennings (Eds.), *Walter Benjamin Selected Writings Volume 1: 1913-1926*. Harvard University Press.

Bentley, B. (2017). I Am A White Woman And I Must Confront My Racism. *HuffPost*. Retrieved 18 June 2018 from https://bit.ly/3ZJYAxi

Bergson, H. (2004). *Matter and Memory*. Dover Publications.

Bernal. (1987). *Black Athena: The Afroasiatic roots of classical civilization*. Rutgers University Press.

Bernard, S. (2012). *Documentary storytelling: making stronger and more dramatic nonfiction films*. Routledge. https://doi.org/10.4324/9780080962320

Besten, M.P. (2006). *Transformation and reconstitution of Khoe-San identities: AAS le Fleur I, Griqua identities and post-apartheid Khoe-San revivalism (1894-2004)*. (PhD Thesis). Leiden University.

Biko, S. (2017). *I write what I like: selected writings*. Picador Africa.

Biwa, M. (2006). *'Toa Tama !Khams Ge.'* Remembering the War in Namakhoeland, 1903-1908. (PhD Thesis). The University of Cape Town, Faculty of Humanities, Department of History.

Bock, B. & Javan, M. (2017). Competition keeps traditional riel dancing alive. *Brand South Africa.* Retrieved 19 November 2018 from https://bit.ly/3LOpYnY

Bradbury, J.D. & Guadagno, R.E. (2020). Documentary narrative visualization: Features and modes of documentary film in narrative visualization. *Information Visualization,* 19(4):339-352. https://doi.org/10.1177/1473871620925071

Bredekamp, H.C. (1980). Die Grondtransaksies Van 1672 Tussen Die Hollanders en die Skiereilandse Khoikhoi. *Kronos,* 2(1):1-10.

Bredekamp, H.C. (1981). Die lewe van 'n Khoikhoi-Kaptein Dorhá alias Klaas 1669-1701. *Kronos,* 4.

Bredekamp, H.C. & Pluddemann, H.E.F. (1992). *The Genadendal diaries: Diaries of the Herrnhut missionaries H. Marsveld, D. Schwinn and J.C. Kuhnel; v. 1, 1792-1794.* University of the Western Cape.

Britz, E. (2019). *Songs in the Dust: Riel Music in the Northern and Western Cape Provinces, South Africa.* Master's Dissertation. University of Cape Town.

Buchanan, S. (2015). *Burchell's Travels: The Life, Art and Journeys of William John Burchell 1781-1863.* Penguin Random House.

Bulhan, H.A. (1985). *Frantz Fanon and the Psychology of Oppression.* Springer Science & Business Media. https://doi.org/10.1007/978-1-4899-2269-4

Burchell, W.J. (1822a). *Travels in the interior of Southern Africa* Vol. 1. Hurst, Rees, Orme & Brown. https://doi.org/10.5962/bhl.title.100911

Burchell, W.J. (1822b). *Travels in the interior of Southern Africa* Vol. 2. Hurst, Rees, Orme & Brown. https://doi.org/10.5962/bhl.title.100911

Butler, J. (1997). *The psychic life of power: Theories in subjection.* Stanford University Press. https://doi.org/10.1515/9781503616295

Cambray, J.A. & Stuart, C.T. (1985). Aspects of the biology of a rare redfin minnow, Barbusburchelli (Pisces, Cyprinidae), from South Africa. *South African Journal of Zoology,* 20:3:155-165.

Cape Nature. (2013). What a land owner should know about the indigenous fish of the Cape Floristic Region: Diversity, Threats and Management Interventions. Retrieved on 7 March 2019 from https://bit.ly/3Q5LRBS

Carstens, P.R. (2011). *Port Nolloth: The Making of a South African Seaport.* Xlibris Corporation.

Castro-Klaren, S. (Ed.). (2008). Writing the Andes. *A companion to Latin American literature and culture.* Blackwell Publishing Ltd. https://doi.org/10.1002/9780470696446.ch6

Cloete, J. (2019). *The Politics of Belonging and/or a Contest for Survival: Rethinking the Conflict in North and South Kivu in the Democratic Republic of Congo.* (PhD Thesis). The University of the Western Cape.

Coetzee, A. (2000). *'n Hele os vir 'n ou broodmes: Grond en die plaasnarratief sedert 1595.* Van Schaik.

Cowden, J. (2020). New Colonialists of Africa? -Tackling the White Saviour Complex in Contemporary Voluntourism. *Critical Reflections: A Student Journal on Contemporary Sociological Issues.*

Daily Dispatch. (1999). Jakes Gerwel and a Home for the Left. In: C. Thomas. (Ed.), *Finding freedom in the bush of books: The UWC experience and spirit.* Wendy's Book Lounge.

Damas, D. (2010). The Power of Dignified Protest. In: C. Thomas. (Ed.), *Finding freedom in the bush of books: The UWC experience and spirit.* Wendy's Book Lounge.

Dapper, O. (2011). Kaffraria Or the Land of the Kafirs, Also Named Hottentots. In: I. Schapera & B. Farrington, *The early Cape hottentots, described in the writings of Olfert Dapper (1668), Willem ten Rhyne (1686) and Johannes Gulielmus de Grevenbroek (1695).* Van Riebeeck Society.

De Beer, C.H. (2002). The Stratigraphy, Lithology and Structure of the Table Mountain Group. In: K. Pietersen & R. Parsons (Eds.), *A synthesis of the hydrogeology of the Table Mountain Group-formation of a research strategy.* Water Research Commission. WRC Report No TT 158/0. Retrieved 19 March 2019 from https://bit.ly/3tjciuO

Deleuze, G. (1986). *Cinema 1: The Movement-Image.* University of Minnesota Press. https://doi.org/10.5040/9781350251977

Depelchin, J. (2005). *Silences in African History: Between the Syndromes of Discovery and Abolition.* Mkuki Na Nyota Publishers.

Derrida, J. (1998). *Archive fever: A Freudian impression* (Pbk. ed.). University of Chicago Press.

Derrida, J. & Prenowitz, E. (2013). "Archive Fever: A Freudian Impression." *Diacritics,* 25(2):9-63. http://artsites.ucsc.edu/sdaniel/230/derrida_archivefever.pdf [https://doi.org/10.2307/465144]

Diop, C.A. & Cook, M. (2012). *The African origin of civilization: Myth or reality.* Chicago Review Press.

Dlamini, S.N. (2015). *The Theory and Application of Consociational Democracy in South Africa: A Case Study of Kwazulu-Natal.* PhD Dissertation. The University of Kwazulu-Natal.

Dooling, W. (2005). The origins and aftermath of the Cape Colony's 'Hottentot Code' of 1809. *Kronos: Journal of Cape History,* 31(1):50-61.

Dunseith, M.H. (2017). *Manifestations of 'Langarm': From Colonial Roots to Contemporary Practices. Masters In Musicology.* Stellenbosch University.

Du Bois, W.E.B. (2007). The World and Africa: An Inquiry Into the Part Which Africa Has Played in World History and Color. *The Oxford WEB Du Bois (Vol. 9).* Oxford University Press on Demand.

Du Preez, M. (2014). Honour Khoisan by learning about them. *Cape Time.* Retrieved 8 April 2020 from https://bit.ly/3FmAI9D

Ellis, W. (2015). Ons is Boesmans: Commentary on the naming of Bushmen in the southern Kalahari. *Anthropology Southern Africa,* 38(1-2):120-133. https://doi.org/10.1080/23323256.2015.1056314

Ellis, W. (2018). Vetkat's Cinematic: Oneironauts of Critique in the Kalahari. In: R. Rinehart, J. Kidd & A.G. Quiroga, *Southern Hemisphere Ethnographies of Space, Place, and Time.* (Eds.). Peter Lang.

Elkington, R. (2016). Studies in Australasian Cinema Arguing the Archive: Reconceptualising the National Film and Sound Archive in a Time of Austerity. *Studies in Australasian Cinema*, 10(2):264-76. https://doi.org/10.1080/17503175.2016.1198448

Erasmus, Z. (2017). The Gene. *In Race Otherwise: Forging a new humanism for South Africa*. Wits University Press. pp. 105-132. https://doi.org/10.18772/12017090589

Fanon, F. (1963). *The wretched of the earth*. Grove Press.

Fanon, F. (2001). *The Wretched of the Earth*. Penguin. https://doi.org/10.1007/978-1-137-05194-3_4

Fanon, F. (2008). *Black Skin, White Masks*. Pluto Press.

Findlay, D.A. (1977). *The San of the Cape thirstland and L. Anthing's "Special Mission"*. Bachelor's Thesis. University of Cape Town.

Fredericks. (2013). *A study of dialectal and inter-linguistic variations of Khoekhoegowab: towards the determination of the standard orthography*. PhD Thesis. The University of the Western Cape.

Freire-Medeiros. (2009). The favela and its touristic transits. *Geoforum*, 40(4):580-588. https://doi.org/10.1016/j.geoforum.2008.10.007

Foucault, M. (1977). *Language counter-memory practice: selected essays and interviews*. Basil Blackwell.

Fuss, D. (1994). Interior Colonies: Frantz Fanon and the Politics of Identification. *Diacritics*, 24(2/3). https://doi.org/10.2307/465162

Gerwel, J. (5 June 1987). *Inaugural Address*. The University of the Western Cape.

Gewalf, J.B., Spierenburg, M. & Wels, H. (2019). *Nature Conservation in Southern Africa. Morality and Marginality: Towards Sentient Conservation?* Koninklijke Brill. https://doi.org/10.1163/9789004385115

Giliomee. (2003). *The Afrikaners: biography of a people*. Tafelberg.

Gilroy, P. (2014). Lecture I: Suffering and infrahumanity. Lecture II: Humanities and a new humanism. *Tanner Lectures*.

Glenn, I. (1996). The Bushman in Early South African Literature. In: P. Skotnes, *Miscast: Negotiating the presence of the Bushmen*. University of Cape Town Press.

Godsell, G., Chikane, R., Mpofu-Walsh, S., Ntshingila, O., Lepere, R., Mofoko, S., Nase, A., Everatt, D., Hewlett, L., Masuku-Mukadah, N., Zandamela, H.L., Kouakou, K., Gumede, W., Bond, P., Satgar, V., Fitzgerald, P., Seale, O., Pillay, P., Miller, D. & Metz, T. (2018). *Fees Must Fall: Student revolt, decolonisation and governance in South Africa*. Wits University Press.

Gordon, R.J. (2009). Hiding in Full View: The "Forgotten" Bushman Genocides of Namibia. *Genocide Studies and Prevention: An International Journal*, 4(1:4). Available at: https://scholarcommons.usf.edu/gsp/vol4/iss1/4 [https://doi.org/10.3138/gsp.4.1.29]

Grootboom, A. (2010). A Decade and More of Activism at UWC. In: C. Thomas. (Ed.), *Finding freedom in the bush of books: the UWC experience and spirit*. Wendy's Book Lounge.

Guerlac, S. (2006). *Thinking in time: an introduction to Henri Bergson*. Cornell University Press. https://doi.org/10.7591/9781501716980

Gusinde. (1953). Anthropological Investigations of the Bushmen of South Africa. *Anthropological Quarterly*, 26(1):20-28. https://doi.org/10.2307/3317048

Haacke, W.H.G. (1999). *Khoekhoegowab is mainly the language of the Damara, Hai||om and Nama*. Macmillan Education Namibia Publishers.

Hahn, T. (1881). *Tsuni-||goam: The Supreme Being of the Khoi-Khoi*. Trübner & Co.

Hailey, W.M. (1938). *An African survey: a study of problems arising in Africa South of the Sahara*. Oxford University Press.

Heese, H.F. (1994). *Reg en onreg: Kaapse regspraak in die Agtiende Eeu*. Instituut vir Historise Navorsing. Universiteit van Wes-Kaapland.

Hegel, G.W.F (2001). *The Philosophy of History*. Batoche Books.

Hepple, A. (1967). *Verwoerd*. Penguin.

Hernandez, B.L. (2001). *The Las Casas-Sepúlveda Controversy: 1550-1551*. San Francisco: Ex Post Facto.

Huysamen, M., Barnett, J. & Fraser, D.S. (2020). Slums of hope: Sanitising silences within township tour reviews. *Geoforum*, 110:87-96. https://doi.org/10.1016/j.geoforum.2020.01.006

Iaga Ramoupi, N.L. (2022). Racism in Higher Education: Privileges and Exclusions at Universities in South Africa. In: *Paradise Lost*. Brill, pp. 123-145. https://doi.org/10.1163/9789004515949_006

Jansen, J., Mbembe, A., Keet, A., Schmahmann, B., Soudien, C., Galant, J., Auerbach, J., Le Grange, L., Lange, L. & Mamdani, M. (2019). *Decolonisation in Universities: the Politics of Knowledge*. Johannesburg: Witwatersrand University Press. https://doi.org/10.18772/22019083351.5

Jordaan, M., Chakona, A., Swartz, E. & Impson, D. (2016). Pseudo burchelli. Red List of South African Species. *South African Biodiversity Institute*. Retrieved on 17 March 2019 from https://bit.ly/3PGqfdQ

Khalfani, A.K. & Zuberi, T. (2001). Racial classification and the modern census in South Africa, 1911-1996. *Race & Society*, 4(2):161-176. https://doi.org/10.1016/S1090-9524(03)00007-X

Khan, F. (1994). Rewriting South Africa's Conservation History-The Role of the Native Farmers Association. *Journal of Southern African Studies*, 20(4):499-516. www.jstor.org/stable/2636969 [https://doi.org/10.1080/03057079408708417]

Killingray, D. & Roberts, A. (1989). An Outline History of Photography in Africa to ca. 1940. *History in Africa*, 16:197-208. https://doi.org/10.2307/3171784

Koven, S. (2004). *Slumming: Sexual and Social Politics in Victorian London*. Princeton University Press. https://doi.org/10.1515/9781400843589

Krog, A. (2004). *The Stars Say 'Tsau'*. Kwela Books.

Kuper, A. (2007). Isaac Schapera (1905-2003). His life and Times. In: J.L. Comaroff & J. Comaroff, *Picturing a colonial past. The African Photographs of Isaac Schapera*. The University of Chicago Press.

Lalu, P. (2019). What is the university for? *Critical Times*, 2(1):39-58 https://doi.org/10.1215/26410478-7615003

Lalu, P. (2022). *Undoing Apartheid*. John Wiley & Sons.

Lalu, P. & Murry, N. (2012). Campus: A discourse on the grounds of an Apartheid university. In: P. Lalu & N. Murray (Eds.). *Becoming UWC: Reflections, pathways and unmaking apartheid's legacy*. Centre for Humanities Research.

Landman, C. (1996). The religious Krotoa (cl642-1674). *Kronos*, 23(1):2-35.

Leftwich, A. (1976). *Colonialism and the Constitution of Cape Society Under the Dutch East India Company*. PhD Thesis. University of York.

Legassick, M. (2010). *The politics of a South African frontier: the Griqua, the Sotho-Tswana and the missionaries, 1780-1840*. Basler Afrika Bibliographien. https://doi.org/10.2307/j.ctvh9vxvb

Lewis-Williams, J.D. (1990). *Discovering Southern African Rock Art*. David Phillip Publishers.

Lindqvist, S. (1996). *"Exterminate All the Brutes": One Man's Odyssey into the Heart of Darkness and the Origins of European Genocide*. The New Press.

Lugard, L.F.J. (2013). *The dual mandate in British tropical Africa*. Routledge. https://doi.org/10.4324/9780203042205

Malherbe, V.C. (1997). *The Cape Khoisan in the Eastern Districts of the Colony before and after Ordinance 50 of 1828*. PhD Thesis. The University of Cape Town.

Mamdani, M. (1996). *Citizen and Subject: Contemporary Africa and the Legacy of Late Colonialism*. Fountain Publishers.

Mamdani, M. (2001). *When Victims Become Killers: colonialism, nativism, and the genocide in Rwanda*. David Phillip Publishers.

Mamdani, M. (2005). *Good Muslim, Bad Muslim: America, the Cold War, and the Roots of Terror* (Reprint). Harmony. https://doi.org/10.1515/9781400851720

Mamdani, M. (2019). Decolonising Universities. In: J. Jansen (Ed.), *Decolonisation in Universities*. Wits University Press. https://doi.org/10.18772/22019083351.6

Manoff, M. (2004). Theories of the Archive from Across the Disciplines. *Portal: Libraries and the Academy*, 4(1):9-25. https://doi.org/10.1353/pla.2004.0015

Marais, J.S. (1939). *The Cape Coloured people: 1652-1937*. Longmans, Green.

McCurdy, J. (2016). The Privileged Guardian Angel: An Examination of White Saviour Complex in Western Media. *Political Science Undergraduate Review*, 2(1):23-32. https://doi.org/10.29173/psur60

McKinnon, J. (2004). *A tapestry of lives: Cape women of the 17th century*. Kwela.

Mellet, P.T. (2020). *The lie of 1652: A decolonised history of land*. Cape Town: Tafelberg.

Mignolo, W.D. (2008). Preamble: The Historical Foundation of Modernity/Coloniality and the Emergence of Decolonial Thinking. *A Companion to Latin American Literature and Culture (Blackwell Companions to Literature and Culture)* (2nd ed.). Wiley-Blackwell. https://doi.org/10.1002/9780470696446.cha

Mkandawire, T. (1995). Three Generations of African Academics: A Note. *Transformation (Durban, South Africa)*, 28(28):75-83.

Moodie, D. (1838). *The record: or a series of official papers relative to the condition and treatment of the Native tribes of South Africa*. Balkema.

Ndelu, S. (2017). *Liberation is a falsehood: Fallism at the University of Cape Town. Hashtag: An analysis of the# FeesMustFall movement at South African universities*. Centre for the Study of Violence and Reconciliation, 58-82.

Nead, L. (2005). *Seth Koven. Slumming: Sexual and Social Politics in Victorian London*. Princeton University Press, pp. xvii, 399.

Nel, E. & Meyer, N. (2011). Kô laat ons riel. *LitNet*. Retrieved on 3 April 2020 from https://www.litnet.co.za/ko-laat-ons-riel/

Nienaber, G.S. (1989). *Khoekhoense stamname: 'n voorlopige verkenning*. Academica vir Raad vir Geesteswetenkaplike Navorsing.

Nienaber, G.S. & Raper, P.E. (1980). *Topnymica Hottentotica B. A-Z. Naamkundereeks nr. 10*. Raad vir Geesteswetenskaplike Navorsing.

Oakley. (2006). Collective Rural Identity in Steinkopf, A Communal Colored Reserve, c. 1926-1996. *Journal of Southern African Studies*, 32(3):489-503. https://doi.org/10.1080/03057070600829591

Odile, G. (2007). The Cinema, a Place of Tension in Colonial Africa: Film Censorship in French West Africa. *Afrika Zamani*, 15 & 16:27-43.

Olusoga, D. & Erichsen, C. (2010). *The Kaiser's Holocaust: Germany's forgotten genocide and the colonial roots of Nazism*. Faber & Faber.

Parikh, S. (2022). Being excess bodies: Shame in the age of climate coloniality. *Review of the African Political Economy*. Retrieved on 15 August 2022 from https://bit.ly/46iM4Hm

Parkington, J. (2013). *Cederberg Rock Paintings*. Kradadouw Trust.

Patterson, S. (1953). *Colour and culture in South Africa: a study of the status of the Cape Coloured people within the social structure of the Union of South Africa*. Routledge and Paul.

Penrith, M.C. (1972). *A historical and critical account of the teaching of English Language and Literature in English-medium universities in South Africa, with particular reference to the University of Cape Town and the South African College*. Master's Thesis. Cape Town: University of Cape Town.

Reynolds, G. (2015). *Colonial Cinema in Africa. Origins, Images, Audiences*. McFarland & Company, Inc, Publishers.

Robins, E. (1953). *This Man Malan*. Van Haren Publishing.

Salzwedel, I. (2013). *Onvertelde stories van Afrikaans*. LAPA Uitgewers.

Schapera, I. & Farrington, B. (2011). *The early Cape Hottentots, described in the writings of Olfert Dapper (1668), Willem ten Rhyne (1686) and Johannes Gulielmus de Grevenbroek (1695)*. Van Riebeeck Society.

Schoeman, K. (2006). *Kinders van die Kompanjie: Kaapse lewens uit die sewentiende eeu* (1ste uitg.). Protea Boekhuis.

Scott, D. (1999). *Refashioning futures: criticism after postcoloniality*. Princeton University Press. https://doi.org/10.1515/9781400823062

Scully, P. (2005). Malintzin, Pocahontas, and Krotoa: Indigenous Women and Myth Models of the Atlantic World. *Journal of Colonialism and Colonial History*, 6(3). https://doi.org/10.1353/cch.2006.0022

Sharp, J. (1984). *Rural development schemes and the struggle against impoverishment in the Namaqualand reserves*. SALDRU, UCT.

Skotnes, P. (1996). *Miscast: negotiating the presence of the Bushmen*. University of Cape Town Press.

Sloan, P. (2019). *"Darwin: From Origin of Species to Descent of Man", The Stanford Encyclopaedia of Philosophy* (Summer 2019 Edition). In: Edward N. Zalta (Ed.), Retrieved on 8 April 2020 from https://bit.ly/3LJ1GvB

Smith, J.D. (2019). *Black Judas: William Hannibal Thomas and The American Negro*. University of Georgia Press. https://doi.org/10.2307/j.ctvfxv9g3

Spivak, G.C. (2012). *An Aesthetic Education in the Era of Globalisation.* Harvard University Press.

South African Biodiversity Institute (SABI). (n.d). *Water Use and Water Transfers.* Part 1. Retrieved on 20 May 2019 from https://bit.ly/3LNK2XH

Stiegler, B. (2011). *Technics and Time 3.* Stanford University Press.

Straubhaar, R. (2015). The stark reality of the 'White Saviour'complex and the need for critical consciousness: A document analysis of the early journals of a Freirean educator. *Compare: A Journal of Comparative and International Education,* 45(3):381-400. https://doi.org/10.1080/03057925.2013.876306

Swartz, E.R. (2005). *Phylogeography, phylogenetics and evolution of the redfins (Teleostei, Cyprinidae, Pseudobarbus) in southern Africa.* Dissertation. The University of Cape Town.

Tachard, G. (1688). *A Relation of The Voyage To Siam. Performed by six Jesuits, sent by the French King, to the Indies and China, in the year, 1685: With their Astrological Observations, and their Remarks of Natural Philosophy, Geography, Hydrography, and History.* J. Robinson.

Ten Thyne, W. (2011). An Account of the Cape of Good Hope. In: I, Schapera & B. Farrington, *The early Cape hottentots, described in the writings of Olfert Dapper (1668), Willem ten Rhyne (1686) and Johannes Gulielmus de Grevenbroek (1695).* Van Riebeeck Society.

The University of Cape Town. (n.d.) *University of Cape Town: History and Location.* Retrieved on 13 October 2021 from https://bit.ly/3LKfZji

Tischauser, L.V. (2012). *Jim Crow Laws (Landmarks of the American Mosaic).* Greenwood.

Truth and Reconciliation Commission of South Africa. (1998). *Truth and Reconciliation Commission of South Africa Report. Volume 1.* The Republic of South Africa.

Tuhiwai Smit, L. (2012). *Decolonizing methodologies: research and Indigenous peoples (2nd edition.).* Zed Books.

Tully, J. (1993). *An approach to political philosophy: Locke in contexts.* Cambridge University Press. https://doi.org/10.1017/CBO9780511607882

Upham, M.G. (2013). *Uprooted Lives: unfurling the cape of good hope's earliest colonial inhabitants (1652-713).* First Fifty Years.

Van der Merwe, P.J. (1988). *Die noordwaartse beweging van die boere voor die groot trek (1770-1842).* The State Library.

Van der Merwe, P.J. (2006). *Trek: Studies oor die mobiliteit van die pioniersbevolking aan die Kaap (1770-1842)* (Spesiale herdruk.). African Sun Media. https://doi.org/10.18820/9781919980775

Van der Merwe, C. (Ed.). (2014). *Die houtbeen van St Sergius: Opstelle oor Afrikaanse romans.* African Sun Media. https://doi.org/10.18820/9781920689186

Van Niekerk, A.A.J. (1979). *Tasāl van die grasvlaktes.* Hollandsch Afrikaansche Uigevers Maatschappij.

Van Wyk, M.M. (2012). [Re]claiming the Riel as Khoisan Indigenous Cultural Knowledge. *Stud Tribes Tribals,* 10(1):47-56 https://doi.org/10.1080/0972639X.2012.11886642

Veracini, L. & Verbuyst, R. (2020). South Africa's settler- colonial present: Khoisan revivalism and the question of indigeneity. *Social Dynamics*, 46(2):259-276. https://doi.org/10.1080/02533952.2020.1805883

Verbuyst, R. (2022). *Khoisan Consciousness An Ethnography of Emic Histories and Indigenous Revivalism in Post-Apartheid Cape Town*. Brill. https://doi.org/10.1163/9789004516618

Villette. F. (2016). The effects of apartheid's unequal education system can still be felt today. *Cape Times*. Retrieved on 15 September 2018 from https://bit.ly/3F62GWV

Wiener, N. (1988). *The human use of human beings: Cybernetics and society (No. 320)*. Da Capo Press.

Wiesel, E. (1960). *Night*. Hill & Wang.

Willemse, H. (2013). Obituary: Jakes Gerwel (1946-2012). *Tydskrif vir letterkunde*, 50(1):126-130. https://doi.org/10.4314/tvl.v50i1.10

Wright, M.M. (2004). *Becoming Black: creating identity in the African diaspora*. Duke University Press. https://doi.org/10.1215/9780822385868

Legal Sources

Ministry of Higher Education. (2013). *White Paper for Post-School Education and Training: Building An Expanded, Effective and Integrated Post-School System*. Retrieved on 16 September 2018 from https://bit.ly/3RHywAD

Ministry of Education. (1997). White Paper 3: A Programme for the Transformation of Higher Education. General Notice 1196 of 1997.

Republic of South Africa. (1959). *The Extension of University Education Act 45 of 1959*. Republic of South Africa Government Gazette.

Republic of South Africa. (1959). *Promotion of Bantu Self-Government Act (No 46 of 1959)*. Republic of South Africa Government Gazette.

Republic of South Africa. (1963). *The Coloured Person's Education Act (No. 47 of 1963)*. Republic of South Africa Government Gazette.

Republic of South Africa. (1965). *Indians Education Act (No. 61 of 1965)*. Republic of South Africa Government Gazette.

Republic of South Africa (RSA). (1996). *Constitution of the Republic of South Africa Act (No. 108 of 1996)*. Pretoria: Republic of South Africa Government Gazette.

Republic of South Africa (RSA). (1997). *Higher Education Act (No. 101 of 1997)*. Republic of South Africa Government Gazette.

Republic of South Africa (RSA). (2019). *Traditional and Khoi-San Leadership Act (No. 3 of 2019)*. Republic of South Africa Government Gazette.

Union of South Africa. (1949). *Prohibition of Mixed Marriages Act (No. 55 of 1949)*. SA Government Gazette.

Union of South Africa. (1950). *Immorality Amendment Act (No. 21 of 1950)*. SA Government Gazette.

Union of South Africa. (1950). *Population Registration Act (No 30 of 1950)*. SA Government Gazette.

Union of South Africa. (1950). *Group Areas Act (No. 41 of 1950)*. SA Government Gazette.

Union of South Africa. (1951). *Bantu Authorities Act (No 68 of 1951)*. SA Government Gazette.

Union of South Africa. (1952). *Natives Laws Amendment Act (No 54 of 1952)*. SA Government Gazette.

Union of South Africa. (1953). *Bantu Education Act (No 47 of 1953)*. SA Government Gazette.

Union of South Africa. (1953). *Reservation of Separate Amenities Act (*No 49 of 1953). SA Government Gazette.

Union of South Africa. (1959). *Promotion of Bantu Self-Government Act (No 46 of 1959)*. Republic of South Africa Government Gazette.

Census Reports

Cape of Good Hope (Colony). *Colonial Office. Census of the Colony of the Cape of Good Hope, 1865 / Cape Town, Saul Solomon, 1866.* Parliament. Annexures to the Votes and proceedings, 1866. G 682 E1.

Cape of Good Hope (Colony). *Colonial Secretary's Office Results of a census of the Colony of the Cape of Good Hope, taken on the night of Sunday, the 7th March, 1875.* Cape Town: Saul Solomon, 1877-1878. Appendix I, vol. 2 of 1877 with 3 supplementary vols. in a box. G 682 E5.

Cape of Good Hope (Colony). *Census Office. Results of a census of the Colony of the Cape of Good Hope, as on the night of Sunday, the 5th April, 1891.* Cape Town, W.A. Richards & Sons, Government Printers, 1892. G 682 A.POPU.1891.RESU.

University of the Western Cape Policy Documents

The University of the Western Cape. (2019). *Who Are UWC's First-Year Students?* UWC First Year Experience: Series 1. First-Year Students' Profiles, Pre-Entry Attributes & Expectations of University Studies. Retrieved on 8 November 2022 from https://bit.ly/3LLXYkX

The University of the Western Cape. (2021). *Five-Year Employment Equity Plan. 1 October 2020 to 30 September 2025.* Retrieved on 8 November 2022 from https://bit.ly/48wu25U

Documentary Films

Ambo, P. & Saif, S. (2017). *Family.* Denmark.

Cloete, J. (Director). (2022). Steek My Weg. [YouTube]

Desai, R. (Director). (2014). *Miners Shot Down.* South Africa.

DuVernay, A. (Director). (2016). *13th.* Netflix.

Gibson, A. & Jemma, J. (Directors). (1992). *7Up.* United Kingdom: [Al Jazeera, 1992].

Gibson, A. & Jemma, J. (Directors). (2013). *28Up.* United Kingdom: [Al Jazeera, 2013].

Guzman, P. (Director). (2011). *Nostalgia for the Light.* USA.

Hoffmeester, D. (Producer). Cloete, J. (Director). (2023). Bergsig. [Abrasive Media & Institute for Justice and Reconciliation].

Jene, B. (Director). (2017). *Bobbi Jene.* Sweden.

Mokwena, L. (Producer) & Cloete, J. (Director). (2022). The Broken String. [Cape Town TV (Broadcast)].

Oppenheimer, J. (Director). (2012). *Act of Killing*. Denmark.

Peck, R. (Director). (2017). *I Am Not Your Negro*. United States: Velvet Film.

Saragas, A. (Director). (2017). *Strike a Rock*. [Film]. Elafos Productions.

Steenkamp, A. (Director). (2013). *I Afrikaner*. Netherlands.

Music

Duckworth, K.L. (2015). *To Pimp A Butterfly*. Los Angles: Top Dawg Entertainment; Interscope/ Aftermath. [Available on Apple Music and Spotify.]

Duckworth, K.L. (2015). Institutionalised. [Recorded by Kendrick Lamar]. *To Pimp A Butterfly*. Los Angles: Top Dawg Entertainment; Interscope & Aftermath. [Available on Apple Music and Spotify.]

Van der Westhuizen, P. (2014). Asbrood En Hardevet. [Recorded by Pieter van der Westhuizen]. *Bokkie sê my reg*. [Available on Apple Music and Spotify.]

Public Lectures and Speeches

Lushaba, L. (2018). *Unpacking Decolonised Quality Education: Student Perspective and Institutional Responses*. Public Lecture. The University of the Western Cape.

Mbeki, T. (1996). I am an African. [YouTube]. Retrieved on 20 April 2020 form https://www.youtube.com/ watch?v=dCeLwTITRoQ

Turok, B. (2018). *Deconstructing decolonization: African perspectives, historical insights & lessons for the future*. Public Lecture. The University of the Western Cape.

YouTube

KJRH -TV [Channel 2]. (2017). Judge releases Betty Shelby's interview with police [Video]. YouTube. Retrieved on 17 November 2018 from https://www.youtube.com/ watch?v=Mn9GDm16zNQ

www.ingramcontent.com/pod-product-compliance
Lightning Source LLC
Chambersburg PA
CBHW050745100426
42739CB00016BA/3440